The Future is Feminine

ALSO AVAILABLE FROM BLOOMSBURY

Deleuze, Guattari and the Schizoanalysis of Trans Studies,
ed. Ciara Cremin (forthcoming)
Lacan: A Genealogy, Miguel de Beistegui
Feminist Theory After Deleuze, Hannah Stark
Challenging Power: Democracy and Accountability in a Fractured World, Cynthia Kaufman
Capitalism's Holocaust of Animals: A Non-Marxist Critique of Capital, Philosophy and Patriarchy, Katerina Kolozova

The Future is Feminine

Capitalism and the masculine disorder

CIARA CREMIN

BLOOMSBURY ACADEMIC
LONDON • NEW YORK • OXFORD • NEW DELHI • SYDNEY

BLOOMSBURY ACADEMIC
Bloomsbury Publishing Plc
50 Bedford Square, London, WC1B 3DP, UK
1385 Broadway, New York, NY 10018, USA
29 Earlsfort Terrace, Dublin 2, Ireland

BLOOMSBURY, BLOOMSBURY ACADEMIC and the Diana logo are
trademarks of Bloomsbury Publishing Plc

First published in Great Britain 2021

Cover design by Charlotte Daniels
Cover image © Camerique Archive / Getty Images

A catalogue record for this book is available from the British Library.

A catalog record for this book is available from the Library of Congress.

ISBN: HB: 978-1-3501-4977-9
        PB: 978-1-3501-4976-2
        ePDF: 978-1-3501-4978-6
        eBook: 978-1-3501-4979-3

Typeset by RefineCatch Limited, Bungay, Suffolk
Printed and bound in Great Britain

To find out more about our authors and books visit www.bloomsbury.com
and sign up for our newsletters.

Contents

Acknowledgements

The author's name mystifies what in any event is a collaborative work. It's the work of all those who influenced and inspired the author. It's the work of those who either directly or indirectly have helped bring works like this to fruition. As such, there are many people I could name and only some of whom are named here. Apologies in advance if on this occasion I do not mentioned you specifically.

This was a difficult book to write. I struggled at times to find my voice. There were many theoretical and conceptual issues to juggle. I was at times in danger of drowning in the voluminous amount of literature spanning the many fields of relevance to the topic. One of the most difficult things was determining what to leave out and what of course to put in. Hye Ji Lee's sharp eye for detail and deft hand at editing helped enormously in bringing the book to its polished state. To her I am eternally grateful. I thank all the people at Bloomsbury and their associates for the work they have put into this project, especially my commissioning editor Liza Thompson. I have several people to thank for checking over sections on Lacan (Matthew Flisfeder, Warwick Tie and Bruce Edman), Deleuze and Guattari (Ian Buchanan) and in the chapter 'Queervestism' (Juliet Jacques). I'd like to thank Dylan Taylor and Jack Foster too for their helpful comments on an article I wrote for their journal CounterFutures on a feminine praxis, parts of which are incorporated into the first chapter. I thank my colleague and friend David Mayeda with whom I have spent many fruitful days at our favourite 'writing retreats', cafes in other words, fired up on caffeine. I am grateful to the University of Auckland for affording me the opportunity to write this book and colleagues / friends such as Bruce Cohen and Adam White for the support they have given me over the years. It's a privilege to have taught and to work with many excellent students. Their unqualified affirmation of my femininity is deeply appreciated. They demonstrate in their commitment to critical inquiry and social justice why education matters.

The heroes of our lives whose many contributions frequently go unsung are so often women. Akiko is neither my crutch nor my absent phallus. It is to her that I am the most indebted. .

1

The general sickness

Masculinity kills. Femininity saves lives. Caring for others, tenderness, empathy, sensuality, a diversity of emotional expressions, qualities such as these are essential to the wellbeing of individuals and to a healthy society. Those, however, with an appendage dangling between their legs are pressurized from an early age to repudiate such qualities because they are arbitrarily associated with femininity, a word also signifying woman. They are qualities that masculinity is defined in contrast to and that the male in particular learns to rebel against. An ego that thrives on competition, society cultivates in so many of us a need for status and power. It rewards those who aggressively pursue it. The premise of this book is that masculinity is a disorder which afflicts each and every one of us. Mapping the disorder to capitalism, the book aims to discover a therapy appropriate to it. The future, if to survive to see it, must be feminine: a femininity that with no reference to the masculine renders these gendered terms and, under radically transformed circumstances, the material consequences of them, obsolete.

The disorder is born from a sick society that none of us, whatever our sex or gender, is immune from. Those who are most afflicted, such as the sociopaths in high office, men in uniform and the predators of women who abuse their power, tend, for understandable reasons, to draw the most attention. But it distracts us from the general condition that, because we are so habituated to it, seems by comparison banal or worse, naturally male. It is not only the worst of men but also the best of men who in this book are in my sights. There is a banality in the routine bullying behaviours of men, their craving for status and power, and their reactions when aspersions are cast on their character. The most aggressive and self-serving of men are sometimes also women, women who also demand in men the very qualities that perpetuate the patriarchy. This should not surprise us. In an androcentric society, the unconscious is also androcentric. We can barely grasp how and to what extent, symptomatic of the disorder, we are invested in and dependent on the masculine. The disorder lies behind the statistics of domestic violence, suicide rates, homelessness and incarceration. But it is also what characterizes an atomized, competitive, warmongering, class-ridden and racist society. In other words, capitalism. Capitalism can no more do without this disorder than it can a class to exploit for profit. Class and masculine domination are braided together so finely that it is difficult to imagine anyone with the sharpness of vision and the deftness of hand skilled enough to unstitch them. Masculinity, to be sure, is a porous term. It is difficult to define but easy enough for people to discern. It is discerned in the negative. In other words, what it stands in contrast to. Its nemesis, its prop – the thing that is most feared and repudiated – what our society labels as feminine is the vaccine to this sickness.

The process of becoming a man is an aversion therapy in anything held as feminine. This is not simply an issue of style. The absence is an index of something more profound, disturbing and destructive. Not only does it limit the repertoire of styles available to men but foundational in this book, what I describe and diagnose as a masculine disorder, is the repression and sabotaging of aspects of the self which are vital to mental health and the wellbeing of others. When tenderness, empathy, sensuality, caring for others – a broad diversity of emotions and affects – are considered feminine and therefore unmanly, it is not only men who are in trouble – it is all of us.

A stylization as opposed to a state of being, forever compensating for feelings of inadequacy, masculinity is born of crisis but only named as such when the veneer of invulnerability is tarnished. A feminine woman, on the other hand, wears her vulnerability. Goddess, slut, scab to the sisterhood and never queer enough, her femininity is synonymous with decadence, frivolity, weakness and fragility. Her adornments, Freud thought, compensated for the absence of a penis. Whereas for the self-righteous male who disdains femininity for its seeming excesses, betraying his misogyny in doing so, they are markers of an enslavement to, and complicity with, the nefarious practices of the beauty and fashion industries. Complicated by class, racial and ethnic differences, doubtless there are as many masculinities as there are men. A barrier nonetheless exists in an overwhelming majority of men that prevents them from making even the slightest sartorial incursion onto women's turf. And as an index of something that goes far deeper than appearance, this, as I suggest, is no trivial matter.

Clothing is the most visible and easy-to-verify example of how closely the masculine gender is guarded. It is not, however, that men are never seen in women's clothes. On the contrary, they daily wear clothes such as shirts and trousers, staples in a woman's wardrobe. Incorporating a multiplicity of styles, the clothes that women wear are, if anything, gender neutral. Inclusive of different subjective orientations, political affinities, gay and queer sexual identities, the failure of a broad diversity of men to cross this trivial sartorial threshold issues from an unconscious dependency in *both* men and women on masculine domination. Men say to me, 'But I have no desire to wear women's clothes.' Women say to me, 'I'm not attracted to feminine men.' There's no reason to be suspicious of such claims; it either does it for you or not. But if there is nothing genetic about the disposition or otherwise towards feminine affect and apparel, it is evident that this androcentric order – one that dignifies the male member with the status of a religious fetish – is remarkably efficient in socializing us into wanting the gender markers that sustain it. Whether male or female, one way or another, libido is wedded to the masculine.

Toxic masculinity is a term coined by Karner in 1996 and that Sculos (2017) defines as a loose set of 'norms, beliefs, and behaviours' that harms 'women, men, children, and society more broadly'. This could apply to anyone. When society is itself toxic, there's every likelihood that the subject brought up in it will inherit that toxicity too. My focus then is the general condition of what I call the masculine disorder. In our society, gender and sex are usually conflated. Typically, those born with a penis are masculinized. Hence why, empirically, boys and men are typically those who are most afflicted. But it can happen to females too. There is a continuum of masculine and feminine traits but which nevertheless, to a remarkable degree, map to a binary notion of gender that man invented. As a person defined male at birth but who presents as a woman, I tend to stand out from the crowd and am a constant source of curiosity. Trans women are the exception that proves the rule of the extent to which styles, behaviours, passions and so forth conform to the erroneous notion of a gender binary which pivots to the masculine. It is a reason perhaps why trans women in particular are subject to considerable abuse.

Phalluses are everywhere. It's a phallocentric (dis)order. Or simply it is patriarchy, a set of structurally embedded conditions that privileges those who are the most emotionally stunted. Aside from class and racial divisions, when one considers the damage that masculine socialization does to the human psyche, the idea that men are 'privileged' works only in the narrowest of terms. bell hooks articulates it well when she says that patriarchy demands of boys and men that they 'kill off the emotional parts of themselves' and inflict such damage on one another. Becoming a man is a process of what she aptly describes as 'psychic self-mutilation' (hooks, 2004: 58). I deploy this phrase as a shorthand in this book when describing a key characteristic of the disorder. Where feminists have sought to recruit men in their struggle against patriarchy, I instead describe it as *our* struggle. By this I don't mean that it is ours because of a common interest in ending all forms of oppression whether we are personally affected or not. It is not out of charity that we fight or, as I suspect is the case, because the 'I'm a feminist' badge has a phallic status. Instead, by underlining the damage it does to the male psyche, it is in the direct interest of men to 'smash the patriarchy' too.

And if men have a material interest in ending patriarchy, it stands to reason that so do trans women. The difference with trans and cis women (women who identify as the gender they were given at birth) is that, depending on factors such as class and race, their interest is often more viscerally discerned and urgent. The only true beneficiaries of patriarchy as I can tell is the capitalist class. While men have committed brutal acts of violence throughout the ages, it is in capitalism that a particular form of masculinity emerges. People describe capitalism as a 'libidinal economy'. It is libidinal in the precise ways that males in particular are socialized to be invested in the phallic ideals and objects that capital valorizes or derives value from.

Yet we're not uncritical of masculinity. A 'toxic' masculinity is, after all, held responsible for many of society's ills. Thus, we might suppose that if men were of a more progressive disposition, patriarchy would end. Describing masculinity as toxic is like describing water as wet. Echoing, though also disavowing Freud, Bourdieu (2001) described how men and women are libidinally and unconsciously oriented to masculine forms of domination and are habitually and unthinkingly reproducing it in everyday interactions, comportments, gestures and tones of voice. In the home, the workplace and leisure time, in our everyday words and gestures, through space and time, such is the power of androcentrism that it is impossible to register the multitude of ways that we are all complicit in the reproduction of these relationships. Being turned into a woman, wrote Bourdieu (2001), is the worst kind of humiliation to be inflicted on a man. Or, as Stoller (1985: 83) said, 'The first order of business in being a man is, "don't be a woman." The male fears 'weakness, dependence, intimacy and closeness', as Segal (2007: 259) writes. What a man fears is to be found lacking and not the man he imagines himself to be. If femininity is said to be a masquerade, even in enslavement to commercial fashion and beauty ideals, masculinity is symptomatic of a fundamental delusion of being whole and in no need of a mask. And this is where the problem chiefly lies. Losing face, their delusions of grandeur are all too frequently exposed.

Women were typically never made to feel entitled in the first place, so typically they have no fear of being exposed or at least are not so reactive when not measuring up to whatever ideals they identify with. A woman can be competitive without being libidinally invested in winning. Being exposed as weak, vulnerable, for being a 'loser', is another matter entirely for men. It is easy for men to feel humiliated. So much violence is committed either to avoid humiliation or when humiliated. This is what it means to be emasculated or feminized, or as Freud would say 'castrated'. 'Castration', in this book, is not the condition of females but a placeholder description of a general state of being in which all of us are vulnerable, in need of others for support and therefore interdependent. 'Phallus' is whatever signifier for the subject represents status, authority and power, in other words, what masks 'castration'.

Freud (1989) called femininity a 'riddle', its 'repudiation' being the principal obstacle to the successful completion of psychoanalytic therapy. Men fear weakness; women labour under its sign. Women are not so much castrated, as Freud averred, but under duress to appear the weaker sex. My mind casts back to the early 1980s when Prince Charles and Princess Diana were featured together on various cheap memorabilia. Although taller in real life, the Princess was always presented diminutive in comparison to Charles, almost as if she was functioning as a crutch to prop up the Prince. This is precisely what she was, like many women. But I doubt women perform this role self-consciously. I doubt they say to themselves 'My man is weak; I best appear smaller and weaker than he is.' We're creatures of habit and feel secure in the familiar. It's not the mortgage paid out of the man's salary that makes women dependent on men, but the purpose for which their femininity is conditioned to serve.

While it's tempting to say that the masculinized ego – not the male as such – is the lynchpin on which the existing patriarchal arrangements depend, if anything it is the feminine that functions as the absolute necessity. Like the capitalist who cannot exist without a worker to exploit, it is the feminine that enables the masculine and henceforth serves as its necessary supplement. Ought we then to abandon femininity? Defaulting to the masculine, were we to do so, we'd be in need of another crutch to function in its place. To end this psychic and sociological disorder, rather than abandon our proverbial crutches, I prescribe firmly holding on to them and recrafting them into weapons: an affirmative femininity that withdraws its support. It would constitute a positive resignification of femininity that negates its patriarchal function while simultaneously putting the subject on a communistic trajectory. Not 'femininity' as such but what femininity has come to stand for in this gendered society.

This is the 'dialectic' of femininity, a femininity that capitalism and a masculinized ego depends upon – in the most material of ways through caregiving, child rearing and so forth – that for this reason affords it the power of negation. Femininity is not a 'thing', of course, but, as Marx said of the working class, as conceived here the androcentric disorder's potential gravedigger. There is no gender 'binary' as such – not only because it reduces gender to two categories but also because the relationship between 'masculinity' and 'femininity' is an asymmetrical one: the former is the gender that patriarchy obviously privileges and also, as conceived here, it is the gender *par excellence* of capitalism. Thus, to occupy a position of 'gender neutrality' is like being 'neutral' in respect to class or racial antagonisms. It simply affirms the status quo. This is why I call for an affirmative femininity. A femininity that, like a class acting for itself, simultaneously stands in negation not of everything masculinity today signifies but of the sickness itself. It is a sickness born from a fear of the feminine and a simultaneous but disavowed dependency on what femininity in contrast signifies.

The problem of masculinity is discerned, as suggested, in those who commit carnage in the classroom, the misogynists in high office, sociopaths in uniforms, chauvinists at the pub. It's discerned in the swaggering, upper-class, public-school-educated bully, one who is distinctly English and of prankster infantilism as Mark Fisher (2017: 351) has observed. These are the most visible symptoms of the masculine disorder but which, as I have also suggested, distract attention from its wider import. The disorder is a general one that varies in intensity and, related to circumstance, effect. But you won't find the entry 'masculine disorder' in the bible of clinical psychology, the *Diagnostic and Statistical Manual for Mental Disorders (DSM)*. Nor, for the same reason, can an entry for 'alienation disorder' be found in such a text. This is because we're describing a disorder that is the society itself, a capitalist society that depends on these twin disorders and whose institutions and economic arrangements are structured to reproduce them. We do not, however, require the recognition of the psychiatric establishment to diagnose the condition. They have done enough damage as it is with their invention and administering of mental disorders.

Freud had already charted the process through which the disorder is reproduced. He called this Oedipalization. But as with the psychologist and their *DSM* bible, the society that produced this form of psychic sabotage was not the subject of interrogation. If to the psychologist (not the psychoanalyst) the individual is like a laboratory rat isolated from society, to the sociologist the individual cannot be discerned except through the social. Were the norms and mores of our time subject to scrutiny and called into question, the psychological profession would perhaps be looking to Marx for guidance on appropriate therapies. They'd be advising their patients to take to the streets, agitate in the workplace, schools and universities – a barricade therapy that irritates the individual and agitates the social; a therapy that concludes when the prevailing order is quarantined to history. Only under a radically transformed condition – the end of class society – will there be a subject who is not out of economic necessity born susceptible to the affliction.

Capitalism is to masculinity what communism is to femininity. Another dialectic, this time of masculinity, the irony is that the very symptoms of the masculine disorder, so essential to capitalism, are the same that may have to be marshalled to forcibly make the future feminine. There can be no other future. The condition can be traced back to the early period of colonization and, exported and settled the world over, is both universal and distinctly European, something I flesh out in chapter 4, 'Vectors of androcentrism'. Class, race and gender intersect in this analysis; an intersectionality not of identity differences but material ones that are structurally determined by the capitalist patriarchy. They are material phenomena washed through with libido, everything in this respect, sexually charged: not sexuality in the mundane sense of practices described as 'normative' or 'non-normative', but impulses, desires, even affects that condition our lives and our relationship to production and consumption that keep the grinding wheels of exploitation in motion.

The masculine disorder will not end under capitalism; only in a communistic society will there be a chance of it withering away. But we shouldn't count on it. Adapted to the situation, prefigurative moves are required – pink shirts, red lipsticks and flowery dresses. Feminine items and affects are the machinery of a praxis that manoeuvres up against the masculine disorder, and, testing for its weaknesses, explores ways to breach it. Both jarring and revelatory of an androcentric unconscious, a *tactical* reification and everyday embodiment by men of feminine signifiers is needed. The substance of this move is determined by what is at stake—whether, for example, the effect is alienating to others and forces a subjective recalibration. A feminine praxis burns. Like that aforementioned crutch, it whips away the material and psychological supports that enable the masculine disorder while also paving the way for an alternative, but importantly collective, mode of being and becoming.

When thinking about the cover image of the book, I wanted something that affirmed femininity. I didn't want an image of men behaving badly nor resigned to the odd cliché, a lipstick, stockings, that sort of thing. But the problem was that, telling of the way femininity is imagined, every image fell into one of several categories. They looked like adverts for products, or, worse, for bodies, and when in a suburban setting, femininity was associated with domesticity. Aside from the camped-up queer, there was one other image category, the one I eventually settled on – though nonetheless cliched, the classic feminine-chic evocative of Hollywood's golden era. Much admired, frequently aped, iconic femininity, a femininity that in my old school sensibilities I could get my head around, and that reflects how I often dress. It was this image that eventually I settled on. Old school style, new school purpose, but don't judge the book by its cover: it's not about Hollywood, the femme fatale, nor glamour. Nor do I even explore in any detail the politicization of femme by those who advocate a queer mode of being, which would distract from the analysis I do want to undertake.

Not everything associated with masculinity is of course negative. Being 'strong', for example, is not an inherently masculine trait nor in itself negative. The problem is when one's self-esteem depends on appearing strong. There's a difference, for instance, between being competitive when playing tennis, and being competitive because one's esteem relies on winning. It is sometimes said that it is of the masculine trait to be singular in one's pursuits, which many artists and scientists are. But if this is so, both for the individual and society, it comes at a heavy price. The problem is sometimes one of signification.

In this book I aim to resignify traits that we think of as masculine and not always negative, such as bravery, strength, even aggression. In a radically transformed reality principle, or what Lacan calls the symbolic order, there would be no barriers, psychic or social, to males expressing themselves in ways considered today to be feminine. No need to 'man up' or display 'strength' through domination. For in such transformed conditions, there would be nothing to fear in the feminine, not least because women would no longer be positioned, materially or symbolically, as the 'weaker sex'.

Feminine praxis

Dresses and skirts are emblematic of a feminine style. What is erroneously called gender-neutral or unisex clothing, though, is neither a sign of progress nor of the victory of feminists. For while in protest against their physical and symbolic impositions, women were abandoning feminine affect and apparel, without the political motive or economic incentive, men were under no pressure to do likewise. Men enacted no equivalent abandonment of masculinity. With a feminine aesthetic subtracted out, the style men were habituated to wearing became gender neutral by default and nothing was or is sacrificed by men to achieve it.

While femininity is an escape valve for the cross-dresser who reserves his proclivity for the home, when taken out of the home, it is potentially an exit strategy. It is potentially a more totalizing and altogether radical alternative to masculine forms of being and becoming and ultimately the violence, whether self-inflicted or inflicted upon others, that is engendered through them. In acquiring the aura of femininity that for a long time has mystified the female body—the 'enigma of women' trope — femininity becomes a free-floating signifier, neither male nor female. Though such moves are sometimes necessary when opposing forced dress codes, this cannot be achieved by women who refuse feminine adornment. As with unisex clothing, a masculine hegemony is not countered by such gestures; if anything, it is reinforced. The various 'crises' of masculinity issue from the fear of appearing weak and with weakness associated with femininity. A way to overcome this fear at a collective level is to openly embrace the feminine; thereby to signal that there is a multiplicity of alternatives to 'being' a man. For feminists such as Irigaray (1993), the female body, however, has the unique capacity for a multiplicity of heterogeneous pleasures. Segal (2005) criticizes Irigaray (1993), and the strand of French feminism with which the latter is associated, for evoking a corporeal idea of woman. This idea, she says, reproduces the patriarchal myth that women are essentially nurturing, non-violent and egalitarian. This is why, for all their positive evocations of femininity, I shall not be developing my argument through these theorists. They are simply incompatible with the position I take. So frequently a touchstone for critiques of gender and sexuality, Butler is largely bypassed too. This angle has I feel been exhausted. The important critiques have too. This is not to disparage the important contributions Butler has made and continues to make in these fields.

From an early age I wanted to dress in women's clothes but only later in life could I do so without risking my job or being isolated from friends and loved ones. But it was still a risk, with many consequences that were impossible to anticipate. Each situation comes with its own challenges and tests, tests that only the subject in their situation can determine and, weighing up the risks, decide to undertake. The most affluent and economically secure are sometimes in the best position to breach gender norms but relative to their situation, such breaches are not necessarily as profound as those without the security of resources, jobs, friends and so forth. There is no single praxis that fits all, but many different ways to approach the problem in the self and in the society that made us. And it doesn't necessarily have to involve a change of clothing.

If there's a feminine praxis for cisgendered women, it's primarily in the denial that femininity is a mark of castration and to affirm it, perhaps even going against the grain of unexamined hostilities, to offer support and encouragement to males, especially children, to cross gender lines, experiment and play. Can there be a feminine praxis for a trans man? I don't imagine that becoming a man for them involves supressing their emotions, committing acts of psychic self-mutilation or practising violence. Likewise, for me, becoming a woman is not about being weak, coquettish or superficial. Liberated from a gender that was imposed upon them, far from being more aggressive, mean spirited and so forth, I am sure that many trans men are happier, more at ease in themselves and kinder to others as I am today as a trans woman. The disorder is not determined by sex. It primarily concerns the aforementioned traits that those defined male at birth are pressurized to repudiate and sabotage. The absence of feminine signifiers on male bodies is symptomatic of the social condition not of anatomy, chromosomes, testosterone levels, genetics or anything like that. As with the cis woman, trans men have an important part to play in encouraging children to experiment with a diversity of gendered signifiers but also in giving courage to those designated as male on their journey of becoming women. With

nary a lipstick in sight, these are some of the ways that trans men
and cis women may enact their own form of feminine praxis and
contribute towards the detoxication of the whole. But there is no
equivalent masculine praxis, for this would involve the opposite,
homogeneity, closure, repression. In short, it would constitute an
investment in the status quo and reproduction of relations of
domination.

Femininity in perspective

Bordo (1995) suggests that the female who feminizes her body must
bear some responsibility for their subordination. Nevertheless, men
and women, she says, are both implicated by conditions they have
no authority to determine, but through 'external regulation, subjection,
transformation' and 'improvement', it is the female body that is
'docile'. Comparing my elaborate and time-consuming morning
routine of applying make-up, and all the vexing questions about which
outfit to wear and what shoes and jewellery to match it with, to that
of the man who was out of bed and out the door in ten minutes, I
would surely agree. But such views must be tempered according to
the greater extent to which men police their own boundaries and the
lengths they go to in disassociating their bodies and their egos from
femininity. While women are also obviously subject to gendered
forms of disciplining, they differ in the key respect that while a man
must disassociate himself from the image of woman, a woman must
partly incorporate masculine traits in order to compete. In view of the
material circumstance and symbolic ordering of gender, a rejection
by women of femininity would appear salutary to a *feminist* praxis
but risks reinforcing the conditions it opposes. It is by now apparent
that the outcomes of such moves are if anything counterproductive.
Women are shamed for being feminine.

Bartky's (2002: 15) description of a stereotypical femininity
underscores the problem with such critiques, at least insofar that,
contextually, she regards the following traits to be negative. The
feminine woman, she says, is 'warm, nurturant, expressive,
unaggressive, gentle and genteel', and, if not for her occasional
lapses of vulgarity, likely mistaken for being upper class. A feminine

woman defines herself in contrast to the image of a stereotypical masculinity and thus, lacking ambition for herself, is ambitious for her husband and children. Acknowledging that there have been changes in the workplace, Bartky claims that a feminine woman still tends to disassociate from activities and professions where the masculine male dominates. Sometimes the feminine woman is courageous, Bartky writes; unlike men, however, she is not ashamed of appearing cowardly.

Femininity is not in itself the problem, but how it is situated in respect to capitalism. In contrast to 'masculine' forms of labour that are physical, 'skilled' and practical, 'feminine' labour is affective and intangible. Like the work that women are tasked to do in the home, feminine waged labour is invisible. It literally cannot be counted. When femininity is equated with being girly, individualistic and materialistic, and this attitude to life equated with feminism—a neoliberal variant to be sure—then Bartky makes a salient point: that to be feminist one has to overcome femininity. But just as it is wrong to conflate feminism with liberalism, so too it is wrong to conflate femininity with patriarchal submission.

If femininity cannot exist without masculinity, it can nevertheless be resignified as an expression of strength and, even further, be incorporated in a mode of resistance. As Barton writes in respect to a queer femininity, 'to be "femme" is to forge a self-made femininity that subverts the gender binary and heteropatriarchy by refusing to be defined in opposition to manhood and masculinity'.[1] But within the queer hegemony, feminine styles and expressions are considered passive and to therefore reinforce gender norms (Brightwell, 2018). Thus, in the LGBTQI+ pecking order, trans men are not subject to the level of criticisms that trans women are. If a feminine woman cannot be queer, what we are left with is a queer femininity – appropriated, caricatured and monopolized by what Duggan (in Castronovo and Nelson, 2002) calls homonormative men: men who are gay, typically white, affluent and liberal in their values, the kind likely to campaign for gay marriage and defend the right of police officers to attend gay pride parades dressed in uniform.

Even amongst those who identify as queer, trans women appear then to encounter the most hostility. Serano (2007) describes this as transmisogyny and links it to sexism. This no more explains the general aversion to femininity, however, than saying that black people are more oppressed than white people because the police are racist. The theoretical perspectives that Serano does not engage with do provide an explanation: those of Freud and Marx and those who in their wake have revised, developed and synthesized their theories. The term transmisogyny is not in itself inappropriate and what Serano has observed is telling but of the general (not universal) repudiation of femininity amongst cis men and women, queer, non-binary and even trans men and women. It tells of how femininity is to this day equated with weakness, an idea that is unconsciously incorporated, the symptoms of which, including transmisogyny, are manifold. The materialist explanation for this is that the masculine ego-formation, which is characterized by the repudiation of femininity, is essential to capitalism.

However egregious the idea in practice, the 'binary' as such is not the issue, at least not one for which a solution can be found by its wholesale refusal. Immanent to the situation, whether that be the material, the symbolic, the identitarian or the affective, it is masculinity that is at the heart of the problem. Masculinity wants queering, it is masculinity trouble that wants causing and masculinity that wants fucking. And femininity is the means by which it can be done.

Androcentric disorder

Rosemary Hennessy (2000: 23) makes the point that the concept of 'patriarchy is a crucial one for any analysis of sexual identity precisely because it allows us to make connections between the ideological formation of identities and divisions of labour'. These structures, she continues, are 'historically variable and complex'. They also incorporate 'several axes of difference: racial, gendered, sexual'. Patriarchy, she avers, is necessary 'to most socioeconomic systems in the world and has been fundamental to capitalism's exploitative human relations'.

The literal definition of patriarchy is 'rule of the father'. Clearly, this needs qualifying. For patriarchy does not depend on actual fathers nor are those in positions of authority necessarily men. It can be described, as Hennessey does, in terms of broader and varying structures of domination that fan out well beyond the familial domain. While not an object in itself that can be seen, it manifests in how we work and play, how we dress and interact with one another. The term is nevertheless misleading and sends us up many blind alleyways: that patriarchy precedes class; that because many households no longer fit the archetypal male breadwinner model or because woman do occupy positions of high office, society is no longer patriarchal; or, that patriarchy coexists with capitalism as a 'dual' system of exploitation which then begs the question is race not another system of exploitation too?

While I don't want to abandon the term, my preference when describing the structural condition is for the term 'androcentrism', a word coined by Charlotte Perkins Gilman at the beginning of the twentieth century. It refers to the priority society gives to the masculine wherein anything that is not masculine is situated as Other. It is no longer then the father as such or the male sex that is at a structural advantage but rather those who adopt, embody and articulate qualities that are associated with the masculine position, who are of course typically male. I think this better describes how figures such as Freud and Lacan work with gendered concepts. For them the feminine position is Other but not as with the masculine one respectively female or male. Anyone can function in the place of the 'paternal' superego authority. There is no division of the sexes in the unconscious. Masculine sexuality denotes a libidinal dependency on and investment in 'phallic' props, a sexuality that originates with language as the means through which we develop a sense of self and relationship to others. By identifying the problem with 'man' as a symbolic position and masculinity as libidinal, and therefore sociological and psychological , a clear line is drawn between the position I take and the TERF (trans-exclusionary radical feminist), or the preferred term 'gender critical', for whom the problem is the 'male' and by this they mean those endowed with penises. According to this mode of reasoning, which conveniently erases those who are intersex, a trans woman is neither a woman nor female and in disguise have the licence to occupy hard fought 'women's spaces' where sanctuary is found from predatory men, making them enemy number one.

As someone who has spent the best part of my life trying to be a man, I inevitably bear symptoms of the disorder. To this day I still feel

uneasy about expressing affection. I'm still competitive – even thrive on competition. But if at an earlier age I were to have opened up to family and friends about my desire to wear feminine things, habits would've been broken, and connections established that would've likely enriched relationships with people I became estranged from. I know this because this is precisely how being a trans woman has affected me. Transgender kids should not be subjected to my fate. We ought in fact to welcome their transgressions; to aid and abet them. I'm, however, making up for lost time. And now as a woman I'm afforded a new perspective on my past and the society that I once viewed from the perspective of a man. Today male friends tend to be less guarded and, perhaps no longer measuring up to me, more relaxed in my company. I affect a change in them and, as with many women, they in turn affect a change in me. If my psyche is nevertheless irreparably 'damaged', like a chair creaking under the strain of repeated use, it is now being handled with greater care and that will prevent it from breaking. The praxis works for me. It can work for others too.

I write then from the standpoint of a (trans) woman, who was born and raised in a working-class family to become a man. The signifiers 'woman' and 'she' are self-consciously adopted in part because of the dialectical implications of the problem I diagnose and the aforementioned asymmetries of the so-called gender binary theorized. I cannot speak for all trans women or for that matter those raised as male. Trans women are as different from one another as any other person is. We come from different backgrounds, have different ideological and political perspectives, experience being transgender, and interpret our feelings, in many different ways. What I would however say is this: regardless of how we are sexed and how we identify ourselves, everyone has a perspective on gender and experience of being gendered but those who are transgender and have undergone a transition have a unique perspective on what it means to live (and be identified) both as a man and as a woman. We do not only theorize gender, we encounter both viscerally and self-consciously in our daily lives the subtle and sometimes profound differences in how people relate to you according to your gender presentation. However many books they have read or documentaries they have seen, a cisgender man or woman does not get to sense these contrasting effects nor how they affect you and your perspective on the self and others. Liberated from the pressures to perform masculinity, more than as a man as society perceived them, by living as a woman trans women gain a deeper insight into the sickness they were infected with and how debilitating it was in retrospect. I could not have written this book had I never come out as trans, not even in the two years writing my first book about presenting openly as a woman, *Man-Made Woman* (2017). What I write is in part informed by the perspective living as a woman for over five years has afforded me.

The term 'trans' is misleading. Adding the 'trans' prefix to man or woman suggests that we're not simply men or women, that we're something apart and that we're transitioning between genders. Stryker, Currah and Moore (2008: 11) suggest adding a hyphen to the word 'trans', making 'trans-', to denote that gender is not a destination but rather a becoming, not a 'transition' as such. Recalling de Beauvoir (2015), who famously stated that one is not born a woman but becomes one, are we not, however, all 'trans' in this sense? In molecular biology 'trans' refers to the other side of 'cis'. What I am suggesting here is that as gender is imposed on all of us, all those who are gendered are in a sense gender dysphoric (a term I oppose as a medical description). Trans people know it. Cis people tend to disavow it. There is a general dysphoria that as a society we need to address. But if I am not adding the hyphen here, it is not out of disagreement with Stryker and co. It's more about stressing the distinctive perspective being/becoming trans- affords, and not being afraid to describe what one sees. But if I'm to be honest, I don't particularly care for these labels. My main reason for identifying as transgender is because I have to identify as something. Better in my view to affirm this label as it registers a position of solidarity with people who are discriminated against. It can, as Feinberg (1996) averred, serve a political purpose (if aligned materially to struggles against capitalism, patriarchy, white supremacy and so forth). It is also a means of survival.

Miles Davis teaches how to do theory

In my 'discipline' of sociology, people balk at the idea of making reductive/totalizing claims about society. They say that society is far too complex to be talked about in general terms. No doubt they'd be saying the same about my description of the masculine disorder. The invocation of 'complexity', however, often functions as an ideological veil to avoid making critical interventions and taking sides. Those who reject the idea that society can be described and analysed as a totality wouldn't think twice about using a map to negotiate a geographical space even though the map is a crude representation of that space. Fredric Jameson (in Nelson and Grossberg, 1990) makes this very point when arguing for an equivalent 'cognitive mapping' of society. The mapping work is essential he says to a socialist project. This is what this book aims to do. It aims to map the masculine disorder and in doing so develop propositions on how it might be overcome. It also does something along the lines of avant-garde jazz. It experiments with theories and concepts to make them dance to my tune and serve the purpose of analysing, explaining and discovering ways to overcome the disorder.

This brings me to a wonderful anecdote about the jazz legend Herbie Hancock, when, back in the 1960s and barely out of his teens, he jammed with an even bigger legend, Miles Davis. In awe of Davis, Hancock describes his horror when he hit the 'wrong' note, his hands frozen over the keyboard. Anticipating Davis's wrath and fearing that his reputation by now in the latter's eyes is shredded, Davis coolly changes the key by blowing a note that suggests what in Hancock's mind was a mistake was, much to the latter's relief, an intentional part of the overall composition. Retroactively, it ceases to be an error and instead signals a new and interesting sonic. While 'errors' may not be intentional, taking a cool perspective, bringing seemingly incompatible theorists together in a kind of syncopated fusion does at times give rise to new and interesting sonics that vitalize the composition and break otherwise intractable theoretical deadlocks. The theorists I draw on do not neatly align, and with shifts in their own thinking that at different stages in the book map variously to my own, there's a certain 'art' to my engagement.

The chapters do, however, trace a coherent line. It begins in the most obvious of places with how in the book I am conceptualizing masculinity and defining it as a disorder. Chapter 2, 'Who's ur daddy', begins with masculine entitlement and the pressures to live up to masculine ideals. Through Freud and Lacan, I describe masculinity in libidinal terms but also, beyond their ideas, in sociological terms corresponding to the notion of gender. Chapter 3, 'Toxicity index', maps all masculinities across a schematic that at one pole is signified by the most extreme, brittle and sociopathic of masculinities and at the other the most flexible, open and experimental of masculinities. Between these poles I situate the masculine norm and ideals that, reminiscent of Connell's 'hegemonic masculinity', vary in time and place. The ideal is calibrated by the push and pull of these opposing poles and which I call a calibrated masculinity. Chapter 4, 'Vectors of androcentrism', traces the disorder back to early colonization and the witch hunts. Here I describe precisely why capitalism needs a mutilated ego to serve its interests. The vectors in question are what I refer to as four interconnected labours: waged labour; consuming labour; repressive labour such as police work; and reproductive labour, primarily the reproduction of the disorder. Reflecting on my own relationship to masculinity and experiences of presenting openly as a woman, chapter 5, 'Queervestism', fleshes out the idea of a feminine praxis. It does so through perhaps the most maligned of transgender subjects: the figure of the transvestite for whom the interest in presenting as a woman is, as deployed here, libidinally motivated. Sometimes described as a pervert, it is through this figure that I queer social norms. The last chapter, 'Obsolescent empire', draws the complex array of arguments and concepts of each chapter together to make the overall case for why, riffing on something that Marx once said but here with a Freudian twist, femininity is the riddle of a masculine disorder solved, and it knows itself to be this solution.

With this I think we're now ready to blow our horn and put this sorry state of affairs to rights.

2

Who's ur daddy?

'**W**iz' Khalifa thinks it's gay to eat bananas whole. 'You gotta break it in pieces bro,' he advises.[1] A phallus is confused with a penis and it's easy to see why. Glass towers probe our city skylines. Billboard ads feature women with mouths wrapped around Magnum ice-creams. Society has deified the male sex organ. But not in its limp pathetic state. Tall, hard, erect, if ever the ideals the phallus is associated with are achieved, those achievements are fleeting at best. All manner of catastrophes issue from these failings. 'Male privilege' is a trap, writes Bourdieu (2001: 29). It 'has its negative side in the permanent tension and contention, sometimes verging on the absurd, imposed on every man by the duty to assert his manliness in all circumstances'. This chapter is about daddy issues. It's about masculine entitlement and the fear, redolent in the general repudiation of femininity, of castration.

The need for men to assert their virility is well documented. It is documented in all those stories of conquest and domination. Directed by Alan Clarke, *Scum* is set in an English borstal (a detention centre for adolescent boys). Played by Ray Winstone, Carlin is the new kid on the block, bullied by fellow inmate nicknamed the 'Daddy'. The latter's reign comes to an end when Carlin rams his head hard onto a ceramic sink and pronounces 'I'm the Daddy now!' The father has a special place in the masculine psyche. He comes under various names and titles, entitlements – and the pressure to justify them. To own the name is to be the daddy and therefore worthy of the title. 'You dis my name?' roars Marlow, the ruthless drug dealer from the TV series *The Wire*, when, finally behind bars, another mocks him. Assured of his notoriety, he stands proud in prison. But being deprived of a name is capital punishment. To dis a man's name is not only to question whatever a man feels himself the equal to. It questions the value of the entitlement itself and thereby all the efforts to prove oneself worthy of it. It is to deprive a man of his very subjectivity. However, perhaps the best and most telling fictional example of the general disorder, and of the tragic consequences of men's need for recognition, is Walter White, played by Brain Cranston, from the superlative television series *Breaking Bad*.

White is the archetypical middle-class, white American husband and a father whose job as a chemistry teacher pays for the family's suburban lifestyle. It all goes awry when he is diagnosed with terminal cancer and cannot afford treatment. A wealthy former business partner steps in and offers to pay for it but White finds the idea of accepting charity humiliating, especially from someone he holds a grudge against. His family insists on treatment for the cancer which, unbeknownst to them, he pays for through a criminal enterprise. Everything he does, he tells himself, is for the family. Everything is to preserve the family name. In other words, his own ego.

An opportunity for a new career arises when White encounters a former pupil and now a meth head and dealer, Jesse Pinkman, played by Aaron Paul. White uses his chemistry skills to cook the purest form of methamphetamine and uses Pinkman's drug connections to distribute it. Becoming an instant hit with junkies, White soon attracts the attention of the big players. But for obvious reasons unable to disclose his actual name, White adopts the moniker Heisenberg. It soon acquires a legendary status. The trouble for White, though, is that those who are closest to him know nothing of this. They think he's getting the money from his son's charity crowd-funding scheme. His brother-in-law, a cop obsessed with the figure Heisenberg, is oblivious to White's alter-ego and regularly puts him down in front of his son. Whatever the consequences, it was obvious from early in the series that sooner or later White would put them all straight and tell them who Heisenberg really is. There are several 'I'm the Daddy' moments, the most memorable of which is when White dispatches ruthless drug lord Gus Fring and meets with a rival in the desert to do a drug trade. The dialogue is worth repeating:

Dealer   'Who the hell are ya?'

White name.'   'You all know. You all know exactly who I am. Say my name.'

Dealer   'Do what? I don't have a damn clue really who you are.'

White Fring.'   'Yeah you do. I'm the cook. I'm the man who killed Gus Fring.'

Dealer   'Bullshit. Cartel got Fring.'

White   'You sure? That's right. Now, say my name.'

Dealer   'You're Heisenberg.'

White   'You're god damn right.'[2]

There are many examples that can be drawn from real life. Such as the 2014 Isla Vista murder spree. Elliot Rodger killed six people and injured fourteen. Prior to committing his crimes, he declared, 'I'll take great pleasure in slaughtering all of you. You will finally see that I am, in truth, the superior one, the true alpha male.' But White is not an Incel (involuntary celibate). He's the respectable white suburban family man whose values are, by American standards, liberal. It's only when tested that White reveals all the worst symptoms of the masculine disorder. It's only then that it becomes apparent that beneath the veneer of suburban decency, wannabe-Alpha-male monsters lurk. The real-life Heisenbergs make the headlines. It's the suburban Whites who are more reflective of the generic problem with men. While I intend no equivalence with the Holocaust, it recalls something Primo Levi once said. 'Monsters exist, but they are too few to be truly dangerous; ordinary men are more dangerous.'

Although Freud never described masculinity as a disorder, one can certainly infer one from his description of Oedipalization and the castration complex. In the following sections of this chapter, I first discuss the place of the father in the masculine and feminine psyche. Terms like castration are useful in my view as descriptions of symbolic positions that males and females occupy in patriarchy. For Lacan, castration is nothing physical, but an effect of language that relates to concepts such as the real and desire. More importantly, the way that

I conceptualize masculinity as a libidinal orientation is how Lacan differentiates between what he calls masculine and feminine sexuality. 'Castration' and 'phallus' are intimately related. But it's through the more sociological descriptions of masculinity that masculinity as a gendered position is derived. I'll be connecting Connell's concept of 'hegemonic masculinity' to the libidinal and the sociological to question precisely what – the daddy of daddies – in today's society represents a masculine ideal.

Death becomes him

Hollywood cinema has perfected the Oedipal formula. Act one: emasculation. Act two: heroism. Act three: triumph. Drug lords, terrorists, sharks, Nazis, alien invasions: the superego enemy is interchangeable. It's been said before but worth saying again, Spielberg works exactly to this formula. In *Duel* the superego is a truck; in *Jaws* a shark, *Schindler's List*, Nazis; and *War of the Worlds*, Martians. In these narratives the father is killed, or in *Schindler's List* wrong-footed, and the protagonist (son) takes his place or becomes the hero. The popularity of the trope in cinema and video games reflects the magnitude of the disorder and its global coverage. It gives the male what is impossible for them to achieve in their alienated life. Walter White's superego adversary was drug lord Gus Fring. Crystal and cash were his phallus. But Heisenberg was only ever a name. Nothing more. Flesh and blood fathers are always eventually found out. Just as White was. But the Real father can never be found out. He's the mythical exception, writes Lacan (1993), that establishes the masculine rule. The Real father is the dead father. Dead fathers are answerable to nobody. They are above the law and, like God, set a standard that no mortal being can match.

The superego authority makes demands that are impossible to satisfy. The star of track and field who breaks the record knows that the record they have broken can also be broken too. And this is the point with the superego. Every demand to be a man fails because the ideal is impossible to embody or maintain. However successful a man is in his attempts to represent a masculine ideal, there is always another waiting in the wings to challenge him and show him up.

Hence, every success is born of failure and every failure born of success. It's a mug's game, so why do men, and some women, play it? Why are they unable to come to terms with their mortal, vulnerable – in a manner of speaking, castrated – condition?

Our libido has no object at birth. In other words, it is not genitally focused and therefore is not primarily heterosexual. There is no intrinsic masculinity or femininity either. This raises a question. If, as Freud (2011) thought, human sexuality is 'polymorphous-perverse' or multidirectional, then what happens in childhood that makes people heterosexual? Why this tendency when there is nothing natural to it? Freud begins with the first object of the child's love: the mother or equivalent who initially satisfies their needs. But then the father enters the scene. Like the shark in *Jaws* and the Martians in *War of the Worlds*, the father is a metonym for society, a force more powerful than us that stands as an obstacle to the object of desire and which threatens to punish us. The first object of love is abandoned to society. To make up for this loss, the male develops a heterosexual need for a mother substitute. But as females are also dependent on the mother in their formative years, why is there no tendency towards lesbianism in them? For this reason, Freud (1989) considered femininity a 'riddle'.

It's no doubt true that Freud's theories were influenced by the conservatism of Viennese society at the turn of the twentieth century and the middle-class women who sought his counsel. The applicability of Freud's theories lies in the flexibility of the terms. As with Lacan who wrote of the many 'names of the father', the paternal or superego authority does not have to be a literal father. The mother of a single-parent household, the teacher or even the hero in the fictional movie can function as a moral barometer and socializing authority. Freud is clear then about one thing. Anatomy is not destiny. Anatomy is key nonetheless to how the castration complex plays out and why the process of Oedipalization tends to differ between males and females. Those in patriarchal society who occupy more dominant and respected roles tend to have characteristics and dress in ways consistent with ideas of masculinity, ideas which are imposed on those with a male anatomy. The boy is raised to see himself as the heir to a largesse those in the image of a father have and also to prove himself worthy of it. The problem is that the ideals he is under pressure to embody can never be attained, but upon coming of age he can at least act as if they have been and thereby represent the paternal authority himself. This, of course, makes him vulnerable to being exposed as unworthy of the father's name and thereby emasculated like the mother. The fear of castration is the fear of the feminine which he guards against by aping the paternal rival. The masculine disorder is a hereditary sickness, not of biology but instead of the desires and demands of those who pre-exist us.

Act one then is castration. It is the paradigmatic moment when, in video game mythology, Bowser captures Princess Peach. This castrating moment is the universal condition of being subjects of society, as Lacan says of language. In other words, for Lacan it is the inconsistencies and inadequacies of language that set us on a metonymic quest for a compensatory phallus. The phallus functions as a symbolic suture of this castrated condition, a kind of crutch even with which to stand tall. According to Freud, the Oedipal process comes to an end for the boy when he comes of age and occupies the paternal position. There's no such closure for the female. The father is a rival too but unlike the boy who's endowed with the same sex organ, what her clitoris signifies is clearly inferior both to the boy and the father. She has no choice other than to give up any claim to the father's largesse. Accepting her subordinated position, she seeks protection and a penis of her own in the form of a baby, preferably a boy, and depends on and demands a paternal authority. Males compete with other males to represent the daddy. The female demands one. As her man is never adequate for the paternal ideal, as in the relationship between Diana and Charles, she functions as his prop or missing phallus.

Anatomy is clothed by styles of dress and activities. The relative positions of men and women under patriarchy can be read through anatomy, but anatomy does not in itself determine anything. In other words, it is not that the female sex organ is 'inferior', but that inferiority is presumed on the basis of how signifiers and signifying practices are mapped on anatomy. This is worth bearing in mind when Freud laments:

> At no other point in one's analytic work does one suffer more from an oppressive feeling that all one's repeated efforts have been in

vain, and from a suspicion that one has been 'preaching to the winds', than when one is trying to persuade a woman to abandon her wish for a penis on the ground of its being unrealisable or when one is seeking to convince a man that a passive attitude to men does not always signify castration and that it is indispensable in many relationships in life.

Quoted in GLOCER and ABELIN-SAS ROSE 2010: 97

Freud's theory is not androcentric. Nor is it one that develops in any detail a critique of androcentrism. But he puts in place foundation stones for such a critique. Far from suggesting that we abandon ourselves to our relative positions in patriarchy, what Freud appears to be saying is that our psychological problems arise from it. The repudiation of femininity in both men and women is the principal obstacle to the successful completion of therapy. On the basis that they are womanly and thereby a sign of weakness, it causes men to kill off emotions that are essential to wellbeing. Identifying themselves as inferior because of their femininity, it leads women to become dependent on men and be hamstrung by a need for a baby as some form of phallic compensation. Demanding a patriarch to care for her, it draws her into a compact with patriarchy. She also makes herself up to masquerade as his inferior. The effect of the repudiation of femininity is thereby doubled. Men feel the need to assert themselves as the superior one and women the need both to aid men in their delusions of grandeur while at the same time goading them into being stronger. Patriarchal forms of domination are unwittingly reproduced because neither men nor women are able to find ways to positively affirm the feminine.

Without naming it as such, in this remarkable admission, Freud not only diagnoses the masculine disorder, but also identifies it as a disorder of society itself. He explains how it arises and how it passes down through the generations. Freud's lack of explicit articulation of this parallel to the societal level is due to his failure to historicize the condition and thereby recognize it as contingent on the patriarchal structures of an historically locatable reality principle. Had he focused his critique on the society we are raised in and the superego demands placed upon us, he may well have concluded that for the subject to be reconciled with the feminine, a radical transformation of those structures would be required. A therapy that succeeds not on the couch but via the barricades. Femininity is the antidote to the masculine disorder. Marx's contribution, discussed in chapter 4, is in explaining why the antidote will not be made universally available under capitalism.

Today the paternal authority is just as likely to be a celebrity as it is a parent. Invoking the image of a child who without a critical filter watches television, Adorno and Horkheimer (1997) pointed out as far back as the 1940s that Oedipalization is no longer strictly a family affair. It raises the question, then. If today, in figures ranging from Bond to Black Panther, Drake to David Beckham, billions of children are exposed to the same masculine ideals, despite society's presumed cultural diversity, is the human subject becoming more homogenized? There is certainly a universalization of Westernized masculine ideals that children around the world are taking their cues from.

Amongst his many gifts to us, Freud offers an explanation for the masculine sense of entitlement and its crippling effects. He offers an explanation for why, to this day, it is rare for men to adopt feminine styles and mannerisms. He offers an explanation for why it is always men who commit school massacres and (nearly always) acts of police brutality. He also offers an explanation as to why women frequently position themselves in the role of the supporting cast who demand from their leads performances that are beyond their ham acting abilities. Freud touches on all these things without essentializing biology or clutching at the proverbial straws of different levels of testosterone, chromosomes or whatever. Psychoanalytical theory explains the masculine disorder and hints at the possibility of an antidote. Whatever pathologies of the individual it observes, the pathologies of the society into which the individual is born must, however, be kept in view. My job here is to ensure this is the case.

At the end of chapter 3 I take castration theory on a journey through Lacan's theory of sexuation which is only touched on here. The distinction he makes between masculine and feminine sexuality is useful for my argument. Much of this is foregrounded in my analysis of masculinity in this and the next chapter. Consequently, the more obscure details underpinning the theory will make more sense located towards the end of chapter three.

Now I want to return to the masculine ideals that boys and men try and fail to live up to: the daddy of daddies. More specifically I want to consider ideals that Raewyn Connell has described as hegemonic.

Dividends for disorder

Passing down through the male line from the early stages of empire, the masculine disorder is our Oedipal inheritance. Conditioned by fear of the feminine, men marshal every possible means to destroy evidence of their castration. The male tragedy is to have mistaken their penis for a phallus; their misfortune to have been born in a society that has made a totem of their member. It is a sick society that privileges the masculine gender but a sickness that is man itself. Males get worst grades at school. They're more like to take their own life: 76 per cent of all suicides according to Men's Health Forum. They make up 87 per cent of rough sleepers.[3] They are in the vast majority of cases the perpetrators of domestic violence.

Masculinity, Connell and Messerschmidt (2005: 836) write, is accomplished 'in social action'. Masculinities are contextually situated 'configurations of practice'. Masculinity is not a thing but an empty signifier, the meaning of which can loosely be derived from the values, behaviours, activities and aesthetic choices that are typically associated with the word. Connell writes about *masculinities* in the plural because, as she points out, there are considerable variations between men, especially regarding the different ways that class, race and sexuality intersect. What she coined 'hegemonic masculinity' (Connell: 2005) is not, she stresses, a statistical norm but normative in the sense of an ideal type against which boys and men judge themselves and others. What is this ideal? How do we know that it's hegemonic?

Hegemonic masculinity, says Connell (2005), commands the greatest respect from boys and men. Amongst the traits she lists are aggression, status investment, entitlement and difficulty in expressing emotions. Such men are hostile to those considered weaker, different, gay or effeminate. They are often sexist, misogynistic and most of all homophobic. But are men really aspiring towards those who are the most brazenly misogynistic and homophobic? Do men see honour in bullying?

Black Americans are often in the position of what Connell (2005) calls marginal masculinities. Their resources in competing with white hegemonic boys and men are more limited, but they still aspire to the same ideals. Complicit masculinities, on the other hand, may not strongly position themselves as dominant but clearly derive dividends from hegemonic men and are also supported by heterosexual women. Connell finally refers to what she calls subordinate masculinities. These are the boys and men who are bullied and marginalized due, for example, to their homosexuality. What I propose is that homosexuality as such is not the problem for a masculinized ego but what historically it has intimated: femininity.

Homophobia appears most pronounced in schools, sport and various other gender-segregated institutions such as the police and military. The problem, however, is not so much with homosexuality but that homosexuality has historically been linked with unmanliness. Writing about gang rape, Karen Franklin (2004) recalls the grim incident at Mepham High School in Long Island, New York, in which a group of upper-class football players subjected a number of younger players to systematic sexual abuse and humiliation. Three in particular endured the worst, including the shoving of billiard balls up their anuses with sticks. Franklin suggests that with these phallic instruments, feminization was forced onto the victims. It was not, in other words, a homosexual act. Feminization was the means through which the perpetrators aimed to humiliate. Whether it is a phallus or a penis, the device achieves the same end, serving, in the words of one author, 'as a concrete symbol of masculine social power and dominance' (Sanday, 1990: 10). In an age when gay men often embody hypermasculine ideals, the idea that masculinization is born out of a fear of homosexuality is increasingly tenuous. In any event, it is not the act in itself that humiliates but whether the act is interpreted as feminine and thereby emasculating. If homosexuality is now largely accommodated in the most Westernized of societies, it is because the successful appropriation of masculinity by gay men has broken the connection. Homophobia is a metonym of misogyny and in turn a fear of the castrating effects of feminization.

In their 2005 article that reflects on criticisms of the concept, Connell and Messerschmidt (2005: 832) describe 'hegemonic masculinity' as representing 'the currently most honoured way of being a man, it required all other men to position themselves in relation to it, and it ideologically legitimated the global subordination of women to men'. The concept has clearly gained traction. This can be explained by the simplicity and elegance of the term but also because there are problems with the concept itself and the presuppositions underlying it. The problems offer a productive space in which scholars can innovate, which is in effect what I'm doing here.

Anderson (2009), for example, notes the rise of 'inclusive masculinities' that challenge institutionalized forms of gender inequality and intolerance of different sexualities. Rather than forming hierarchies based on exclusion, the mostly white and heterosexual young men of Anderson's study were inclusive and non-hierarchical in their interpersonal relationships. Masculinities, he suggests, are becoming less monolithic and, in accordance with Connell and Messerschmidt's (2005) description, more 'hybrid' in their masculinity. The problem with this analysis, as others, such as Demetriou (2001) and Messner (2007), suggest, is that appearance belies practice. Toughness and tenderness combine in what Messner (2007) calls an 'ascendant hybrid masculinity'. Giving the example of Arnold Schwarzenegger, such displays serve to veil the patriarchal structures of inequality and strengthen the position of men under pressure to appear tolerant and inclusive. There is a 'dialectical pragmatism', Demetriou writes, in how hegemonic masculinities incorporate aspects of 'otherness' to reinforce their status. In these various respects, and as Messerschmidt (2010) observed in presidential figures such as George W. Bush, feminine traits such as empathy and compassion are appropriated to manipulate opinion, diffuse critique and obscure structural inequalities.

Acknowledging class and racial intersections on top of the pressures that males are under to measure up to masculine ideals, critics of masculinity tend nevertheless to default to the idea that men enjoy, as Connell (2005: 79) puts it, a 'patriarchal dividend' at the expense of women. It is the notion of a 'dividend' that I take issue with. While I don't think this will be lost on Connell, there are as already explained many disadvantages, including psychological, in being a man. Moreover, there are too many variations between men in respect of class, race and so forth that, if not stressed, establishes a false dichotomy between men and woman either as dominant or subordinate. This is not to suggest that men do not typically hold positions of authority over women, earn higher wages or commit acts of violence against them. All things considered, however, men no more benefit from patriarchy than a worker with a handful of shares in the company that exploits them benefits from capitalism. They are still, in sum, losers who are psychically damaged. The winners of the capitalist patriarchy are clearly not women either. The primary division that determines who the net beneficiaries are is class. Hence, why it is important when describing patriarchy to stress, first and foremost, its capitalist dimension.

The dividends are accrued, Connell (2005: 82) goes on to claim, 'in terms of honour, prestige and the right to command', through which a material dividend is secured. But honour on whose terms? Prestige in relation to what? And who exactly feels they have a right to command? Men of a certain class and education may well feel they have a 'right to command', but the problem of masculine entitlement that Freud traces through Oedipalization operates at the level of the unconscious and is just as likely to be disavowed at the conscious level. Is Connell, then, referring to ideas that men consciously identify with or how the unconscious is aligned with phallic signifiers that the capitalist patriarchy valorizes? While we both perhaps value different ideals, the way in which we are psychologically staked to them may nonetheless be reinforcing the conditions we are critical of.

The popularity of 'Battle Royale' games such as *Fortnite* is evidence that pleasure can be derived from simulated acts of violence. As with the Hollywood Oedipal formulas, they are a virtual form of the death drive in which castration or loss is staged, the phallus recovered and cathexis afforded. They are visual manifestations of how unconsciously the ego is libidinally oriented but, despite the popularity of narratives that glorify American power, the ideological content does not straightforwardly reflect actual values and beliefs. As a player of video games, the pleasure in killing the virtual avatar of my friend in *Titanfall 2* is always greater than when killing the computer-controlled 'grunt'. However symptomatic of our masculinization, I don't think either of us would derive pleasure or whoop in delight if a calamity had befallen either of us in real life. My point being is that if, as Connell claims, we are talking about ideals that are consciously strived for and bragged about, this is different from the unconscious dimension of masculinized sexuality theorized by Freud and later Lacan. Sometimes they do align. But as I have suggested in respect of the games I play with my friend, there is often a disconnect between what enjoyment is derived from and what is represented. One can sense arousal when a woman is put in her place, but still nonetheless be repulsed by idea that one was aroused. The disorder can be detected in our feelings and responses to winning or losing, but are not necessarily reflective of attitudes and aspirations. Connell's theory accounts for the unconscious dimensions of masculinity. The question for me is whether the ideal types that males consciously strive for are so palpably negative. How hegemonic masculinity is conceived has implications for how the problem and its negation is conceived too.

All that glitters is not gold

The term hegemony is commonly associated with the Italian Marxist and Communist Party leader Antonio Gramsci, who was imprisoned under Mussolini. Hegemonic ideology reflects the interest of a dominant class and therefore relates to the capitalist economy. As per Gramsci, the term does not neatly align with appropriations that do not stress the class or economic dimension. It is not through force, however, that the ideology derives its efficacy, but rather through consent. The ideology appears to reflect self-interest. The United States is typically described as a 'hegemonic' power that is legitimated through the consent of its allies. Together they form the 'international community' and in the name of 'freedom', 'democracy' and 'human rights' impose a 'world order'. These values do not reflect reality, but they do reflect how allied states like to see themselves and want others to see them. There is honour in this, but not in bragging about how many people your military has murdered.

Trump is an interesting figure in this regard. As he himself makes clear, he does not represent the hegemonic ideology, which according to him is represented by the 'metropolitan elites' who he claims wield considerable media influence. Likewise, the 'cultural Marxists' (a pejorative and misconceived term favoured by Jordan Peterson) who act conspiratorially to undermine traditional American values. Trump's position is counter-hegemonic but also closer to the truth of American power which it crudely lays bare. He also shamelessly expresses what most men would disown and disavow in themselves, namely sexism, racism and misogyny. He represents masculinity in its most toxic, destructive, sociopathic and narcissistic form. While it would be wrong to suggest that this is the masculinity Connell has in mind when describing the hegemonic ideal, it aligns more closely with this representation than the one I want to suggest does reflect the ideal today.

Continuing with Trump, who after all did hold the highest of office and is therefore a symbol of power and authority, it is his principal rival and nemesis Barak Obama who, despite being black, is the closest embodiment of hegemonic masculinity in the current ideological constellation. It's the ideal that Trump obsessively compares himself to and, unable to compete, constantly puts down. The qualities that Obama embodies are those which can be considered the most honourable and which are held in the greatest esteem. It is the man who is respectful towards others who are different from himself, who welcomes cultural diversity, prides himself on his education and cultural sophistication, is articulate and sensitive and is comfortable displaying affection. He regards women his equal and, if asked, would describe himself a proponent of LGBTQI+ rights. It is a masculinity whose feminine veneer obscures the disorder and legitimates androcentrism. He represents the best of men but is best good enough?

Just as there can be no masculine without a feminine against which to distinguish itself, there cannot be a hegemonic masculinity without its opposing one. In a phoney cultural war, Trump is the emblem of the religious and white supremacist right-wing defending 'traditional' American values against 'woke' 'left-wing' Democrats for whom Obama is emblematic. It is a struggle for cultural hegemony that, however much the far right appears to be in the ascendency, is, from the broader perspective of America's traditional allies, nevertheless an aberration.

We have all encountered bullies, racists and misogynists. Many of us, including myself, work at institutions dominated by privileged white men in which self-interest does indeed pay dividends. The

#MeToo movement did not expose anything we did not already know about men or how they prey on, bully and manipulate those they have institutional power over. In reality, nothing changed when men were called out. It had the effect nonetheless of reminding people of their complicity in turning a blind eye to such behaviour, quickly atoned for through a superficial joining in a chorus of condemnation. Ideology, as Žižek (1989) frequently reminds us, functions through disavowal. We can recognize that Trump has a weak ego and Obama is a war criminal but still hold them up as respective paragons of strength and virtue providing they themselves nor those in a position of authority do not point out the fiction and what really lies underneath it. When in response to a question from a shareholder about how their prices are so low, chief executive of the British high street chain Ratner's jewellers Gerhard Ratner stated the obvious by declaring the jewellery to be 'total crap'. The value of the firm plummeted by a staggering 500 per cent, bringing it close to collapse. Hegemonic masculinity operates according to this logic. Whoever occupies this position declares the other 'total crap'. This is the problem with the discourse on toxic masculinity. It registers that certain men have a problem with masculinity but not that masculinity is itself a disorder or that the critic himself bears many of its symptoms.

The economy, said Althusser (1994), is 'overdetermined' by a range of 'ideological state apparatuses' like that of the family, school and media. What in a particular moment constitutes a hegemonic masculinity is determined by a range of institutions and social 'influencers', in Gramsci's less jarring terminology 'organic intellectuals'. It cannot be discerned solely therefore by who is president. In discerning, therefore, what in any given moment represents the masculine ideal – the daddy of daddies – a constellation of forces must be taken into consideration. Althusser also refers to 'repressive state apparatuses' such as the military, police and prison that the most brutalized of men are recruited into. But whatever goes on inside of them, even these institutions advertise themselves as inclusive and humane. The repudiation of femininity that lies at the heart of the disorder is sustained by the superficial appropriations of femininity within these various apparatuses and by the organic intellectuals that comprise them. The likes of Obama are not only a more accurate reflection of the hegemonic ideal than the hard men and chauvinists who wear their masculinity on their sleeves – they also alert us to the problem in its more generic, disarming and deceptive form. This is the problem with the kind of hegemonic masculinity that Connell, here with Messerschmidt (2005: 853), does in fact support. It is one that would be 'open to equality with women' but unattainable in the present context. Being 'open to' is not the same as being 'in favour of' equality. Aside from being vague and unambitious, what's to say that this isn't already normative? This is why definitions matter.

In the next section, further examples are provided of what I am suggesting is in fact the hegemonic masculine ideal (in the next chapter I substitute in its place the concept of 'calibrated masculinity').

The best is not good enough

Men are full of bravado. They like to boast about their 'conquests', disavow homosexual desires and hide their frailties. This description would fit many of the men I have spent time with over the years. Men recognize when to serve their bigotries in jokes and when it is safe to serve them on a plate. My friends today are mostly university-educated. They don't fit Connell's description of hegemonic masculinity. Nor, with their liberal outlook and critical take on patriarchy, are they complicit from her point of view in silently reaping dividends from the power of hegemonic men. The educated class have a lot, in fact, to feel smug about. They can easily, and fairly, tell themselves apart from those who in the discourse on masculinities are usually singled out for critique. Rarely does the critic reflect on their own phallic investments in masculine domination. From a position of relative privilege, critique itself functions as a phallic suture of their afflictions. Through recourse to examples, I propose a different definition of what today constitutes the normative ideal. As in my description of friends above, casting normal men in a better light than Connell does, a more uncompromising perspective is ironically at the same time afforded.

Connell (2012: 14) qualifies that 'a pattern of masculinity may be hegemonic that does not mandate personal violence, but is systematically open to violence'. This could certainly be said of

Obama, who normalized drone warfare and presided over the disintegration of Libya. As one report notes, ten times as many people were killed on Obama's watch than that of the much-vilified George W. Bush.[4] An openness to violence can be documented in public figures but through which manner of procedure can such openness be observed in the average man?

When the ideal that men are supposed to be modelling themselves on is so evidently bad it should come as no surprise that the alternative is so patently modest. This is the case with Connell and to some extent even hooks (2004), who calls for an anti-patriarchal masculinity. Such men would be empathetic, emotionally expressive and supportive of women. This comes easier for a certain class of men, and however positive such qualities may be, they can never be universalized as long as the structural and unconscious dimensions of androcentrism persist. In the absence of any systematic attack on the apparatuses themselves, what this attitude does is simply cement the privileges of those, typically the white educated middle classes, who need not confront in themselves their own investments in androcentrism, which is either obscured or trivialized. As I have maintained, traits associated with masculinity are not necessarily in themselves negative. Aggression, as I later argue, can often be ethically motivated. The context, and what drives the aggression, is crucial.

In defence of aspects of masculinity, Connell evokes the 'participatory pleasures such as neighbourhood baseball' through to the hero stories from the Iliad and Twilight of the Gods, or the 'beauty in fields such as pure mathematics' (Connell, 2005: 233). Segal (2007: 242) approvingly restates Connell's position that far from being, in Connell's words, an 'impoverished character structure', masculinity is 'a richness, and plenitude'. I do not disagree with this. But I do take issue with the conflation of signifier (the action) and signified (gender) which, from reading their work, does not strike me as either Connell or Segal's intention. Some of the most heroic of people, for example, are trans women who daily brave a society that is hostile to them. Are they masculine? To declare the pursuit of scientific knowledge or the beauty of maths masculine risks reinforcing a fundamental misconception that males are better suited to these activities. Rather than defend masculinity on the basis that such activities and traits are positive ones, it is more salutary to an emancipatory procedure to resignify or degender them.

Connell (2005) states her opposition to what she describes the 'degendering' of masculinity. This refers to a debate amongst feminists about eliminating gender differences but which, as feminists in the late 1970s pointed out, would mean women becoming more like men. This is not what I am arguing. What instead I am proposing is the negation of the negation of the feminine in men but also women. It is the unconscious and conscious repudiation of femininity in which the problems with men resides. Rather than affirm what is positive in masculinity, the primary task is to remove the psychic and institutional shackles that contain and repress a repertoire of emotions vital to mental health and a well-functioning society. This is what I am proposing by a feminine praxis or negation of masculinity − not the essentializing of traits arbitrarily associated with the word femininity and the stifling of those that are indeed individually and socially enriching associated with the word masculinity, but rather the removal of those metaphorical shackles. Only in this way will the potential to experience life in the fullness of our capacities be realized. This corresponds more to the ideals propagated by people such as Mario Mieli (2018), who, as Connell notes, saw a liberation in the improvizational articulation of masculine and feminine signifiers and affects. Connell is sensitive, however, to the fact that men feel threatened by the questioning of masculinity. Thus the 'goal is not to abolish masculinity, as some right-wing commentators claim, but to create a hegemony for forms of masculinity that already exist in the lives of men' (Connell, 2012: 15). But the question that ought to be asked here is why do right-wing commentators make these claims? They are clearly in fear of something and maybe it is what they fear the most that needs to be affirmed. To stress the point again, to abolish masculinity is to remove the shackles on our personal and collective enrichment. Femininity functions as the supplement to masculinity, but it can also function in semiotic terms as a vanishing mediator. A key to unlock those shackles can, like the shackles themselves, be discarded once its purpose is served. The point of a feminine praxis is to free ourselves of the negative consequences of our gendering and thereby deprive these signifiers of their material and psychological effects.

In his *Hidden Persuaders*, Vince Packard (2007) describes a survey of housewives who were given the same laundry detergent in different colour containers. Those who received the detergent in a blue container thought the product ineffective; those in a yellow too powerful; and those in blue and yellow thought the liquid washed the whites just right. The lesson is that people base their purchasing decisions on irrational feelings, not on how the thing functions in reality. The invocation of environmental sustainability by oil companies works for the same reason.

It would be irrational to claim that oil extraction and the burning of fossil fuels does not cause environmental harm. We are likely to feel better, however, in filling our tank at a petrol station painted green than one featuring large murals of birds covered in oil. The green signifier registers the problem that neither the company nor consumer is in a position to do much about – but also the solution. Both company and consumer are guilty for the damage caused by the burning of fossil fuels but at least in recognizing that there is a problem they can both feel good about themselves. This is also the prospectus on which companies such as Gillette today criticize masculinity and various forms of bigotry. They acknowledge their contribution in manufacturing impossible ideals for men to live up to and present themselves as part of the solution to the toxic forms of masculinity that arise. Once upon a time performance anxieties were provoked through images of rugged white men conquering preternaturally beautiful women to sell a product. Now the product is sold on the prospectus that having bought into these sexist tropes the male is complicit in the subordination of women. It plays to and appropriates discourses on toxic masculinity and the #MeToo movement. The better man recognizes the problem and, in purchasing the newly branded product, demonstrates his openness to equality with women. Here, as elsewhere, the critique of masculinity turns feminism into a phallus, and a phallus, as we all know, is a masking effect. Coca-Cola, Gillette and Heineken have in various ways held a mirror to the consumer to show them who they are, the ideal-ego, and how they could ideally be, the ego-ideal. In buying Gillette you're buying the ego-ideal, the best a man can get. But let's start with Coke.

Discovering that men were put off buying Coke Light because of the feminine association with 'light', the Coca-Cola Company introduced Coke Zero. Packaged in a black can, words such as 'Bro', 'Wingman' and 'Legend' featured in their branding. None, as far as I know, are emblazoned 'Castrated', 'Insecure' or 'Hate Women, Love Coke!' But for all their misgivings about the adjective 'light', these days the Bros and Legends are more at ease in their gender and sexuality. Coca-Cola timed their pro-LGBTQI advertising campaign in Hungary to coincide with a popular music festival. The billboard ads featured smiling homonormative (self-satisfied, affluent, etc) gay people and couples and were accompanied by slogans such as 'zero sugar, zero prejudice'. Supporters of the nationalist Fidesz Party, which opposes same-sex marriage, took issue, and the deputy leader of the party, István Boldog, called for a boycott of the company. Effective in generating free publicity for the company, the Coke Zero campaign aimed to appeal to a new generation of consumers more open in their gender and sexual orientations and perhaps less likely to associate the brand with its support for right-wing death squads in Colombia who targeted and killed trade union leaders.[5] Coke is not suggesting that you are queer if you buy Coke. Queer is commodifiable because whether you identify as queer or not, those who drink it are comfortable with gender and sexual differences and therefore confident in their masculinity. As with 'feminism', 'queer' is likewise a phallic supplement.

Playing on their own famous slogan 'The best a man can get', razor brand Gillette confesses to the part they played in promoting a white, muscular and chauvinistic masculine ideal. It recalls a past complacency with sexism that, by extension, anyone purchasing its product was complicit in. They have moved on. The question is whether the consumer has. 'Is *this* the best a man can get?' Gillette asks. In asking the question they position themselves as agitators goading the bystander into joining the protest. The video clip they produced was widely shared on social media. Adding to its notoriety and proving its point, some men predictably reacted badly. However, the progressive press loved it (itself misleading, I deploy the term 'progressive' because of how the word 'liberal' has negatively been appropriated in the US by the right). With explicit references to the #MeToo movement, the clip depicts various examples of male aggression and behaviours considered masculine. The most striking image is a panning shot of men of different ethnicities lined up next to one another tending individually to their barbecue sets. It is a distinctly suburban image of average working-class men that those more educated and urban would comfortably be able to distance themselves from. More poignant still is a series of images of men looking at their reflection in the mirror, as if to ask of it whether, invoking Connell, they do indeed embody the most honourable way of being a man. A man can never be man enough nor can he ever atone enough for his guilt. But he can at least purchase a Gillette razor and shave that toxic masculinity clean off. It'll all grow back, of course; so, unless, like me, he gets it lasered and does away with the problem altogether, there will always be demand for the product and the palliative. The point, as this makes plain, is not to rid society of the problem, for that would require a transformation of the very conditions in which capitalism thrives. The point is to offer men a way to shore up their ego when masculinity is in the spotlight. That the actual razor being sold is in navy blue packaging and branded 'Power' underscores the tokenism of this move and why it is so easy for men to support it. Not even the best of men thinks twice about the choice of razor and why they wouldn't purchase for themselves the functionally identical Venus razor.

Man is interpellated masculine through the hard edges of the Power razor and affirmed as the best of men through Gillette's new marketing strategy. Power stands at variance with the curvaceous Venus razor for women, the Goddess of Love. On the one hand, the razor functions as a phallus, giving man the clean shave that brings him closer to the masculine ideal. On the other, in its Venus variant, it threatens castration. Gillette is the world's leading brand of men's razors, selling $6.2 billion worth in 2018.[6] But with their market share slipping, tapping into the zeitgeist, the new approach was an acknowledged attempt to extend sales to the more elusive 'generation Z' and 'millennials'. Does hope then lie in the rising generation? Not if these marketing strategies do their job. Perhaps when Power and Venus razors can be mocked by Gillette without it producing the 'Ratner' effect we may by then have turned a corner.

In the same vein as Coke and Gillette, Heineken rolled out its 'Open Your World' theme, in which bigots are forced into a dialogue with their nemesis, while Snickers satirized sexism by showing construction workers calling out to female pedestrians to talk about gender inequality. This is happening simultaneously with a counter-hegemonic narrative being constructed by the resurgent conservatives. It is a cultural war that critics of masculinity line up on the other side of, but which plays in the order of the hyper-real. The battleground is androcentrism, but the struggle is for the ego and its embellishment. However, if those on either side of this struggle are united on anything, it is in their shared admiration of James Bond. His antics plays to the narcissistic fantasies of every boss and would-be hero. He plays to those nostalgic for a time when Britannia ruled the waves and now also the progressive who wants a change of representation if not a change in the order itself.

The real man in the film *Goldeneye*, argues Halberstam (1998), is Bond's shadowy female boss, 'M'. Bond requires gadgets, fast cars, sexy women and so forth. But M has no need for such phallic props. She is in this sense the real embodiment of a masculine ideal. I'd put it differently. Were this the case she'd simply be the impossible exception that no man can measure up to. Instead, her more muted but nonetheless enunciated femininity is the perfect suture for the cold-hearted masculine instrumentality necessary for anyone working in the secret services. Such celebrated examples of 'strong women' are entirely in the masculine register. They are not the negation of men and masculinity, but rather a reinforcement of the idea that the noblest of traits are those that come easy to men, their strongest advocates. Like the mother in a household without a father, the female protagonist of the formulaic Hollywood Oedipal narrative is simply playing the man. The exchange is not entirely trivial though. For at least it provides girls with role models in how to be men – which in a society dominated by men is not necessarily a bad thing. M in *Goldeneye* is a more effective man and consistent with what I am suggesting is the hegemonic ideal because, comparable to Messner's (2007) take on Schwarzenegger, in its feminine drapery the most egregious of acts are veiled. Cis women are sometimes 'ascendant hybrid masculinities'. M portends the hegemonic masculinity that corporations like Gillette have helped and subsequently fashions what Daniel Craig's Bond in the film *Casino Royale* was eventually to embody.

Bond is larger than life, more than just a fiction. In Britain he is emblematic of empire, and whoever plays him must bear the weight of a myth by representing the very best of men. He must be virtuous, courageous, a man of conviction, have a passion for justice, be willing to sacrifice himself for the greater good, as well as being rugged, handsome, charming and open to being equal to women.

In *Casino Royale*, Bond, who this time was played by Daniel Craig, had all the usual gadgets. Only now they were no longer fit for purpose. The signature car chase ended abruptly with a crash. His customary wit escaped him. But most of all, the female lead had personality. As an object to love rather than an object to conquer for sex, she is lost forever at the end of the film when brutally murdered. She survives in his heart as the object cause of his desire for revenge, which is satisfied at the end of the more routine sequel, *Quantum of Solace*. Ultimately, she does function as a more traditional phallic prop who, while not as such rescued, by being avenged adds another notch to Bond's triumph-over-adversity belt. However, it's in *Casino Royale* that Bond proves himself a man for all people, the truly hegemonic masculine male who isn't sexist nor the self-satisfied arrogant and boastful womanizer his detractors liked to paint him as. He's the white Obama. Strong but not afraid to show his vulnerability, sophisticated and sensitive. He's still an agent of the capitalist state, but as always, violence is deployed in defence of liberal values, against rogue states, terrorist organizations and psychopathic billionaires.

The offscreen image parallels the onscreen one. Coinciding with International Women's Day and realizing a common fantasy amongst men, Craig features in a short clip wearing a blonde wig, make-up, a dress, sheer tights and heels. Judi Dench, who at the time played M in the Bond films, is heard asking 'For someone with such a fondness for women, I wonder if you've ever considered what it means to be one?'[7] A voice and nothing more, she is Bond's conscience. The reactionary *Daily Mail* was full of praise. Craig is not the exception. He is the calibrating device of a default masculinity I define at the start of the next chapter.

According to Halberstam (1998: 269), if masculinity was the default gender category, more young girls would be 'running around and playing sports . . . building things . . . and so on'. Furthermore, masculinity, she claims, is 'reserved for people with male bodies and has been actively denied to people with female bodies'. But whatever truth there is about games girls are encouraged to play, this misses the pivotal function of femininity as the disavowed structuring principle of the masculine. A girl who builds things 'and so on' acts in contradiction to a stereotypical femininity but not androcentrism. By contrast, all masculinities are defined by the relative degree to which the feminine is repulsed and phallic props consistent with a masculine ideal are relied on. If there is no equivalent spectrum of femininities, it is because femininity cannot be defined by a relative repulsion of the masculine and need of (feminine) phallic props, while in the context of patriarchy, ideals are by definition masculine and women do to an extent have to affect masculinity in order to compete and also defend themselves against predatory men. In the typology of masculine forms that I propose in the next chapter, the norm, default masculinity, is what I call avoidant / restrictive masculinities, the avoidant and restrictive incorporation of the feminine. Here also I drop the concept of 'hegemonic masculinity' and propose in its place the alternative 'calibrated masculinity'. My typology of masculinities is dialectically arranged to afford a way to conceptualize how, dynamically, meanings and behaviours change.

3

Toxicity index

Toxic masculinity is in vogue. The dividing lines are drawn. Piers Morgan, on the one hand, criticizes Daniel Craig for his unmanly behaviour – not for wearing a dress but carrying his baby daughter while shopping.[1] In their aptly named *The Care Manifesto* (2020), Chatzidakis and colleagues stress, on the other hand, how fundamental caring for one another is to a well-functioning society. Whether it is caring for a child or caring for the environment, to care is to be emasculated. As welfare provisions erode away, the impact of Covid-19 intensifies and the climate crisis becomes catastrophic, more than ever we will come to depend on one another for survival. It is not a question that men of toxic masculinity exist. But the focus on this kind of masculinity detracts from the more banal but nonetheless destructive impacts of this ego-formation. This chapter introduces a toxicity index that defines all masculinities in relation to the relative repudiation of femininity. Those at one extreme repudiate anything that even vaguely connotes femininity – caring for others being an example. At the other extreme are figures like Prince, who, by adopting a feminine aesthetic, reimagined masculinity as something altogether more joyous, expressive and colourful. This chapter is about monsters but also minnows, the Whites who would be Heisenbergs. Finally, it is here that I eschew the hegemonic masculinities concept altogether and replace it with the more conceptually robust (for my analysis at least) 'calibrated masculinity'.

The standard dictionary gives no clues on how to be a man, and the entry on masculinity raises as many questions as it answers. With no definitive answer to what it is, it is possible at least to say what it is not. The index of toxicity is discerned according to the relative degree to which femininity is repudiated and inadequacies overcompensated. These overcompensations can be anything from the purchase of sports cars through to a PhD and mass murder. On a continuum of masculinities, the most toxic have the most difficulty in reconciling themselves with the feminine and are most in need of the compensatory phallus to mask their fears and inadequacies; the most prone to violence when exposed as lacking. Recall, 'You dis my name?!' I call these reactive/aggravated masculinities (RAMS). At the other end of the continuum are reflective/experimental masculinities (REMS): those who are reflective and critical of their masculine gendering, and crucially, experiment with and adopt feminine modes of expression, be they stylistic or affective. This is precisely the sort of man or otherwise who might experiment with make-up and, short of fully adopting a feminine mode of being, put themselves out there in a way that those making gestures towards equality with women do not. To be clear, I am not suggesting that those who do this are necessarily any the less toxic than those who don't. It's more a question of how in their doing, they affect a gradual dissolution of the blockages to femininity that masculinization has erected and, testing the very concept of masculinity, do things that are in a given context considered unbecoming of men. It is not by wearing a dress that one necessarily stretches the meaning of masculinity. Everything in this respect is culturally and historically contingent. As with a feminine praxis, there are multiple ways, both individual and collective, to stretch the meaning of masculinity beyond its culturally determined limits and also thereby to negate the sickness.

Becoming increasingly prevalent amongst young people, avoidant/restrictive food intake disorder, or ARFID, is a recently diagnosed disorder linked to the consumption of junk food. As one expert says, 'The children resist, object or throw a tantrum, and the parents avoid that behaviour by giving them the diet they want . . . It's hard to get out of habits when they have been established.' Starved of nutrition, one teenager who would only eat 'chips, crisps, sausages, processed ham and white bread' even went blind.[2] Drawing from this concept of a disorder, it is possible to diagnose masculinity in a similar manner. Starved of femininity, avoidant/restrictive masculinities (ARMS) are the default of masculinities. ARMS are not the ideal types. They denote, instead, a continuum of masculinities that are sandwiched between two opposing poles: reactive/aggravated masculinities, or RAMS, and reflective/experimental masculinities, or REMS. The hegemonic ideals, the calibrated masculinity, of any given time and place fall within the ARMS continuum.

My point is that, in contrast to RAMS who hold to a rigid concept of masculinity, REMS stretch the definition of masculinity. RAMS and REMS are therefore at the two opposing extremes of a masculinities spectrum between which float the majority of men who are in what I call the avoidant/restrictive masculinities (ARMS) category, avoidant of femininity and restrictive in this respect. The two opposing poles function like the gravitational pull of the moon to drag the hegemonic ideals situated in between them one way or the other. RAMS and REMS are, relative to ARMS, the respective reactionary and progressive counter-hegemonic positions to which those ideals are calibrated. RAMS–ARMS–REMS. This is the formula for all masculinities.

As every masculinity drifts out of tune, at certain points ARMS require recalibration to be with the times, which they do so through recourse to a provisional calibrated ideal. Trump is exemplary of RAMS. Prince is exemplary of REMS. Obama is the exemplary calibrated masculinity today that the ARMS in between are pressurized to calibrate their masculinity to. But with RAMS in the ascendent, even the modest ideals that Obama represents are on the defensive in the current constellation. Thus, what at any given time constitutes this ideal is determined by the degree to which the tide moves one way towards RAMS or the other way towards REMS. The calibrated masculinity reflects the mores of the time. So, for example, while resistant and resentful towards the idea of addressing those who consider themselves non-binary 'they', under increasing pressure men (and also women) eventually fall into line and address people according to their preferred pronoun. The masculinized sex is not necessarily male. As masculinity is the dominant form, it follows that women will to lesser degrees likewise be pressured to recalibrate themselves to changing mores reflective of men. This is why it makes no sense to describe a calibrated femininity.

Hypothetically, a female could be socialized to develop the same complexes as those socialized to be men. However, their relationship to others in a society that is gendered according to sex would differ. Unlike the male, by experimenting with feminine signifiers and affects she would be conforming to social norms. The relationship of a trans man to masculinities also differs. Their rejection of femininity is a self-conscious affirmation of the positive aspects of masculinity their gendering has denied to them. In the existing conditions of the capitalist patriarchy in which all of us are raised and compelled to negotiate within, the formula is more useful to the mapping of the sexed male to masculinities. In qualified and more superficial ways, it could also, however, apply to those who are not unambiguously male, but I've leave this matter for another time.

RAMS, ARMS and REMS are all on the continuum and inclusive of all masculinities. REMS may appear more ambiguous in their gender and reject gender categories altogether but would not be mistaken for trans or considered to be cross-dressing. It would not be awkward for them to use changing rooms and toilets designated for males in the way it would be for a trans woman. They may identify as 'they', but if venturing a guess as to their preferred pronoun, people would likely err to 'he'. I'm sometimes addressed as 'Sir' or 'he' but much more frequently as 'Madam' or 'her'. While she is likely to bear symptoms of the disorder elders passed down to her, a trans woman removes the shackles of masculinity and, reconciled to the feminine, is open to a feminine mode of becoming. She is off the spectrum. Laverne Cox is one of many famous examples of this category. She negates masculinity and affirms the feminine, categorically embodying a rejection of the idea that anatomy is destiny.

Boundaries that delineate the masculine and feminine are blurred, but not to the extent that these terms are not descriptive of how gender is signified. Our lightning-quick ability to discern gender differences testifies to the relevance of these terms and the need to explain the degree to which the sex of a person can be predicted through them. Some of my physical features signify male. Judging by how people react to me, these are easily spotted. I embody a contradiction in terms: a dialectical unity of opposing genders that produces an uncanny effect. There is something about me that is 'not quite right', not normative and therefore a source of interest and fascination. My appearance affects a different dynamic between people that affords men, in particular, the opportunities to reflect on their gender. Sometimes this reveals a tenderness and vulnerability they may otherwise previously have hidden from me when I identified as a man. Masculinity and femininity can be visualized. The problem with non-binary and agender is that there is no equivalent third image in the Westernized imaginary by which this difference can neatly be delineated. Prince came close. It is possible to appear ambiguous, to be in the border zone, but impossible within the current symbolic constellation to inhabit a style and affect a way of being that cannot be referenced to masculinity or femininity. So, the question I first want to ask is when is a male not masculine and instead feminine? What, in other words, is the threshold that one has to pass in order to be considered ambiguous or trans and thereby off the masculinities spectrum altogether?

Masculinities and the capacity for veering towards the feminine are socially conditioned. Circumstance is everything. Deleuze and Guattari's (2003a and b) theory of the assemblage helps conceptualize the limitations and potentialities of the socially situated forms of masculinity I describe.

Tables and chairs

We can probably all agree that a typical table has four or more legs that support a flat surface perpendicular to the force of gravity, upon which you can rest objects such as plates. When does a table cease being a table? Is it when the surface is sloped and can no longer support objects? Would it be a table if the surface was square, the height of one's knees when standing and had a backplate raised above its surface to roughly the height of one's chest? Or am I now describing a chair? What is a chair capable of that a table isn't? How would your relationship to it change? This same procedure can be carried out when thinking about gender. What had to change before it was appropriate for me to use the women's lavatory instead of the men's? Or for people to address me as 'she', adapt their behaviour and relate differently to me? Was it necessary for me to dress openly in a conventional feminine style? What if the only difference from before was that I wore full colourful make-up? What if I only dressed as a woman on special occasions, as a stated 'sociological experiment', or 'just for fun'? Would I be a man in women's clothes? Would it be reasonable for people to insist that I am a man and use the men's lavatory instead? Was it necessary to construct a narrative about why my feminine presentation is more authentic to how I feel inside? Is familiarity with the discourse on transgender or exposure, even if only through the media, to people who define themselves as transgender a prerequisite for people like me being identified and accepted as a woman? Without familiarity with this category would people simply pass me off as a 'cross-dresser'? What if I was living in a country where people are more hostile to trans women such as the UK? Would I even have plucked up the courage to present openly?

Whether table or chair, masculine or feminine, these forms can be thought of as assemblages. Assemblages are composed of bodies, objects, languages, desires, histories and social relationships. It's not so much a question of what constitutes an assemblage but how we produce and enter into one and what is afforded by their form. Tables and chairs, for example, are the product of human labour and are utilized by humans. Assemblages are composed along with what Deleuze and Guattari call abstract machines. Capitalism is such a machine that connects with labour whose power, a force, it subtracts to make profit. Tables are produced for profit. There is a context and there is a subject of desire that has connected with objects that, like a machine, produces and utilizes the 'assemblage'. There would be no masculine assemblage, or any assemblage for that matter, without desire. Desire, as Deleuze and Guattari (2003b) see it, is affective. Affect here corresponds to force rather than emotion, a productive unconscious force or intensity, and stressing the productive, the unconscious they say is a factory.

Assemblages are also composed, according to Ian Buchanan (2020), along with Bodies without Organs (BwOs). This is an obscure term that Deleuze and Guattari adapt from Antonin Artaud, but which is useful in thinking about masculinities. To simplify, it concerns the capacity of the subject to enter into an assemblage – a working arrangement – and also exceed one. It is about making bodies that are not reducible, defined by or limited to organic capacities. These are not organs as such, but rather identities and the mode of subjectivity we are burdened with – including how through Oedipalization we are gendered according to anatomy. People are defined by anatomy and labelled 'man' or 'woman'. But we do not have to be reducible to these categories. We possess the capacity to exceed these definitions or rather what is imposed by them. This depends, though, on how invested we are in the assemblage itself. RAMS, it could be said, are heavily invested in the masculine assemblage, which is predicated on a highly prescriptive idea of masculinity and gender relations. Their BwOs is highly restricted and incapable of exceeding it. Their BwOs is a cancerous one that eats away at them. It blocks their becomings and, through their actions, deprives others of their vitality. The question, which is really what a feminine praxis is all about, is how do we make ourselves a Body without Organs adequate to the task of exceeding the limitations imposed on us or that we impose on ourselves and on others?

There are internal and external boundaries to every assemblage, Buchanan explains – boundaries, as he puts it, 'which cannot be crossed without becoming something different from what it was' (Buchanan, 2017: 468). If the surface of a table was sloped, for example, the assemblage would have exceeded its internal limits. By openly and consistently presenting as a woman I breach the internal limits of what representationally is considered masculine. But the external limits, relating to the socio-historical context in which the actions occur, are crucial. The implications, for example, of dressing as a woman in Aotearoa are of an entirely different order of magnitude to doing so in the United Arab Emirates.

In Aotearoa, for example, Maori people have invoked a taboo on sitting on tables. The conditions allowing for the use of the table for this purpose differ to that of the UK, where no such taboo is invoked. This again can be mapped to gender and the conditions that afford breaches of gender norms. In Aotearoa I can dress openly as a woman and maintain my job as a university lecturer. In my situation, there was no external boundary as such to prevent my exceeding of the masculine assemblage. I wasn't breaking the law, my job was secure and I have no children to complicate matters. Unlike trans people for whom the obstacle is often the external boundary, for the most toxic of masculinities it is the internal boundary that is overwhelmingly the obstacle: their own investments in and dependency on a narrow concept of masculinity that prevents liberation from its egregious effects. Whether due to the social conditions or the condition of the ego, when the obstacle appears insurmountable, suicide can seem like the only means of escape. Not being a man is another.

I am describing the masculine assemblage of a particular form, but, thanks to colonialism, commodification and the cultural penetration of Westernized values on a global scale, also a form that is universalized. The capacity of the BwOs to exceed the internal and external limits of the assemblage is thwarted by the weight of this history, the discourses through which man and woman are defined and regulated, and our own desires. Many variables have to be taken into account, such as the person's race, their social class and the people in their lives and within their community. But it is Oedipalization that, according to Deleuze and Guattari, has turned desire against itself. It instils feelings of guilt and shame for desires that are associated with signifiers of femininity. As such, the masculinized ego comes to desire the repression of their desire and identify with the objects and activities from which capital can profit as their mode of salvation. Masculine desire is a connective force that fuels the abstract machine of capital. I return to this point in the next chapter.

Femininity is the road less travelled. It is the place that few men are prepared to go. The extent to which femininity is repudiated and the historically specific castration complex overcompensated for is what most of all defines the boundaries of each of the aforementioned masculine assemblages or forms. Exceeding these forms is no easy task. As Deleuze puts it:

> It is not easy to be a free man, to flee the plague, organize encounters, increase the power to act, to be moved by joy, to multiply the affects which express or encompass a maximum of affirmation. To make the body a power which is not reducible to the organism, to make thought a power which is not reducible to consciousness.
>
> DELEUZE and PARNET, 2007: 62

So, to be clear, assemblages do not exist independently of the subject of desire. A chair, in this sense, is only an assemblage if the labour involved in making it, the consumer who uses it, and various other intermediaries are taken into account. Like that of the table and chair, the condition of possibility for masculine and feminine assemblages also differ. The limitations of the former can be defined in relationship to the possibilities of the latter. These centre on the capacities for expression and affect, the extent to which they are delimited by the subject's investment in the father's name, the kind of phallic substitutes such investments demand and also, crucially, the socio-historic circumstances.

What we identify and come to accept as man or woman, masculine or feminine, is clearly contingent on a range of factors. But it doesn't require extensive research or deliberation for conclusions to be drawn and snapshot decisions to be made as to whether you are a man, woman, cis or trans. Those at one end of the masculinities spectrum, RAMS, are the most brittle of men. They are the most restricted in terms of their capacities. A 'table' for them is a table. There is no ambiguity, no deviation from the standard formula. There is no condition of possibility for decorative flourishes or quirky designs. To add them would be to break the assemblage. A RAM would no longer be a RAM in other words, and it would have happened under specific social conditions. These breaching effects would constitute what Deleuze and Guattari call a line of flight or escape. The inverse of a productive line of flight is a destructive line to oblivion or suicide, which is precisely what happens when all avenues of escape except into death are closed. This is why such men are so dangerous to themselves and others. They are restricted in their capacities to committing acts of violence or taking their own life. To care would be to negate and stretch the idea of themselves beyond the form they embody. At the other end of the continuum, REMS possess the capacity to add such flourishes without breaking the assemblage or, metaphorically, without it still functioning as a table. The trans woman, on the other hand, is no longer subject to the conventions of masculinity and completely at liberty to incorporate and affect feminine modes of expression and becoming. They compose from the given assemblage and the possibilities both individual and collective it affords to them as new BwOs. Whatever I felt inside, instrumental to taking flight or embarking on this process of becoming was the discourse on trans. But more importantly, it helped considerably that I live in a country and have a job that affords opportunities to do so without either being arrested or losing my employment. One can exceed the internal limits of an assemblage only to encounter the external ones of prejudice, discrimination and a legal apparatus that blocks the flows of desire and their vitalizing effects. To be fully appraised of the implications and to ensure what from the point of view of the individual is appropriate for them, in Aotearoa you have to meet with a consultant for access to hormone treatment. Unlike in the UK, you do not have to convince them that you suffer from a clinically defined gender dysphoria.

Having made that break I am no longer directed by a need to maintain a functioning 'table'. The sickness that was inside me may not have entirely been purged, but pathways have at least now opened through which progressively to break down and dissolve obstacles residing in my psyche. A trans woman may not be entirely free of the disorder, but they are no longer subject to it either. Although sometimes unregistered, there is no blockage to prevent a feminine praxis, only an opening that may or may not be passed through. A feminine praxis is about experimentation, not necessarily in a literal sense but an experiment insofar as the internal and external limits are being tested. It is what REMS do and trans women have done to the point of being able to live on a different plane of existence. A feminine praxis is about testing the limits of masculinity, liberating the potentialities that your ego has blocked, opening up new pathways of becoming for yourself and for others. Whatever we do individually is, to stress the point, also by extension social.

Calibrated masculinity

Companies referred to earlier, such as Gillette and Coca-Cola, advocate a version of masculinity that has more in common with the editorials of the *Guardian* newspaper than they do *Fox News*. The meaning of masculinity and the kind of masculinity society ought to encourage has become a political issue, over which the competing interests of capital fight. Obama is the masculine figurehead of a more 'liberal' wing of capitalism. Toxic by such analysis, Trump's masculinity is a phoney counter-hegemonic posturing. His rebellion, in turn, is not against the kind of masculinity that Obama represents, but rather those that Obama and many corporations hold up as ideals that he cannot compete with. As confirmation that they themselves are not toxic, a calibrated masculinity is notionally accommodating of REMS and trans, sometimes even celebrating the latter because they are 'different' but only when not antagonistic in their politics. RAMS, REMS and trans (men as well as women) are categories of cognition through which ARMS can be triangulated and pathologized.

ARMS are the most invisible of masculine formations. They are invisible because they are generic. The most toxic of men and the most feminine of masculinities are by comparison easier to discern, but for this reason their positionality affords a perspective on the norm. By undergoing periodic calibration to changing mores, ARMS normalize the repudiation of femininity which is the repellent/propellant of every calibration. The calibrated masculinity today is cognizant of, though possibly confused about, gender diversity. They recognize that women have suffered multiple injustices at the hands of predatory men. They recognize that open displays of sexism and utterances that denigrate women may get them in trouble. Those who are closest at a given moment in time to the calibrated ideal, what pejoratively those critical of 'political correctness' call being 'woke', act themselves as a calibrator for those in their company to adjust themselves to. By recognizing themselves as distinct from RAMS, whom they disdain, and REMS, whom they either tolerate or welcome, their disorder is largely decentred. In their affirmations and embodiments of femininity, and declarations that they are women, trans women are sometimes harder for ARMS to accommodate. They, more than any category of cognition, expose the depth of the problem that many, including those who are REMS or self-identifying as queer, have with the feminine.

RAMS are the useful idiots that put ARMS in a positive light. They are counter-hegemonic in the manner that Trump is. REMS, on the other hand, are counter-hegemonic in another sense. They function in their difference as confirmation that masculinities are fluid and thereby lend legitimation to the idea that in their openness and reflexivity, ARMS too are fluid, or at least are free to be. ARMS are thus sandwiched between RAMS and REMS, but the boundaries are not clearly delineated. Perhaps at the pub with the kind of mates they'd not want to introduce to work colleagues and that their partner are unable to tolerate, the most regressive of their character traits are displayed. The difference with the RAMS whose company they may sometimes entertain becomes more marked out over time as they calibrate their masculinity to changing mores. Friendships may, for this reason, over time become increasingly strained and difficult for either party to maintain. This also happens in more abrupt ways when, as a trans woman, you negate masculinity altogether.

To affirm and defend the right of trans people to live and identify with the gender that feels authentic to them is proof positive of an enlarged capacity to accommodate difference. Rather than questioning gender categories or reflecting on one's own aversions to femininity, it can have the effect of reifying those differences and reinforcing a need to reaffirm them. Even though trans people sometimes hold to specific notions of gender, they not only sow confusion, they question the meaning of man and woman and the dependency of the cisgendered on signifiers and signifying practices that masculinity and femininity delineate. The masculine disorder is particularly sensitive to trans women and the need to establish clear definitions of what it means to be cis or trans. Affirming that cis women are categorically different to trans women ensures that woman remains a category apart from men: that only cis women are female and that those who are female are the categorical victims of patriarchy not trans who according to such definitions are male. Trans women threaten not only to confuse these terms, they threaten a specific critique of patriarchy that relies on this delineation, but by affirming femininity, the androcentrism upon which men and women rely on is called into question. To declare, on the other hand, that a trans woman is female positively affirms that gender is not the given of anatomy. However, by defining their gender orientation as one of dysphoria, the clinical establishment helps put to rest in the minds of those who regard gender to be a fixed natural condition any confusion as to whether their gender is socially contingent, permeable, vulnerable or even appropriate for them. Femininity is the 'other' to the masculine. Trans women are the 'other' to the normative androcentrism wherein masculine means strength and feminine means weakness. It is why, unable to come to terms with the many implications of this relationship, the various discourses 'on' trans are literally and metaphorically 'all over the place'. I return to this in chapter 5.

Men's self-reflexive critique of masculinity serves the fetishistic function of revealing their inadequacies while at the same time suturing them. In other words, by gesturing to your flaws you at the same time show that you are less flawed than those who do not gesture to them. Being cognizant and reflective of one's flaws is obviously important but what I am referring to here is something more cynical: the sort of gesture made instrumentally to deflect an appropriately placed criticism. Women become the categorical victims of men that men identifying as feminists can offer support to. Masculinity is called out, but, heroes to women, their masculinity is reaffirmed by such moves. This false dichotomizing of patriarchy, wherein women are its victims and men are not, lends weight to the notion that patriarchy's victims are cis women. This is precisely what former *Guardian* columnist Suzanne Moore, self-proclaimed leftist feminist, insists on and why, according to her, when trans women are considered real women, the dividing lines are confused.[3] What is ultimately being defended when the term 'woman' becomes an antagonistic category inclusive of all variations – such as ethnicity, race, sexuality, and class but not trans – is white privilege. It is the white elite 'liberal' who speaks and gets to decide who's the victim of patriarchy and on which terms, terms that invariably reflect well on their own status and compromised class politics. Again, I return to this in chapter 5. My point is not that we are all equally, and in undifferentiated ways, victims of patriarchy. What I am arguing is that the detrimental effects of patriarchy are not reducible to birth sex. They are experienced at multiple levels including the psychological. But where there are victims, there are also profiteers. To take one of those banal and everyday examples, Carl Cederström, who wrote a piece for the *Guardian* exhorting men to do the right thing and embrace feminism, provides an exemplary instance of the calibrated masculinity.

Cederström writes of how the Harvey Weinstein revelations spurred him to 'sit down and read about women's experiences'.[4] He spent a 'month reading the feminist classics' such as De Beauvoir's *The Second Sex* and 'nodded his way' in agreement through all the books he read. Equating the love of shoes and bags with being a 'flawed feminist', Roxane – the 'bad feminist' – Gay is Cederström's cue for being a flawed feminist too. It is a classic example of fetishistic disavowal. As with the charity contributions of Bill Gates, gestures such as these are easy to make when you're a cis white man with a tenured professorship at a prestigious university. Relying on the very thing he is critical of, Cederström is able to enhance his academic profile, make an 'impact' that the academy will recognize and position himself as an example of good masculinity. The article functions as a mirror for the earnest and well-meaning *Guardian* reader to look hard at and ask of the image: 'Am I as good as Cederström?' Is the reader's phallus as big as the author's? Probably not. But if you recognize yourself as a 'flawed feminist' too, you might be able to persuade yourself that it is.

In a twist on this critique, I met Cederström when visiting Stockholm on my sabbatical and raised these issues with him. He claimed that feminists attacked him for the sort of reasons I do here, but also men who felt they were under attack. His subsequent disowning of the piece itself may be more of a case of having been found out than anything else. I guess this is the point – that ambassadors of a good masculinity need to be found out, again and again, until no credit can be taken, no phallus earned or kudos cashed in, for their gestures and the disorder itself centred on them and how they aid and abet it. The same can be said of anyone irrespective of their sex or gender advancing their academic career through phoney gestures of solidarity with those they position themselves as organic intellectuals for.

Recalling hooks and Connell, if what Obama, Craig, Gillette and Cederström enunciate and embody is a positive (anti-patriarchal) masculinity, it is because the bar is set so low. The reader could be forgiven here for thinking that with my sweeping claim that masculinity itself is a disorder I am being far harsher on men than these authors are. Quite the opposite. What Connell, in particular, has done is, having painted such a negative caricature, made it so easy for men to disown and position themselves above it. Thus, it provides them with a phallus through which to shore up their position as good men and also deflect criticism away from the masculine ego formation. I'm not so hard on normal men. I credit them with the capacity for reflection, sensitivity towards others and the fairness of mind to recognize when an injustice against women is committed. This is no trivial thing and in fact ought to be welcomed. But it is not enough. Critique comes easy when you create straw men. The more difficult task, which is one I'm attempting, is to map the entire circumference of the disorder inclusive even of women, cis or trans, and examine the formation not at its most vulnerable (RAMS) but where it is strongest and most resilient to critique because so normalized it appears benign (ARMS). That said, the most reactive of masculinities present the most immediate and apparent danger to the rest of us. Their condition is simply more aggravated.

Reactive/aggravated masculinities (RAMS)

RAMS are exhibit number one in support of the claim that masculinity is a disorder. They are the kind that makes headlines for driving trucks into protesters at Black Lives Matters demonstrations and write manifestos of hate. They are the infamous Incels (involuntary celibates). But also, they are the men in our midst, not necessarily racist or ideologically on the far right, but who nevertheless lash out at the slightest provocation. The disorder is also discernible via exhibit number two. Trans women do not embody the disorder in the way that ARMS do but like the REMS who wear unambiguous feminine clothing, they stand out. In doing so, they put the norm into relief: that the absence of feminine signifiers on the majority of men demonstrate that, while not necessarily true of all men, the majority have a problem with femininity. I know from experience that people are surprised when they see a 'male' going about their everyday business in women's clothes. It would be shocking, however, if after hearing about a school massacre the perpetrator was revealed to be a cis woman or trans man or woman. Those who commit such acts identify as male and are cis gender. The cis woman does not have a name to defend. The trans man was never made to feel entitled in the first place and thereby prone to commit acts of violence to prove themselves worthy of the entitlement. The trans woman has refused the name and has nothing thereby to prove either. A third exhibit could be added: the sheer abundance and popularity of films and video games that stage the Oedipal drama. Exhibits one, two and three: these are truths that no jury will quarrel with – the *extreme*, the *exception* and the *fantasy*. In the next chapter I add a fourth, the (libidinal) *economy*.

Why single out religion, ethnicity or race, when the masculine gender is the common denominator of mass killings asks *Guardian* columnist Gary Younge. There are moral panics about Muslims, not about men. So why no equivalent call 'for moderate men to denounce toxic masculinity?'[5] I would say that Younge is wrong about the latter and the problem with this, as suggested earlier, is that critique is decentred. The problem at the core of RAMS is the same as that at the core of ARMS. But while the symptoms of the former make headlines, those of the latter do not. They can be just as corrosive and debilitating, but often in more subtle ways or behind closed doors. The worst of men appear to have a high pain threshold. They can take the knocks. What they can't take is the humiliation. This is what struck Bonnie Mann (2014: ix) about the testimonies of the men tortured by the Americans at Abu Ghraib. As one victim put it:

> They were trying to humiliate us, break our pride. We are men. It's OK if they beat me. Beatings don't hurt us, it's just a blow. But no one would want their manhood to be shattered . . . They wanted us to feel as though we were women, the way women feel and this is the worst insult, to feel like a woman.

Actions are not in themselves humiliating. The problem is with how actions are interpreted. A man can be forced to commit an act against himself by those who consider the act humiliating but he cannot be forced to find it humiliating or be libidinally invested in whatever the act deprives him of. The disorder cannot be discerned on the basis of the act itself, only in terms of whether the act is libidinally and unconsciously invested in. The latter can sometimes be extrapolated from the former but the former can sometimes be misleading. As this distinction is crucial, I'm going to have to inflict Jacques Lacan on the reader, a primer for an exegesis on sexuation at the end of this chapter. Now, while sport is to analogy what sarcasm is to wit, sport is here the perfect way to elucidate this distinction.

Three dark crosses on my school timetable marked the games period which took up half a full day a week. On the morning I would pray for sickness in order that I could miss it. Rarely was I so fortunate. It always started with the roll call which involved standing in a line, frozen in my shorts, as team captains picked us off one by one. I was always the last to be chosen. In football this meant being consigned to goal. Whatever humiliation I suffered was nothing to what could be suffered on the pitch if I let a ball get past me into the back of the net. There was at least the sporting chance of recovering some dignity by placing my frozen body in its way as it travelled at alarming velocities in my direction. The open goal was to my castrated condition what my body was to masculinity, the means to block it and save face.

For Lacan, castration is born of signification. It is the condition of being subjects of language, and language the flawed means through which we make sense of ourselves. Masculinity is a case in point. What it means is guesswork. Can we ever fully embody it? Obviously not when the term itself is so slippery. Something is always lost in translation – a gap of signification. To man up is to acquire the phallic means – a signifier – that closes that gap which is of course impossible. No such signifier exists to complete us and thereby put paid to the need to prove ourselves 'the' man. Castration – the gap born of language – and the desire for a phallus – the signifier to close the gap – go hand in hand. My body as a signifier of masculinity was not of equal dimensions to the goal mouth, dimensions that only an impossible Real (dead) Father who exists only in myth fills. No matter how many pies I ate, how much effort I put into improving my skills (not much), I was never going to be the equivalent of the goal mouth (the hole at the core of being that the subject as signifier aims to cover). Sometimes I caught the ball and momentarily recovered my dignity. Sooner or later, though, I was bound to let one in. The ball itself functions as a metaphor for what Lacan calls *objet (petit) a*, the object cause of desire. It is the object or signifier that is absent from our grasp and going through various contortions and all manner of somersaults, we dedicate our lives to capturing. It is this absence that motivates us to improve our skills and, even if it causes pain, throw ourselves endlessly at that metaphorical ball. The big Other here, the team constituting the superego authority, demands that I capture the ball. But the demand can only fail because as soon as the ball is captured it's placed back at the centre of the pitch. The process repeats endlessly until death – in this case, of the game.

Of crucial importance is the meaning invested in the game. A keeper who, standing aside from the goal, refuses to play by the rules is not only going to let his teammates down, he'll likely suffer the ritualistic whipping with wet towels in the shower room afterwards. We can't independently escape or change the symbolic order – the rules of the game Freud referred to as the reality principle. To do this requires the whole team to stand down. Sometimes the game is played for self-preservation, sometimes to protect others, sometimes because it is everything that we stand for and in which meaning is invested. Born of failure and frustration, with the repetitive process of missing and catching the ball becoming itself a source of libidinal gratification, that is when the subject is wedded to the game. Lacan (2004) calls this kind of pleasure *jouissance*, a pleasure in pain whose object is not the ball as such but the aim of catching it. By prolonging the game, death is delayed. So, although Lacan compares *jouissance* to the Freudian death drive, the aim is not, as the term would suggest, death as such but the prolongation of life: to play the game endlessly.

In truth, being consigned to goal or failing to save the ball never really felt humiliating to me because I was never invested in the game in the first place. I played the game out of necessity not because of any libidinal drive. Hence why I never developed my skills. I simply wasn't motivated. Lacan describes subjectivity as the unconscious fantasy that gives form to desire. In terms of the football analogy, this would be the rules of the game that are introjected or internalized into the unconscious. They are thereby performed without consideration of why we're following them or take them seriously. In such instances, like a natural inclination or impulse, catching the ball, *objet a* or phallus is the be all and end all. Thus, it is no longer through external pressure that the game is maintained but by the subject's self-propelling drive to play it. They themselves become the cause of their own frustrated attempts to catch the ball: the pleasure in the pain. The masculine disorder can thus be considered both a condition imposed on us and one that, having internalized the condition, we come to depend on and derive satisfaction from.

An important point to be taken from this is that whatever the extent to which the violence of those who are the most afflicted by the disorder can be attributed to the external pressures to mutilate the psyche, they do not in themselves explain or justify the violence. The psychoanalytic therapy is about recognizing how we ourselves are invested in the condition and, however destructive it is to us, derive enjoyment from it. To 'traverse the fantasy' is to rid ourselves of those proverbial rules that unconsciously have gotten us hooked on the violence that is symptomatic of it. This is the stage when a game we are so passionate about that everything else in life is an afterthought loses all meaning and is now seen from a radically different perspective: a stupid exercise in which, in the game of football, grown men act like idiots chasing after an inanimate object. Desires, pleasures and passions often do seem stupid from the point of view of others. Many women are no doubt perplexed that I love wearing sheer tights just as I am perplexed as to why anyone would enjoy watching or playing rugby. Whatever gives form to my desire to wear tights is not one I care to overcome. We can love football, hate racism and feel no compulsion to lash out at someone when our team is defeated. It is a question of what the subject is staked in, how and the degree to which they are staked in it and the consequences for themselves and for others, especially when the object to which their lives are staked falls from their grasp.

I stopped playing football the moment I left school. But when subjectivity is conditional on playing the game, the only way out of the predicament from a Lacanian perspective is to 'traverse the fantasy': to recognize that our pain and suffering is due to the stake we have in the game, not because of any external pressure. The stupidity of this drive to catch the phallus is then seen for what it is. When the game itself has no value to us, the object has no value either. RAMS, it seems, would rather take their own life or the life of another than face this. Kiebold and Harris, the Columbine killers, saw themselves as subjects proportionate to the metaphorical goal mouth. It meant everything to them. Their classmates thought otherwise. It was only in death that their masculinity was no longer tested, only in death that they became Real impossible men. As the authors of a study on the Columbine massacre put it, you humiliate a boy and 'you take away his manhood' (Kalish and Kimmel, 2010: 454). You can't humiliate what no longer exists.

'Most of the guys I meet are good guys,' Kimmel writes in *Guyland* (2008: 22). 'But far too many are easily influenced by the bullies and the big shots, the guys who think they are making up the rules and, in any event, are the most committed to enforcing them.' Under pressure to prove their manhood, boys drink more alcohol than they can handle, shirk studying because it is seen as girly, engage in ritualistic bullying of classmates, lie and brag about sexual experiences and make defamatory jokes about girls and women they are attracted to. Such boys, bell hooks (2004: 42) says, 'know they must not express feelings, with the exception of anger; that they must not do anything considered feminine or womanly'.

The frame of the goal can be thought of as the circumference within which all masculinities lie. RAMS stake their masculinity to the posts that stand rigid on either side. If the goalposts of RAMS are brittle and the distance between them determined by some officially sanctioned measure, still involved in the game, REMS, by contrast, improvise with movable jumpers for goalposts. As a boy I had no choice other than to put up with and inexpertly play the game, to work on my masculinity as the only protection from the cruelty of others. It was only later when the circumstances themselves had changed that I could with a reasonable degree of safety reject the game. As a boy I had no agency to up sticks, to improvise with jumpers for goalposts, to leave home or escape my class situation or my classmates. So instead, I would hope for sickness or for the coach that took us to the playing field to crash on the way. We learn the hard way though, that there is no *deus ex machina* to get us out of such predicaments. This is what those total institutions such as the school and prison do to you. The boys and men who find themselves in them may not be RAMS but they are often under pressure to appear as if they are. They do not have to be libidinally invested in what Connell calls hegemonic masculinity to do exactly what is normative to it.

My characterization of RAMS recalls the landmark study conducted by Adorno and his colleagues (1950) on the susceptibility of the German personality to fascistic persuasion. It led to the conclusion that nothing less than a new kind of subject had emerged. Characteristics included feelings of grandiosity, a prurient interest in the sexual activity of others and, making them susceptible to flattery, a weak ego. Their pathological form of narcissism is reflected in a lack of empathy and projection of their inadequacies onto others who become either objects of love or hate. Adorno (2005: 142) clearly had figures such as Hitler in mind when describing how in their 'startling symptoms of inferiority' and resembling 'ham actors and asocial psychopaths', the leader is able to cast himself in the follower's image and, confirming the latter's feelings of grandiosity, gain popularity. In a carefully crafted narrative, the immigrant, the Jew, the Black Americans, the feminists, the metropolitan elites, the unemployed or whoever function as figures who have robbed the follower of his entitlement. Incels fit this description.

If women's desire is, as the standard narrative goes, an enigma for men, then Incels know precisely what women want. The only mystery is that women do not appear to want them. Messaging one another on 4Chan, 8Chan and Reddit, Elliot Rodger became a poster boy for this nascent loose association of adolescent boys and men. Rodger had his own video-log or vlog on which he called for a 'War on Women' and hit the headlines after going on a rampage. He killed six people, three of whom were men stabbed in his apartment, two women, shot outside on the street, and finally a male student. Fourteen people in total were injured. His declaration is worth repeating: 'I'll take great pleasure in slaughtering all of you. You will finally see that I am, in truth, the superior one, the true alpha male.'[6] In Rodger's 140-page manifesto, *My Twisted World: The Story of Elliot Rodger*, women are represented as flat and faceless. Men, on the other hand, are described in detail. Rodger provides their names and offers rich descriptions of their personalities. He notes their race and even describes their hobbies. The boyfriend of the woman he had a crush on is described as a 'tall, muscular surfer-jock with a buzz cut'.[7] The woman herself is hardly mentioned.

Such men are textbook examples of what Freud tells us about the male castration complex. Here's alt-right blogger Matt Forney:

The vagina is the perfect representation of the nature of females. An empty vessel, a hole, a void with no identity of its own. Without a man to fill her with his essence, she is as useless as a crab apple rotting on the sidewalk. Alt righters and other white supremacists frequently refer to women as 'thots' which stands for 'that ho over there'.[8]

'Gamergate', which began in 2014 with the harassment of an indie video game developer Zoe Quinn, is one of the more notorious examples of the castration anxieties of adolescent boys and sometimes men. Anita Sarkeesian was at one stage threatened with rape and murder and even hounded from her home. Her crime was to criticize gender representations in video games in her YouTube series *Tropes vs Women* (see Cremin, 2016). The 'manosphere' is replete with examples such as these: 'I'll rape you and put your head on a stick'; 'It would be funny if five guys raped her right now'; 'I violently masturbate to your face'; and 'Tits or get the fuck out'. 'The pain of relentless rejection,' Nagle (2017: 89) writes, 'has festered in these forums and allowed them to be the masters of the cruel natural hierarchies that bring them so much humiliation.'

The castration anxieties of the adolescent and the adult are a mirror of the nation. England, the country I was born in, was once an empire that colonized Aotearoa (New Zealand), where I now live in. In the latter, the Queen is the figurehead whose birthday is celebrated with a day off work. There is a thing here called the 'Tall Poppy Syndrome' which reflects a cultural unease with those who, through their own merits, appear to stand above the crowd. In a country that is intensely anti-intellectual, like tall poppies, they are cut down to size. It is a reflection not so much of the diminished and emasculated status of the white Pākehā 'Kiwi' from whom this attitude derives, but rather an attempt to shoot down pretenders who aspire to the throne. A kind of cutting of the nose to spite the face, it is in an inverted means to legitimize the (post-) colonial order and who by rights commands power and authority in it. Not the indigenous Māori population whose name for 'New Zealand' *Aotearoa* has not been made official. The 'Make America Great Again' slogan intimates both castration and potency and functions in much the same way as the Tall Poppy Syndrome. It has the same effect as the self-deprecations of the 4Chan 'beta' boys. Suicide rates in Aotearoa are some of the highest in the world. When it comes to toxic masculinity, the United States, however, is the world leader. The slave trade, racial segregation and the structural racism that Black Lives Matter is protesting against help to explain this. Names, flags, celebrations and statues are, in the final analysis, symbols of a white supremacist masculine disorder.

American masculinity, according to Gail Bederman (1996: 234), was shaped from the early colonial period by white supremacism. For her, the figure who encapsulates this is the mythical Tarzan, the 'King of the Apes':

> Combining the ultimate in Anglo-Saxon manliness with the most primal masculinity, Tarzan is violent yet chivalrous; moral yet passionate. Above all, he has a superb body. If manhood is a historical process that constructs the male body as a metonym for power and identity, Tarzan's cultural work was to proclaim that the white man's potential for power and mastery was as limitless as the masculine perfection of Tarzan's body.

Authoritarian tendencies, the need to dominate and control others, and investment in signifiers of status and power are not entirely monopolized by those who are racist and identify with right-wing ideologies. There are RAMS on the left too. I will return to this point in the next section.

In amongst all of this are 'good kids', as Kimmel puts it. Sure they jostle with their peers on the football field, engage in 'locker room' talk, pick on those deemed effeminate, but they are constrained by their material circumstance: the external as opposed to the internal limits to taking flight. Perhaps, as I did as a child, they went through the motions of chasing the phallus without being fully invested in it. These kids need different ideals to inspire them and provide them with the opportunity to branch out in new and vitalizing directions. Prince, an archetypal REM, did this for me. I saw him live multiple times as a teenager in the 1980s. Through his appearance, the symbols he adopted, his lyrics and the refusal to define himself through gender categories, he demonstrated that there was another way. Despite wearing overtly feminine clothing and make-up, he still nonetheless had masculine appeal and also, as those close to him testified (see Garcia, 2017), (inevitably) displayed some of the negative traits associated with masculinity. Short of negating man, he did then as he does now in death: stretch the definition of what signifies masculinity to the absolute limit.

Prince represented an ideal but was he in fact a masculine ideal? Do boys need, as Kimmel suggests, masculine ideals or is it more accurate to say they need males in their lives who, like Prince, are feminized? Don't we already have plenty of masculine ideals? It's the feminine ideals that are missing. The so-called good kids need feminine ideals that they themselves can proudly embody. But it is not enough to rely on media celebrities, pop icons and fictional heroes to serve this function. Prince was never there in the shower-room to protect me from a whipping. Trans celebrities will not be on site when kids questioning their gender are bullied.

A REMS/trans entryism is required. By this I mean that those on the cutting edges of the masculinities spectrum who experiment with feminine apparel and affects, and of course trans women, need to embark on a long march through the institutions and be on site in precisely those places where a nascent masculinity is forged – to take up frontline jobs at creches, primary and secondary schools, at youth community centres and even in universities when many kids for the first time are living away from home and have an opportunity to experiment; to be the teacher of physical education and organize the sports team: this is what is required to usurp the positions that RAMS and a superficially calibrated masculinity occupy. It is to deprive the guardians and gatekeepers of the androcentric order of their phallus and to declare 'I'm the daddy now', your daddy and your momma too. Incorporating aspects of femininity, REMS are a stepping stone, but a stepping stone only, to the dissolution of the disorder.

But it's worth stressing the point that it's easy to be a good guy when you're relatively affluent, successful by any standard measure, when you've survived the playing field without knocks, bruises or, naked and exposed, ritualistic whippings with wet towels in the shower. It's nice when a middle-class trans woman offers an olive branch to *Harry Potter* author and infamous commentator J. K. Rowling.[9] It's not so easy to be calm and empathetic when you're at the raw end of daily discrimination. In our sick society, the righteous anger and aggression of trans women is read as proof that they are men. Whatever the motive and whoever the target, a violent cis woman – worse, a violent trans woman – is the paragon of evil. A split is in order but also a resignification. It's not enough, however, simply to assert that traits people think of as feminine, such as tenderness, compassion and sensuality, are positive ones. Liberating ourselves from our masculine constraints is a struggle demanding strength, assertiveness, power, aggression, sometimes even violence. But this doesn't mean being a man. It's important both to cis women fighting the patriarchy and trans women fighting TERFS, that terms such as these are demasculinized, and even feminized. Focusing on the most masculine of traits, aggression, this is what I aim to do in the next section.

Degendering aggression

I want to start with an example, a fictional depiction of reality for many people in Britain today. Fiction does what reality never affords. It provides clarity of context and insights into personal psychology on which the rights and wrongs of an action can reliably be determined. The fictional example in question is a film that belongs to the genre of social realism.

It was a packed house at the 2,300-seater Civic Theatre in Auckland for the premiere of Ken Loach's film *Sorry We Missed You*, released in 2019. It's a story of a working-class family from Newcastle upon Tyne, struggling to make ends meet. It showcases the brutal reality of zero-hour contracts. Ricky, played by Kris Hitchen, persuades his partner Abbie, played by Debby Honeywood, to sell the car she needs for her job as a care worker visiting elderly people in their homes. He uses the money to buy a van to deliver parcels for a firm at which he is contracted as 'self-employed'. Tight delivery times, which prove impossible to meet, are enforced by penalties. The situation worsens when thugs beat him up, steal his parcels and smash the electronic device for tracking, which he now has to pay for. Intensified by a bizarre incident in the theatre, the most dramatic moment is when Kris punches his adolescent son, Seb, in the face, after falsely accusing the latter of hiding his van keys. It was precisely at this moment that, coinciding with what happened onscreen and suggesting that an assault had occurred, I heard a scream from somewhere in the audience, a woman's voice: 'Don't touch me!', 'How dare you!', and 'I'm calling the police!' Without any idea of what had triggered this outburst, people across the theatre yelled 'Shut up!', 'Be quiet!', and various other phrases to that effect, some of which were more colourful. With social realism, the audience gained the perspective to evaluate the righteousness of Kris's aggression. There was no such perspective here, no way of knowing whether the outburst was ethically motivated or contextually justified, whether there was a history to the altercation, or the mental health condition of either person.

We did have insights into the circumstances leading up to Kris punching Seb. The audience had the perspective by which to judge the righteousness of the act which, as the hushed response intimated, like me it considered completely wrong. By contrast, when, towards the end of the film, Abbie snatches Kris's mobile phone from him and shouts abuse to his boss on the other end of it, the audience burst out in a spontaneous cheer. Both actions can be considered aggressive. The context in which they occurred was the same. But the gender of the aggressor differed. Kris channelled his anger and frustration against an innocent minor; Abbie against a culpable boss. Had she hit the boss, the righteousness of the act would be open to debate. We can know that Kris's action was ego motivated. We cannot be sure of the extent to which Abbie's aggression was, but can be sure that it was ethically proportionate to the situation. The family eventually forgave Kris, if not primarily because of the circumstance but through tacit recognition that, comparable to the forgiving of a Tourette's suffer for issuing expletives, he is a sufferer of the masculine disorder and his capacity to express himself in other ways is limited. If the violence of a woman is harder for society to accommodate, it is because there is no readily available alibi. Those who are likewise repulsed on the rare occasion that a trans woman is aggressive is unconscious acknowledgement that the latter is a woman.

Whatever injustices Kris experienced, it was the classic situation that Engels himself observed, of the proletariat dealing with the humiliations he experiences at the hands of the capitalist boss by acting himself as the boss at home. It was no coincidence that the act occurred soon after the son had mocked Kris's job and status. In this Oedipal drama, Seb had exposed his father's adequacies and for this reason had to be taken down. Kris's violence was therefore an unambiguously ego motivated and libidinally gratifying act. Consistent with the conventions of social realism, whereby the film aims to provide an unvarnished and accurate depiction of reality, his reaction was plausible. It would have been unrealistic or seen as misrepresentative of women had Abbie acted in this way instead but all the more repulsive for it.

Social realism aims to provide the audience with a God's-eye perspective on the lives of those who are marginalized, disenfranchised and made scapegoats for the crime and social disintegration engendered by regressive government policies. Set in a Yorkshire mining town, in Loach's earlier masterpiece, *Kes*, a Kestrel bird is a metaphor of a young boy Caspar's dream to escape his class predicament. Those dreams are dashed when, in an act of revenge for not placing a bet on a horse he was given money for, the elder brother kills the bird. Both *Kes* and *Sorry We Missed You* illustrate how material circumstances can have an aggravating effect on the masculine disorder. The psychic disorder further compounds and complicates the difficulties arising from the material situation and the attempt to escape the class position. If the middle classes appear at times to be less prone to aggression, it is because, thanks to their affluent, well-connected and educated parents, they are afforded the breaks that are simply not available to those at the sharper end of the class and racial divide. They are also more likely for these reasons to be convinced of their own naturally given superiority. Psychopaths are just as likely to be found in penthouses and palaces as they are in slums and on sink estates.

My proposition is that whoever the target is and whatever the circumstance, aggression motivated by the ego is defined as masculine. In contrast, aggression that is motivated by injustice and aimed at those who aid and abet class, gender and racial forms of domination and discrimination can be defined as feminine or gender indeterminate. These are not mutually exclusive of course. However, while it is never entirely clear whether someone who strikes down a fascist is doing so to gratify their ego, whatever skewed notion of justice they may harbour, there's no ambiguity when, for example, Incels commit acts of verbal and physical aggression or husbands beat up their wives in the home. A distinction is easier to make with acts of political violence committed by figures on the right than it is by figures on the left. The most visible of RAMS are usually right wing. However, as many women know, being a socialist is no antidote to the disorder. The hero who punches a fascist on the streets is sometimes the same man who punches his wife in the home and bullies his way into leadership positions in movements.

It is easy, Deleuze and Guattari (2003a) say, to be anti-fascist on the outside, translating as identity, the molar level of representation. In other words, this is how you see yourself and want others to see you, without recognizing the fascist within you, which you yourself nourish and sustain, the molecular level of affects that can be sensed but which are not seen. For example, due perhaps to unexamined feelings of inadequacy, a committed activist in a movement or party opposed to capitalism may, without being conscious of it, intimidate others, bully them and be emotionally cold to those whose gender, sexuality, race or class background differs from their own. Driving people away, the movement becomes increasingly uniform, masculinist in tone and authoritarian in nature as only those in their image remain. This is the kind of scenario that Deleuze and Guattari warn against, and why, whether we are talking about a socialist party, a feminist group or LGBTQI+ activists, it is not only the card-carrying fascist but also the 'micro-fascist' that poses a threat. It is why, as difficult as it is, discerning between masculine and feminine/ degendered forms of aggression matters.

The preponderance of masculine aggression amongst sexed males relates to the Oedipal process but women are no less violent, though often for different motives, and historically have played instrumental roles in armed movements for liberation. The attribution of aggression to the masculine gender or, as Connell does, describing heroism and a passion for science as masculine traits, legitimates the positions that men occupy in party and movement hierarchies, as well as obscuring the role of women in the history of class struggle frontlines. Guerrilla warfare, uprisings, riots and revolutions that women have been at the centre of are still nonetheless presented in the image of men. Che Guevara's silhouetted image is sported on tee-shirts. Rosa Luxemburg was never accorded such iconic status. The only benefit to women of this gendering of aggression is that, in contrast to the guerrilla movements, it is typically men that imperialists recruit to fight their wars of aggression.

If the answer to the problem of masculinity is femininity, it is not to be attained by ridding the self of every trait symbolically defined as masculine and adopting those that the patriarchy defines as feminine. The effect would be to promote cowardliness over heroism, weakness over strength, frivolity over seriousness, superficiality over depth. There is nothing inherently good or bad about such traits, it is how, in Deleuzian/Spinozian terms, they combine in different situations either to have an augmentative or diminutive effect on the capacity of others to act individually and collectively, here in respect of struggles for emancipation from class, racial and gender oppression. And it is in this respect that I propose a rejection of the idea that strength, power, authority, even aggression, are masculine and resignify these as feminine or non-gendered traits depending on how they are operationalized relative to the situation, what purpose they serve and whether they are ego-motivated.

Žižek's (2020: 19) warning about anti-Semitism applies in respect to masculine aggression, which returns to my earlier point that however many blows a male has suffered, it is not an excuse for his aggression and the need to dominate. Žižek makes the point that, while many Jews in the Weimar Republic did, as the propaganda suggested, occupy positions of high office, were affluent and also influential in the cultural sphere, the defence of anti-Semitism on this basis is still absolutely false. Whatever justification is given, that is never the reason why such a perspective is taken. However true it is that some trans women have behaved aggressively in spaces designated for women, the rationale for excluding them from such spaces is also, for the same reasons, absolutely invalid. However true that the capitalist exploits the worker or that the police are a racist institution, when aggression is motivated by feelings of inadequacy and the need to prove oneself to others, the individual is not only a danger to the agents of oppression, they are also a danger to partners, friends, children and the movements themselves. The revolution doesn't require men or women like these. It doesn't require the subject of a disorder to fight oppression. But in view of their numbers, the class struggle cannot be won without them. This is why the interpersonal dynamics of parties and movements are often so unpleasant. Feminists in the 1970s were well aware of this when confronting the sexism and misogyny of the trade union groups and socialist parties that marginalized them. These, unfortunately, are the conditions in which we fight.

Now I want to pick up on where chapter 2 began, with the castration complex. Lacan's take on it differs slightly from Freud's and works better, with the emphasis placed here on resignification. The way he differentiates between masculine and feminine sexuality is also instrumental to my thinking, which, without naming it as such, has already informed my analysis. My football analogy is a useful primer for this theoretically dense section of the chapter, which provides the additional background and detail that is needed to complete the task of explaining by the end of the book why society can cope well and even thrive without a masculinized phallic-oriented subject; that, seemingly against the grain of Lacan, the removal of any referent to masculinity (and therefore femininity) is possible, thereby liberating desire from gender.

Meet the signifiers

I learnt when researching HRT (hormone replacement therapy) that one of the side effects of the procedure was a lowering of the libido. This immediately brought to mind the long days struggling to find the motivation to write, listless deliveries of lecture materials, indifference to albums that once inspired me and an inability to be roused by economic and social injustices. It did have a deleterious effect but not thankfully in any of these respects. The lesson of psychoanalysis is that human sexuality is not about who you like to fuck, whether you have any desire to or are capable of doing it. Sexuality, as Alenka Zupančič (2017: 35) puts it, 'is the problematic territory of being that seems to throw us out of joint, disorient us, and make us indulge in things characteristic of human society', the sort of things I thought HRT might jeopardise. As with the general dysphoria that issues from our initial gendering, sexuality is fundamentally queer.

If Freud is ambiguous about the symbolic nature of 'castration', Lacan is emphatic: castration is the real effect of signification. Lacan's point is that because we are beings who rely on language as a means to communicate and forge an identity, we encounter the problem with language that meaning is always ambiguous. With a dress, heels, tights and make-up on, I represent an image of femininity, perhaps in my ego even identify as a woman. However, what is being signified here, 'trans', 'woman' or 'femininity', is not the equivalent or sum total of who I am. Like the irksome exercise that students are tasked with at the start of a course or by a panel at a job interview, when asked to describe ourselves, there's the stuttering realization that words are never enough. We reduce ourselves to a blathering set of clichés, or worse, default to a jargon out of a managerial textbook. Consistent with de Beauvoir's dictum that one is not born, but rather becomes, a woman, as with the ego itself, gender is fashioned through a process of interpretation, learning from the utterances and behaviours of those around us as to how to enter into the symbolic order. We learn how to be recognized and desired as a gender. We also learn through this process how to desire. Through a process of identification and displacement, introjection and projection, we become recognizable to others as having a gender. Life is made liveable when behaviours, style of dress, interests and passions correspond to social conventions. Entry is thereby found into the symbolic order of society, a symbolic order that in their being and becoming a transgender subject threatens to unravel. They remove the certainties on which others depend and which others, reliant on these certainties, are keen to defend. Our desire to represent a gender corresponds to a need to be loved, to represent to the other what they desire – a boy(!) or a girl(!) – which suggests of course that they lack something too. It's the unconscious aim to represent what the other lacks and demands. Every transgender subject has to contend with these demands and risk being unloved and ostracized.

The unconscious is a swirl of signifiers forming metonymic chains and clustering around metaphors, an unconscious structured like a language. Lacan (1991) gives the example of hieroglyphs to illustrate his point. They meant something, but what they meant was a mystery until the Rosetta Stone was discovered. The letters themselves are the Real to the stone's Symbolic means of decipherment. The letters have a materiality to them that both precedes and defies symbolic inscription. Hieroglyphs are illustrative of Lacan's point that the signifier precedes the signified, that meaning is never entirely transparent and always after the fact.

Signifiers do not, as per Saussure, straightforwardly derive their meaning through the concept or signified. Unloved on our shelf, had I as a boy thumbed that familial dictionary to the entry 'man', all I would've found is a bunch of signifiers none of which would provide the definitive answer. There is always a remainder, *objet (petit) a*, after signification. The lesson of Lacan is that the thing (Real) is never what is said on the tin (Symbolic). What makes a man's man? If there was a key that could be used to peel away the lid of the tin and discover what's inside of him, nothing would be revealed. The subject does not exist outside of the signifying chain, rather they *in-sist* within it. There is no Real man. Real men are always manning up and in their libidinal attachments to phallic supplements they cannot help themselves. It is their 'nature' born of language and the position foisted onto them by the desires and demands of others to which they ultimately conform.

If desire was, as Foucault seemed to think, a product of discourse, we would have to conclude that Saussure was correct and that the signified (concept) precedes the signifier (acoustic image). Desire for Lacan is both symbolic and real. At the symbolic level, desire wants a phallus. At the level of the Real, desire wants to desire. Mapping this to the LGBTQI+ signifying chain, desire wants a letter but, attached to the undecipherable rem(*a*)inder, the object of drive is +. This the materiality of sexuality: the Real is what remains when signification fails, but is not, as Zupančič (2017) stresses, the 'product' of language.

Castration then is Real with a capital R, a material lack in the core of being, a lack *of* being. Castration is now no longer the anatomical condition of females but the condition of everyone (though, adding a further complication, 'woman' is not all castrated). Phallus, a signifier that brings closure, is what is presumed to have been lost and which the masculine subject spends their lives futilely trying to recover. The status and authority that he craves or the thing that would cement his reputation as the daddy, the phallus is what eludes every male and to which their desire is oriented. What makes men delusional and their masculinity fake is their inability to accept their ontological castration and need through phallic signifiers to obscure it. Women in their feminine orientation are not delusional. Accepting of their ontological condition, they are not burdened by the need to prove themselves as a socially sufficient authority. This is the difference between masculine and feminine sexuality, which I return to momentarily.

Language, then, splits us apart. When an animal sees something, as Lacan (1993) avers, it relies on sense. Indicating perhaps danger or food, signifiers are not subjected to a reflective process of interpretation or, mercifully, deconstructed. The relationship between the signifier and what is being signified, its meaning, is bi-univocal. A straightforward example is the proverbial red rag to a bull. The bull sees red and charges. Signifiers for animals are significant. For humans, in contrast, they are signifying. Meaning is always in doubt and subject to conscious, and also unconscious, mediation. This relates to Lacan's (2004) cryptic comment that 'A signifier represents the subject for another signifier.' The subject as conceived through language is what is positively put in the place of the minus (the castrating or negative effect of the introduction of the signifier that produces the gap of the Real).

When referring to someone's gender we tend now to use the phrase 'gender designated at birth' or, more simply, 'given gender'. This suggests, in line with Lacan, that gender originates from outside of us, in the symbolic order (of language), but erroneously that gender is imposed rather than demanded. We are gendered before we are born in the desires of parents. But there is no ready-made gender to give away. We have to do the work of tailoring a gender, a process of testing social conventions (the reality principle in Freudian terminology), and through our experimentations discovering what others deem appropriate. We present ourselves as a signifier of gender. Language, Lacan (2007: 124) says, 'cannot be anything other than a demand, a demand that fails'. It fails insofar that the demand cannot be satisfied. A demand itself suggests that those making it are, as already pointed out, lacking something. And this is Lacan's point: the Other lacks too.

Femininity is a form of masquerade, declared Riviera. But masquerade, notes Zupančič (2017), neither disguises nor reveals castration. As castration is the condition of being subjects of language, it is real and therefore cannot 'be exposed or seen as such'. Castration is, if anything, being staged. Like the infamous photos in which Prince Charles (diminutive in real life) dwarfs Princess Diana, the latter plays her part by acting as his inferior. It suggests that the feminine woman is dependent on her man and like a crutch enables him to stand tall. The myth is perpetuated that the male is the stronger sex. This is how women function as the man's missing phallus. In respect of Lacan's (1999) theory of sexuation, though not necessarily male, masculine sexuality is about *having* the phallus. The function of the phallus here is to mask castration. Feminine sexuality is by contrast about being the phallus as a way to compensate for a masculinized subject's deficiencies and need of ego embellishments. 'Woman' is not all castrated, however. This means that she is not entirely, as in the case of men, in the phallic function. *Jouissance* is an excessive and derailing pleasure in the frustrating attempts to acquire the missing phallus or *objet (petit) a*. Whereas masculine *jouissance* is unidirectional, because there is no Other to measure up to, and become the equivalent of, feminine *jouissance*, comparable to polymorphous perversity, is open and thereby multidirectional. When Lacan provocatively declares that there is no sexual relationship, what he means is that masculinity and femininity are not opposing terms relating to one another. The relationship is to castration or the lack of being and these two possible responses to it. A point worth stressing here is that because feminine sexuality is open, it is therefore inexhaustible, not an either/or that reduces sexuality to the phoney concept of a binary. There are feminine ideals of course that the advertising industry manufactures to evoke and manipulate the anxieties of women. But there is no equivalent sense of entitlement or need for a name equal to that of the father's name. If women are not missing a phallus then, in a sense, it is because they already have it.

In these gender sensitive times, words such as 'castration' and 'phallus' are clearly loaded terms, but are not, as every Lacanian theorist will insist, terms differentiating between genders. I don't have a problem with these terms. After all, they could easily be substituted for others and do denote how normatively people in patriarchy are situated. Gender differences are not, however, the primary concern of psychoanalysis, Zupančič (2017: 57) writes. Its concern, rather, is to show how sexuality is inscribed 'in the constitutive minus of the signifying order in this order itself'. In response to feminist critics of Lacan, Barnard points out that for Lacan the Real of sexuation has no gender or sexuality. As nonsignifiable, the Real is not susceptible to biological, phenomenological or cultural interpretation. Accordingly, all attempts to identify gender differences in these ways can only fail (in Barnard and Fink, 2002).

All too frequently, however, Lacan and those who follow in his footsteps slide into gendered terminology without qualification. They insist that Lacan's sexuation theory is not a sociological take on gender, yet it is the sociological conditions under which we are sexed and directed along bifurcating pathways that, to my mind at least, makes the theory relevant and not just the stuff of philosophical inspection. In respect to the terminology, I have to agree with Segal (2005: 184) when she writes:

> We can accept the historical primacy given to the 'phallus' as symbol of male power in language (and the related notion of the fantasy of 'castration' imposing a narcissistic 'wound' on the female body even as it orchestrates fear around the male body), while at the same time questioning – rather than insistently reproducing – its singular primacy in the Symbolic.

To summarize, there are two possible ways of relating to the phallus: the masculine 'having mode' and the feminine 'being mode'. The (real) father is the fantasy of unlimited *jouissance*, the exception who is not castrated, placing the male, who by comparison is inadequate, entirely in the phallic function. His *jouissance* is thereby phallic oriented. Feminine sexuality, on the other hand, 'Other *jouissance*', is not wholly in the phallic function. Her *jouissance* is real in the sense that it does not depend on a phallic supplement. In proximity to the real and *objet a*, feminine *jouissance* traces multiple pathways – cathects in a multiplicity of ways – a supplementary *jouissance* inaccessible to the male whose *jouissance* is more singular.

Lacan puts signification centre stage. Resignification is what I close this chapter with.

Refusal through resignification

Channelling its power through the narrow straits of the capitalist patriarchy, the masculine ego-formation is a dam to the polymorphous libidinal drive. A feminine praxis is no dam buster. It is rather more like a gradual process of unwinding by opening new channels to enable libido for a multi-directional catharsis. At one extremity of the masculinities spectrum are the most toxic of subjects, often right wing but sometimes left wing. I called these reactive/aggravated masculinities (RAMS). They are wound up so tightly that the only way they appear to be able to liberate the flows is by catastrophically bursting the dam: destroying themselves and everyone in the wake of the subsequent torrent. REMS, on the other hand, reflective/ experimental masculinities, are not afraid of the feminine. They unwind the taps. They unwind them through their experiments with feminine accoutrements and affects. They may identify as non-binary, but due to the conservatism of dress would not be presumed to be a trans woman. Never presumed transgender, Prince, who frequently subverted gender boundaries, would be an exemplar of such a masculinity. Analogous to an elastic band, such men, non-binary and genderqueer, stretch the meaning of the word but not to the point that, at least as others are likely to perceive them, they are off the spectrum altogether.

The feminine is not opposed to the masculine. It is a dialectical means through which, in an ongoing process of separation, blockages in the ego are removed, thus enabling libido to flow in multiple directions without causing catastrophes. Without this dialectical reading of the feminine, the obstacles to, and potential for, liberation is impossible to theorize. The allusions to a progressive masculinity do not cut it. In Connell, there is no equivalent to REMS, no concept of agency as such or theory of how the meaning of masculinity can be stretched and ultimately the term abandoned altogether. Connell's offerings are just the banal statement that meanings differ in space and time and according to the intersections of class, race and so forth. When the repudiations of femininity, which theorists do acknowledge, is a passing thought and not central to the analysis, there is nothing to say about the disruptive force of being trans and why there is so much hostility towards trans women in particular. Critics are mute. Their utopias are the ones of a society that sustains masculine domination because no alternative is conceivable or because their horizons so limited. We need to do more, however, than speculate on a utopia of a classless society in which the institutions of Oedipalization have been dismantled. We need to formulate ways to test the reality principle and stretch it beyond its limits in the here and now. Even if this proves impossible to achieve, our attempts to do so can have the effect of turning the tide towards REMS and a progressive recalibration of masculinity. There is no end point at which masculinity is sufficiently recalibrated, such as the anti-patriarchy masculinity hooks speaks of. If there is an end point, it is when the term 'calibrated masculinity' is as redundant as the term 'calibrated femininity' is. In other words, it is only in a patriarchal androcentric society that, conceptually, the former has explanatory value and the latter does not. The disorder will not be ended under capitalism. The next chapter explains why.

4

Vectors of androcentrism

Capital's incessant drive for surplus value lays the world to waste. A wasteland in which, monuments to man, gleaming glass towers are erected. Exhausting the soils of their nutrients, extracting deep from beneath the surface, capitalism fashions a world and its peoples in its image. From what we know about the masculine disorder, it should be of no surprise that sociopaths such as Donald Trump, Boris Johnson, Jair Bolsonaro, Viktor Orban and Vladimir Putin become leaders of millions. Their flaws are all too evident for their masculinity to function as a calibrated ideal. They are beyond the point of calibration but clearly nonetheless have pulling power. It is no mystery as to why RAMS like these get into such positions, run multinational corporations and become vice chancellors of neoliberalized universities. In a system in which profit matters more than planetary life, they are the sickness of capitalism personified. The sociopaths in high office whose cold and callous ruthlessness is an asset are evidence of this chapter's central thesis; the masculine disorder is necessary to capitalism. Just as there can be no capitalism without a working class to exploit, there can be no capitalism without a psyche that rebels against anything held as feminine.

'Capitalism is such a macho force', director Jane Campion despairs in a recent interview.[1] She has a point. In prior chapters, three pieces of evidence in support of masculinity as a disorder were offered. The first of these was that it is nearly always men who commit extreme acts of (ego-motivated) violence. The second, made visible by the trans exception, was the almost total absence of feminine signifiers on the bodies of the vast majority of men. The third was the popularity of the Oedipal drama in entertainment media. Westernized culture is

thoroughly androcentric. To this can now be added the fourth piece
of evidence: how the mode of production aligns to masculine traits.
The extreme; the exception; the fantasy; and now the economy. My
claim in this chapter, which is neither original nor controversial, is that
for capitalism to exist, a particular subject is required: one who is
psychically mutilated in advance of their alienation as workers,
consumers, caregivers and agents of the repressive state apparatuses
– the vectors along which, for the reproduction and expansion of
capital to occur, the androcentric subject must travel.

To be sure, capitalism didn't invent androcentrism. Patriarchy and
the violence of men precede it and were present in societies before
the European invaders laid them to waste. However, the capitalist
mode of production requires a particular form of masculinity that this
book diagnoses. Capitalism is a 'man-made' libidinal economy. Not
only does it require of the subject that they labour under the condition.
It requires a libidinal investment. The wanderlust of the mongrel
invaders draws from the same libidinal reservoir as those who
slaughtered the Mai Lai villagers and today gun down schoolchildren
from behind the wall that contains and imprisons Palestinians. But
capitalism taps this reservoir in other ways too that are quite
distinctive from any other mode of production. Even if comparisons
can be found, only in capitalism is it imperative that on a societal wide
level libido is also invested in waged labour, consumption for
consumption sake, and the reproduction of the species. The libido is
really and fully subsumed by this mode of production. And in respect
of species reproduction, this is not for the pleasures of sexual
congress or the need to put children to the fields but because a child
fulfils a manufactured gap in the psyche. Coming later in the chapter,
its centrepiece, is the four aforementioned, though perhaps not
exhaustible, intersecting vectors along which a masculinized libido
travels. I describe these as the four labours: waged labour, consuming
labour, repressive labour and reproductive labour. These alight on the
historically specific, interconnected and materially determined form
that I diagnose as the masculine disorder.

The eponymous figure of Werner Herzog's *The Enigma of Kaspar
Hauser* asks a poignant question that this chapter reformulates. Isolated
in a tiny dwelling in the remote countryside for the first twenty or so
years of his life, Hauser's only interaction was with the man who looked

after him and held him captive. When finally set free, Kaspar goes for the first time to the city and finds himself in the company of society. He views it with all the open-eyed naivety of a young child. In the scene, he reflects on his observations of women. He asks in earnest, 'What are women good for?' 'Why are women allowed only to knit and cook?' In the absence of prejudice, it was an unvarnished observation of how things materially are. As adults, we lose sight of this. Conditions that might be noted by an alien are abstractions to those whose thoughts are trained on dinner or a clean pair of underpants. What would Hauser have said of men? That all they do is argue, fight and compete? Men are good for capitalism. In this chapter I draw on Marx's method of abstraction that distils from what appears concrete or a naturally given the multiple factors that engender and ensure capitalism. Marx's method does for this chapter what Freud's theory of Oedipalization has done for the earlier ones. Marx's method of abstraction is first elucidated – not for the sake of it but because it helps to explain precisely why capitalism requires the masculine form I describe.

Cups and sorcerers

The term 'gender' was not part of Freud's vocabulary. However, he discerned in the givenness of heteronormativity the source of its bifurcation in drives, the Oedipal complex and the superego–ego–id triad. These concepts enabled him and us to view human sexuality from a radically different perspective to those who presume our sexuality and gender a natural given. Marx's dialectical method enables us to do likewise with the commodity and the relations that their exchange for money mystifies. Explaining Marx's method, Floyd (2009: 27) writes that he frames it 'in terms of an ongoing movement between the concrete . . . and the abstract'. Think again here of gender. It appears concrete or a naturally given but in actual fact is an abstraction of the relationships that Freud elucidated. The pleasure principle is an abstract concept but when related to the superego a concrete determinant of the bifurcation of sexuality into two discernible though ideologically mystifying genders.

What Marx does is take objects that appear concrete to us and examine how they came to be. Marx calls the commodity the imagined concrete. Like the givenness of gender, what appears concrete to us exists through complex processes and relationships that are obscured. Marx's dialectical method begins with what appears concrete but is essentially an abstract phenomenon and peels away its many different layers to reveal its multiple and interconnected concrete determinants. One such determinant is the exploitation of labour power. As with feminist theory that shows us gender is not determined by sex, when you arrive at such points the world appears differently to you. Marx affords a different and more complete perspective on the conditions under which we labour and consume. He shows that the commodities we daily depend upon are the product of exploitation, oppression and plunder.

Profit is not the end for capital but merely its means for the 'ceaseless augmentation of value' (Marx, 1982: 254). What makes capitalism such a destructive force is that 'the capitalist must by necessity, throw his money again and again into circulation' (1982: 254). As an expression of this, Marx introduces the formula for capital M–C–M'. The M stands for money, the C is commodity, the second M money (return on initial monetary investment) and the dash or prime the value capital extracts from the worker in excess of what they are remunerated for. The dash stands for surplus value or the self-valorization of value.

Unpacking this a little, money capital (M) is essential for kick-starting the process of accumulation and expansion. It is invested in the means of production (MP) and labour power (LP). Labour power is crucial to the production of the commodity (C). It works the machines, crafts the materials, does the paperwork and hawks the product – a thing, service or whatever. Labour is the source of value. What Marx means here is that profit, realized in exchange, can only be generated by exploiting waged labour, not by the machinery involved in the production. If, as Deleuze and Guattari say, capitalism is an abstract machine, as with every assemblage, it requires libidinal energy to electrify its circuits. The extra 'value' that is reaped by the capitalist increases when they increase what they steal: the value the labourer generates in excess of the value of their wages. Machinery reproduces its value. Unlike labour, it cannot be made to augment value by autonomously improving its efficiency. Labour, on the other hand, possesses the capacity to work for longer hours (absolute surplus value) and, perhaps through training now undertaken at the labourer's expense, improve its efficiency (relative surplus value). Machinery (MP) is fixed capital. Labour is in contrast variable capital. It varies in value according to its capacity to add value. Without a trade union to fight for their collective interest, labour is under constant pressure to produce through these means more surplus value for the capitalist which in turn the latter must maintain in order to compete with other capitalists. Whatever moral position we might take in respect to capital's drive for profit, like the worker compelled to compete with other workers, for its own survival capital is compelled to reduce the costs of the labour it exploits. Household labour, which involves replenishing and revitalizing the workforce, is also of course vital to capital. But it is not directly exploited and does not produce commodities that the capitalist can take to market and when purchased by a consumer derive profit from. I'll return to this later.

Marx famously wrote that a 'definite social relation' that exists between 'men' appears only in a 'fantastic form' as a relationship between commodities whose language of communication is money (Marx, 1982: 165). This is what Marx means by commodity fetishism. It is through his dialectical method of abstraction that the 'secret' the commodity obscures is revealed.

In volume one of *Capital*, Marx begins with the commodity, like the cup that you're perhaps currently holding in your hand. A cup and the purpose for which it serves would be as recognizable to a child in twenty-first-century America as it would a peasant in the time of the Shang Dynasty, some 2,000 years before Christ. The cup made by a factory worker serves the same material function as that produced by an artisan in the Shang Dynasty, but that's where all comparisons end. Unlike the artisan who independently produces commodities to sustain their livelihood, the worker's livelihood is conditional on the capitalist who employs them for whom the commodity is produced for its exchange value. In contrast to the production of artefacts in peasant societies, capitalist production requires massive infrastructure and complex supply chains – in other words, an entirely new form of distribution. It requires a labour force whose only asset is their capacity to labour. It requires the commodification of land, labour and money – a different form of exchange – and the total subsumption of society in the service of capital's historically specific purpose.

Thanks in part to the ethical marketing strategies of corporations, it could be said that today we're all aware that commodities do not appear magically from nowhere. However, by marketing the product on the basis that the workers producing it are not as exploited as those produced by the competition, they appear to have done what Marx has and 'demystified' the conditions under which commodities are produced. In *Capitalism's New Clothes* (2011), I described this apparent inversion as another form of mystification. There is sorcery here. It taps knowledge that things are not always as they appear – that coffee in its polystyrene cup is environmentally destructive and that the beans are harvested by impoverished farmers in the so-called developing world. But this misses the point. It does not mean that as consumers we have 'demystified' the matter and that when purchasing the commodity are now cognizant of the real relations that exist between people in the production chain, not least the role of women in the sphere of social reproduction. It is impossible to be fully cognizant of all the labour that is required in order for the consumer to have their coffee. Irrespective of our grasp on the totality, money is the medium through which the consumer evaluates the value of the commodity. Exchange value does to sensual activity what a name does to the person. It obscures all the complexities of life. Exchange value quantifies what is qualitative and incomparable. Thus, the value of an artwork can be compared to the value of a film, a loaf of bread or the labourer. Is it any good? It made a zillion dollars at the box office, so what do you think?! It is the labour power (LP) that gets lost in translation. Labour power is itself quantified and, obscenely, thus renders the human comparable to a product.

By delving beyond the world of appearances and inquiring into the processes through which the commodity arises, different moments in the circulation and expansion of capital are revealed. Connections can be made between the raw materials mined in regions long ago colonized by the Europeans, tariffs on commodities exported from those countries, cargo ships with their massive carbon emissions, the harsh conditions of factory workers, through to the immigrant on a low wage taking your money on behalf of the company that employs them . The worker produces use-values, things that the consumer deems useful and desirable, but the capitalist's only interest is exchange value. In other words, the purposes for which the commodity serves are of no interest to the capitalist, only whether the commodity will be purchased at a price and in sufficient quantities to generate profit. No matter how important it is to life, if there is no profit in it that product will not be manufactured. The capitalist is in the business of manufacturing articles and services that a sufficient number of consumers will see value in and have the wage capacity (or access to credit) to afford. In other words, a mass market is needed in order for production to be justified. It is social use-values that capital caters for, not individual needs as such.

'Consumption,' Marx (1973: 91) writes, 'creates the motive for production'. Production, in turn, 'mediates consumption; it creates the latter's material'. Thus, were it not for production, the consumer would lack an object to consume. Without an object to consume, there is no consumer. It follows from this, then, that production is not only dependent on a consumer. Anticipating the so-called consumer economy by almost 100 years – think here of the person who identifies themselves with the brand and measures their status in terms of what they own – consumption 'alone creates for the products the subject for whom they are products' (Marx 1973: 91). In Bourdieu's terms, if a thing has 'cultural capital' there is use in it. I'd put this differently. In late capitalism the social use-value of an article is not principally in its utility – whether, that is, it satisfies a material need. The value is in its phallic function. This qualification corrects a misconception that Marx was only referring to utility. If that were the case, his theory would not be able to explain why commodities that serve no material need have social use-value. It would have no explanatory value to an economy in which production is geared to desire not need. His theory would have to be abandoned. Where consumption serves a phallic function, consumption can be said to be masculine. I return to this later.

To summarize this brief outline of Marx's method and understanding of capital, in Marx's own words:

> Use-values must . . . never be treated as the immediate aim of the capitalist; nor must the profit on any single transaction. His aim is rather the unceasing movement of profit-making. This boundless drive for enrichment, this passionate chase after value, is common to the capitalist and the miser; but while the miser is merely a

capitalist gone mad, the capitalist is a rational miser. The ceaseless augmentation of value, which the miser seeks to attain by saving his money from circulation, is achieved by the more acute capitalist by means of throwing his money again and again into circulation.

MARX 1982: 254

Marx enables us to grasp in the totality the many different determinants of it. His method is exemplary of the cognitive mapping Jameson said was essential to a socialist project. By knowing what drives capital, we also know what hurts it and thereby what needs to be done to end this cycle of an ever greater magnitudes of destruction. Marx does not have much to say about the state or gender, and does not to my knowledge question the masculine ego-formation. The bourgeois family is, for example, one of those hidden determinants that feminists have rightly factored as a concrete determinant within the totality of capitalist accumulation. Drucker (2015: 52) calls the family 'integral parts of a gendered capitalist totality'.

The next section takes Marx to where capital appears at its most progressive. It shows, through recourse to Marx's way of theorizing the totality, that, taking Amazon's CEO Jeff Bezos as an example, the strongest advocates of LGBTQI+ are not evidence that capitalism can fully accommodate a diversity of genders and sexualities nor that capitalism no longer has a use for patriarchy.

Bezos on the barricade

Herbie, flower power, all things to all people, a friend more than a motorcar – we all loved the original Volkswagen Beetle. The 1998 redesign ought to have been a sales sensation. But instead it was a flop. Men, a segment of the market that is not exactly a niche, were put off by the feminine curves of the car. Should Volkswagen have anticipated this reaction? Would things have been different had they read Freud? You can't blame them. If men had no problem driving the same vehicle in the 1960s and 1970s, why wouldn't they be lapping it up like the dogs they are in this more gender-fluid age? There's nothing like demand, or lack thereof, to force a rethink. A retrograde step by some measure, Volkswagen returned to the drawing board and launched their more gender conservative redesign in 2012. It had a bigger trunk, flatter roof, less bulbous shape and, underlining its utilitarian credentials, a navigation system. Men were so tickled that Mars Bars shot out from anuses, and sales, for a while at least, jumped fivefold.[2]

The gender binary does matter to business but not as one might think. Businessmen do not gather in dark rooms devising schemes for how to reinforce it through marketing. What matters to them is how the punter sees themselves and the image they want to project, to which the product is aligned. Volkswagen was naive. Gillette had the sense at least to recognize that it is one thing to link a brand with progressive ideas, quite another to design their product to reflect them. Ideas and practice rarely coincide. It's the companies whose products are gendered that I feel sorry for, the sort that would have most to gain if men were not averse to femininity. Tights UK (they sell tights), for example, would like nothing more than for the taboo on men wearing tights to be lifted. Boasting that they are the largest online retailer of hosiery in the world, they reassure that 'gender . . . is not an issue'. And to normalize what in some people's mind would be considered a fetish, in fact 'a large part of our customer base are men and we welcome them'.[3] What might be good for an individual business is no measure of what is good for capitalism as a whole. This distinction between individual capitalists and capitalism in the abstract is a crucial one that I will return to momentarily.

In a celebratory video, 'award winning' LGBTQI+ advocate Jeff Bezos, CEO of Amazon, is thanked by company employees and celebrities. Star of the show *Transparent*, cisgender Gaby Hoffman, who plays transgender Ali Pfefferman, describes Bezos as a 'total liberator'. A gay woman adds that Amazon is an 'easy place to be myself.' As if to deflect the view that all this is a cynical branding exercise, another explains 'why diversity and inclusion' is 'important to business and as a community'. Ticking the intersectionality boxes, a self-defined queer, transgender, Jewish, mixed race and female employee agrees. Hoffman adds, 'We need leaders like Jeff and Jeff is a leader.' 'Thank you, Jeff, for being a huge advocate, a leader, a strong voice', chimes another and adds that Amazon is 'a company where people can bring their full selves'. We're reminded of Jeff and McKenzie Bezos's 'gift' of $2.5 million for Washington State's marriage equality 'initiative' and the '1000s of articles' thanking them for their generosity. The five-minute sequence is interspersed with clips from Amazon-sponsored gay pride events featuring company-emblazoned flotillas and rainbow-dressed staff, beaming photographs of Jeff and his wife with Michelle Obama and other famous people who share his inclusive vision. We don't need reminding that their donations are a fraction of their wealth rapidly approaching a trillion dollars, nor of their near total domination of retail, the precarious and low paid labour of many of the workers it employs directly as well as those that it doesn't. As an exercise in impression management it says nothing of course about class divisions, structural racism or the many transgender people barely surviving in a society in which violence is daily meted out to them.

This is one of many examples that could be provided to support James Penney's claim that there is nothing political in queer identities and sexualities which academics in these fields, he adds, trade on and derive considerable kudos from. Rather than the trite assertion that queer is political, Penny (2014: 1) makes the point that 'politics is inherently sexual'. Recalling the polymorphous perversity of the drive, the idea of a queer universalism, he says, 'is compromised by both an identitarian gesture of self-privileging and a reference, tending towards paranoia, to the quasi-omnipotence of heterosexism or "heteronormativity"' (2014: 5). And I would agree, hence why, aside from what psychoanalysis tells us about sexuality, a class perspective on LGBTQI+ grounded in the material conditions of existence is essential.

Žižek (2020: 257) claims that the 'true representatives of global capitalism are figures like Tim Cook who fully support LGBT+'. They are what I called in the previous chapter the calibrated masculinity that in this ideological constellation have the biggest phalluses. But do they signal that capitalism can, as Žižek claims, fully accommodate these differences and have no interest in sustaining patriarchy, such that it is even considered to exist in any material sense? What Žižek suggests in the above quote is right, but the conclusion drawn from it is wrong. I shall explain why through recourse to a formula for sexuality introduced in my previous book, *Man-Made Woman* (2017). The example is especially poignant as Žižek critiqued it in *Sex and the Failed Absolute* (2020).

The formula is LGBT+[]/. If I were to formulate this now, I would add QI. The + sign was introduced (by others) as a shorthand to register all those sexualities that the letters themselves do not apply to. So, in this respect the Q and I can be inferred. In solidarity with those who identify with labels, I added the brackets to denote a registration that one's sex or gender is 'non-normative' but without an identity. This was not to suggest that one can go about life without depending on significations. Rather it was to intimate, in Marcuse's terms, a Great Refusal of the idea that one is reducible to a label and affirmation of a future prospectus in which labels such as these are no longer necessary either for material survival or political purposes. One of Žižek's favourite references is Fritz Lang's answer in Godard's *Le Mepris* (he plays himself) to an invitation to 'include me, out'. This is essentially what the brackets register. But there is nothing political in itself in being 'queer' or 'trans'. Hence why to politicize the chain I added a forward slash. This registers an antagonism to the capitalist patriarchy and a political orientation towards ending it. Hence, we are not reducible to a particular sign. I, for example, identify with three of them. T for trans, [] for the ideal of identification in no identity, and, because of my politics, /. Better still, rather than refer to myself as a trans woman or, denoting a trans becoming, trans-, the brackets can be put to another use. I am a [trans] woman. [T] woman or man is an affirmation of our identity as real women or men but which at the same time denotes a minimal difference relating to process, perspective and positionality in a society that genders sex. My own identity reads therefore as [T]/.

Žižek's charge is that in respect of the [], it is impossible to exist outside the law of signification. This, for the aforementioned reason, misses the point. Žižek also says that by desiring a name, trans women are masculine in their sexuality. Because for Lacan all demands for a name are in the masculine register, it follows that a trans woman is masculine. We're damned if we do and damned if we don't. I can't exist without a name, but in 'demanding' one I am masculine.

Obviously, in respect of /, the likes of Bezos and Cook are not fully accommodating to the idea of self-eradication. The main point, however, is that whatever the 'values' of an individual capitalist, capitalism in the abstract cannot embed the values that Bezos and

Cook amongst others espouse. Such calibrated men may not regard the gender division of labour positive. Nevertheless, for the replenishment and revitalization of the workforce, they depend on women to get pregnant, raise children and care for loved ones. They would vigorously oppose a political party whose manifesto declared that if voted into power they would make them pay for it. They may not celebrate and advocate chronic levels of poverty, but in order to access raw materials and cheap labour, they depend on chronic levels of poverty and oppression in the global south. When the values of the individual capitalist are considered evidence that capital can fully accommodate the dismantling of the institutions of patriarchy, there is a mystification of the multiple and interconnected concrete determinants vital to it. Marx does indeed demystify appearances – which is why his method of abstraction is essential. He was able to discern through this method the chief and sordid origins of capital. I index this in the next section to those who also stress how patriarchy and white supremacy were braided together in the formative years of capital.

Dawn of the disorder

Once it has laid down its roots, like that of a weed, capital spreads across the earth and deprives it of all the nutrients on which life depends. The seeds of accumulation for accumulation's sake appears to have been sown in Britain where capitalism in its modern form flourished. It sprouted from the Calvinist doctrine of predestination, Weber writes. Those destined, one might say entitled, to an afterlife were known by their industry. Unlike the hedonist who blows money on pleasure or the miser who hoards their gains, the Protestant found a motive in religion for throwing money after money. Hence, for Weber, an elective affinity between Protestantism and capitalism was forged. Lacan identified a different kind of elective affinity – that between the subject for whom lack is the ontological condition and the ontological need of capital to ceaselessly expand value. The trick of the latter was to persuade the former that the object to end dissatisfaction could be found at work and in phallic consumption. What Marx called labour power is for Lacan the gift of *jouissance*, or a surplus of libido. Whereas for Deleuze and Guattari, desire is simply a productive force, not a condition arising from an ontological lack, that functions like a cog in the machinery of abstraction. Though never stated by Marx, in these accounts the economy can be described as a libidinal one. If there is such a thing as a work ethic, it lies from the Lacanian point of view in the enjoyment of the dissatisfying effects of being exploited. Lacan does not explain the origin of capitalism, but Marx, on the other hand, traces capitalism's formative years to plunder, pillage and slavery. His description of primitive accumulation is both poetic and devastating:

> The discovery of gold and silver in America, the extirpation, enslavement and entombment in mines of the indigenous population of that continent, the beginnings of the conquest and plunder of India, and the conversion of Africa into a preserve for the commercial hunting of blackskins, are all things which characterise the dawn of the era of capitalist production.'
>
> MARX, 1982: 915

Armed with their commodities, the European invaders transformed the world but did not entirely determine it. As Cedric J. Robinson (2000) reminds us in *Black Marxism*, the regions that capital colonized also, in turn, transformed Europe. Not only was slave and a racialized immigrant labour foundational to the development of capitalism in Europe, their values, ideas and distinctive social practices inflect and refract on Europe and the world. Violent expropriation of communal property, expulsion from their lands, enslavement and the creation of a massive reserve army of 'free labour', what Marx calls a 'primitive accumulation', is theft by any other name. It continues under different guises. Austerity, imperialism, privatization, property speculators pricing people out of their communities, and the hiving off of public services to private contractors are instances of a modern form of primitive accumulation that David Harvey (2007) describes as 'accumulation by dispossession'. Neoliberalism is anticipated by Marx (1982: 873) as 'those moments [in class history] when great masses of men are suddenly and forcibly torn from their means of subsistence, and hurled onto the labour-market as free, unprotected and rightless proletarians'.

By the late nineteenth century, 'civilization' and white male bodies had, in the United States, according to Bederman (1995: 55), become synonymous with notions of manhood. Presumed the natural leader, white males were endowed with hegemonic power. This idea, Bederman says, was promulgated at the World's Columbian Exposition of 1883 held in Chicago. It was also during this time that, linked to the Darwinian idea of the survival of the fittest, primitivism became a byword for masculinity. The aforementioned Tarzan of the Apes was the perfect myth through which to conflate the notion of Anglo-Saxon manliness with the most 'primal' of masculinities. The Tarzan figure represented the power and identity to which the white male felt themselves capable of embodying.

Drucker (2015: 99) adds to this narrative the imposition of a hetero/homo binary. It took shape towards the end of the nineteenth century and the classical period of imperialism. This was prefigured by the enforcing of patriarchy within the colonies. He writes that (2015: 131) 'Imperialism entailed the spread not only of the new category of homosexuality, but also of its official persecution.' Thus, many of the 'laws against sex between males on the books in much of Africa and Asia today are copies of an old British law repealed in Britain in 1967'. It is this 'hetero-gendered social matrix' that the bourgeois patriarchy depends on, writes Hennessy (2000: 25). It is a 'social matrix that includes imaginary identifications with opposite and asymmetrical masculine or feminine positions' as naturalized expressions of males and females. It makes the precariousness of these identifications fixed opposing categories, turning those who do not neatly fit them into outcasts.

These discourses are examples of what Spivak describes as 'epistemic violence'. It is a mode of domination legitimated through a process of naming and 'othering'. The proliferation of names, writes Bannerji (1995), serves to isolate, dehumanize and delegitimate those that by definition do not represent the hegemonic norm or ideal. But this, Bannerji makes clear, cannot be disassociated from class history and processes of primitive accumulation. The idea that class, race and gender 'intersect' at a cultural level can, however, have the effect of mystifying class relations and also dehistoricizing colonization, conquest and domination. This effect is also achieved, according to Bannerji, with the concept of 'woman' as an undifferentiated category of person subordinated under patriarchy. Returning to this point in the next chapter, the universalized notion of 'sisterhood' flattens class and colonial history, centring patriarchal oppression on the experience of white liberal feminists. 'Race', as Robinson shows, also became a category through which class relations were organized.

The witch hunts of the sixteenth and seventeenth centuries also portended the establishment of a white hetero-patriarchy and generalized masculine disorder. They served to exclude women from waged labour and ensure their subordination to men (Mies, 1994). The subsumption of women's labour within capital occurred through another form of primitive accumulation, Federici writes, that was just as instrumental to its development as the colonization of the New World. The persecution of those deemed witches forced the peasantry from the land, divided the household and, with no other available resource, threw them into competition with one another for jobs. It was instrumental not only in affording capital a plentiful supply of cheap labour, but helped create gender divisions and the 'full-time' proletarian housewife. With the support of the state in caring for the worker and through childbirth replenishing the labour force, the housewife became fully subsumed under capital.

Feinberg (1996) also describes a pre-history of trans oppression. Trans oppression, hir [sic.] writes, can be traced back to the overthrow of the matrilineal kinship networks found amongst tribes in Asia, Africa and Australia. Marx and Engels, Feinberg notes, saw evidence in a study by Morgan of the roots of women's oppression. The persecution of witches also coincided with the Church's demonization of transgender which goes back as far as the sixth century. However, it wasn't until the nineteenth century that the gender paradigm came into vogue in the West and as late as the twentieth century, as hir observes, when pink in the United States was considered a girl's colour where previously it was considered a boy's one.

In the global south, neoliberal ideology informed the so-called Structural Adjustment Programmes, imposed through their different mechanisms, by the World Bank and IMF. Drucker (2015: 227) points to the additional stress these programmes imposed on households already struggling. He draws comparisons with monetary policies in the European Union enshrined in the Maastricht Treaty to justify decades of imposed austerity. 'Worldwide neoliberal policies,' writes Drucker (2015: 227), 'have thus made the family more crucial than ever to the reproduction of capital.' It has created further divisions between genders, adding support to Federici's claim that feminine labour is fully subsumed by capital. At a time when gender and sexual diversity is being celebrated as an established fact, parents, Drucker (2015: 227) continues, are being further incentivized to 'encourage and discourage different behaviours in boys and girls'. Scholz (2009: 130) claims the male gender is 'the gender of capitalism', predicated on a 'dualist understanding of gender' but one that is nonetheless the predominant way in which gender in late capitalism is formalized. 'Subject and object, domination and subjugation, man and woman are thus typical dichotomies, antagonistic counterparts within the commodity-producing patriarchy.'

Thus, as Arruzza et al. (2019: 68) put it, capitalism today is 'inextricably braided' by two 'mutually opposed imperatives'. One is profit through the exploitation of labour power, and the other, the 'social reproduction' of the workforce. This label serves as an umbrella term for activities that sustain human life. This includes the servicing of biological needs, but also giving birth, raising children, tending to the emotions and the supporting of the community.

Given what we know about men, it is of no surprise that, in the time of Coronavirus, a highly masculinized society such as the United States is the world leader in infections and deaths. At the time of writing, an estimated 40 million[4] Americans have lost their jobs as a result of Covid-19. But unlike other leading economies, in the US medical and welfare provisions are wholly inadequate in supporting those who have been hardest hit. Brenner (2020) notes that corporations were offered, with the support of both Republicans and Democrats, a 'no strings attached' $4.586 trillion bailout. By comparison, $603 billion was the sum total allocated to individuals and families in direct need of support. The result of this is that 'between 18 March 2020 and 4 June 2020, the wealth of US billionaires increased by $565 billion, reaching the level of $3.5 trillion in total, up 19 per cent in the interval' (2020: 19). It is difficult to conceive of the suffering and desperation of so many Americans as a result of this, but also, as the two are connected, the work of previous administrations, both Republican and Democrat, in shifting the balance further and further in favour of the elites whose wealth has increased exponentially over the last several decades. As Nancy Fraser (2016) reminds us, when the state provides no assistance, it is left to women in the community to hold society together.

Now to the centrepiece of this chapter: the four vectors along which the masculinized libido travels and through which, taken together, the (fully subsumed) form of masculinity specific to capital is theorized.

The four labours of masculinity

Capitalism, Marx (1982: 481) said, 'seizes labour-power by its roots'. It converts the 'worker into a crippled monstrosity by furthering his particular skill as in a forcing-house, through the suppression of a whole world of productive drives and inclinations'. This crippling effect of specializing in tasks, like that of an 'automatic motor of a detail operation', parallel the crippling effect of masculinization, which alienated labour compounds. Nowhere does alienation itself sound more like a psychological disorder than when Marx says that capitalism 'attacks the individual at the very roots of his life, it is the first system to provide the materials and the impetus for industrial pathology' (Marx: 1982: 484).

Gendering is a form of specialization. The more towards the RAMS end of the masculinities spectrum, the more limited are the range of operations. If not reflected in the work that such men do, it is reflected in the repertoire of emotional expressions available and their destructive effects. However, the principal benefit to capital of this form of psychic mutilation is to engender a need for phallic supplements that are found in alienated labour, consumer products, state-sanctioned violence and, casting women in a supporting role, the reproduction of the disorder itself. These are the four vectors of androcentrism discussed presently. The damage is already done before or whether the subject enters into the workplace, their psyche already made plastic to capital. As per the formation of the subject, psychoanalysis offers a systematic account for what Marx only describes in general terms and which, for the latter, centres on what happens when the subject enters the workplace.

Marx describes four kinds of alienation, each of which are related to exploited waged labour, and so quite narrow in this respect. The first of these is alienation from the object of labour. It is not merely that the object itself is owned by the capitalist but also that it is produced for the purpose of an exchange whose social benefits are questionable at best. The second aspect relates to the division of labour and specialization of tasks, alienation from the act itself. Work becomes monotonous, unfulfilling, sapping and, in many instances, soul destroying. Work appears as a form of indenture to free ourselves of at the first opportunity. Hence why we have the notion of 'free-time'. 'Free labour' is unfree. The third kind of alienation, alienation from species-specific capacities or species being, is closest to the description of the effects of masculinization on the capacities of the individual, which I'll come back to in a second. The fourth is alienation from one another: the worker identifies their kind as competitors rather than comrades on the same side of the class struggle. This is especially apparent in anti-immigration sentiments and xenophobia.

What distinguishes the activity of the 'worst of architects' from that of the 'best of bees', wrote Marx (1982: 284), is that the former crafts in their mind the image of their creation before embarking on its construction. We possess the species-specific capacity to observe the bird in flight and figure the means through which to fly too. In such ways, we fashion nature into the image of thought. Whereas animals adapt to environmental changes, humans change the environment. In the space of a single generation, they themselves change. Thatcher famously said that neoliberalism was nothing less than a project to change the soul. It was its principal triumph and proof that our 'nature' is socially-determined and adapts rapidly to changes in the material conditions. This is not to say that we are entirely 'determined' by these conditions. If this were so there would be no prospect for collectively changing them. We become alienated from our species-specific capacities because of how thought and creativity are marshalled to the singular activity of augmenting value for the capitalist. It is not only nature itself that becomes victim to the overriding logic of accumulation here. The capacities inherent to us all are atrophied in mind-numbing routine labour and, if tapped at all, stand opposed to us as belonging to the capitalist. The tragedy is that we are all capable of 'being creative' but few have the opportunity to nurture this capacity. Only a few put their abilities to use other than in these highly specialized ways. Even the work of so-called 'creatives' and 'intellectuals' is determined, more or less, by the logic of exchange.

It is a standard motif of critics of patriarchy such as Cixous (in Bray, 2004) that capitalism is phallocentric. The Westernized imaginary of scientific reason is presumed masculine and sensuality feminine. Cixous argues that the economy needs to be framed in feminine terms in order to overcome the idea that the female body is inferior to the male one (the essentialism here and exclusion therein of trans people in this reasoning is clear enough). The hidden abode by which society holds together, the feminine, is, however, worth stressing as a signifier (not anything essential) of the collective. It is what is signified by it that we depend upon to survive in this atomized society – namely the care we provide for one another that is frequently taken for granted and which ensures that a system organized for profit does not descend into chaos. Capitalism appears only to be individualistic. At base it is social through and through. While exchange value is an inextricable mystifying force; in comparable measure the masculinized economy mystifies and devalues the feminine in all its forms and manifestations. A capitalist economy that priorities use-values is a contradiction in terms. An economy that prioritizes the feminine is likewise a contradiction. For to do so would be to put people before profit.

Heidi Nast (2015) claims that in the early industrial period the inordinate power of the machine was something that the working class handled and took pride in. The machine was an extension of the ego. It was, in other words, their phallic supplement. This had a twofold effect. It instilled in men a feeling of superiority over women and those from the colonies where production wasn't as developed. Neoliberalism, however, robbed the worker of their phallus. The scaling back of industry in countries such as Britain, which was made possible through the defeats inflicted on organized labour, had an emasculating effect. One can see here how the working class, trade unions, even socialism, came to connote masculinity. 'Service work', which by comparison doesn't rely on brute force and is typically more fragmented, comes by the same token to connote femininity. With no option available other than to work in a call centre, the once proud pit worker is emasculated.

From the top of the labour hierarchy where tenured professors are perched, to the bottom where casualized workers eke out a living, often under the professor's supervision, the alienated and the masculinized are one and the same person. The neoliberal myth that the subject is by nature self-serving is not one that psychoanalysis propagates. Due to the combinatory and historically compounding effects of being raised and compelled to live under capitalism, the concept of a gender binary and individualistic self-interest only appear as a reflection of nature. Economy is married to a psyche whose libido is repressed and channelled along pathways – Freud would call it a desexualized sublimation – that are both individually and socially destructive. Industries in which a premium is offered to those who instrumentalize their smile and warm persona rely on what Hochschild (1983) called 'emotional labour'. This type of labour is in certain respects even more alienating. For not only does it draw on capacities that are considered feminine and which are healthy to any society, it turns them into instruments of capital. They become another set of objects that the subject is alienated from and are also thereby phallicized. The effect is to degrade and eviscerate the qualities that must be nourished if an alternative compact is to be forged. Once again, the dialectic of femininity can be invoked as both a prop to capitalism and, withdrawn, a potential gravedigger. The four labours I now describe are dialectically connected to the feminine, but can nevertheless be described masculine.

Political action, Bourdieu (2002: 62) says, must account for 'all the effects of domination that are exerted through the objective complicity between the structures embodied in both women and men and the structures of the major institutions through which not only the masculine order but the whole social order is enacted and reproduced'. A mutilated ego is necessary to capital. This I trace along four libidinally charged vectors. To grasp the point that capitalism is libidinal, it is worth recalling Lacan's concept of *jouissance* and the distinction he makes between desire and drive.

Adorno and Horkheimer (1997) diagnosed the role of commercialized culture in training desire towards the instrumental ends of capital. They drew inspiration from Freud, Weber, Lukacs and Marx. Like the movie that never lives up to its trailer:

The promissory note of pleasure issued by the plot and packaging is indefinitely prolonged: the promise, which actually comprises the entire show, disdainfully intimates that there is nothing more to come, that the diner must be satisfied with reading the menu.

ADORNO and HORKHEIMER 1997: 111

In Lacanian terms, desire, if I can put it this way, imagines that there is a tasty meal to satiate one's hunger. Drive is satisfied simply by the whetting of the appetite. Drive in this sense is under no illusion; it is Real.

Whereas desire is an imaginary relationship to a symbolic lack, drive is oriented to what remains unaccounted for after signification. Drive is a kind of madness, a fiend that endlessly tickles. It makes us fidget. It puts life out of joint. To chase the ball endlessly, it's the well-spring of every endeavour to exceed what is given. And there is no better example of desire-as-drive than the one Lacan gives in respect to Marx who, as he says, 'invented the symptom', the symptomatic torsion that puts life and capital in motion.

Alongside the formation of subjectivity, capitalist appropriation and expansion are the positive responses to a formative negation, the lack of surplus value. For the capitalist, it is the crises that affect value production that create a need to innovate and undermine the capacities of the worker to act in their class interest. For the subject, it is the failure to achieve closure. In other words, to end dissatisfaction by being the equivalent of the Father who does not lack anything: for the subject-cum-goalie to be the metaphorical equivalent of the entire goalmouth. The lack of profit necessitates in the capitalist the ceaseless need to generate it. The lack of an ontological core to subjectivity necessitates phallic substitutes. A compulsion to repeat the process anew and with every repetition to innovate. Drive repeats but does not return to a point of origin. It repeats differently.

Each of the four interconnected vectors of androcentrism as I here conceive them are labours of acquisition, the acquisition of an object to bring closure but which, both for capital and the subject, does not exist. Closure for capital would mean the end of a need to ceaselessly throw money after money, its ontological condition. Closure for the subject would mean the end of desire. Recalling the earlier point, the death drive as *jouissance* does not aim at death but in the endless repetition of the failure to bring closure the prolongation of life (to prolong the game ceaselessly). The catastrophe is that under capitalism these two drives, one for surplus value, the other for the object cause of desire, *objet a*, become bound together. From the point of view of capital, the object of waged labour is surplus value; the object of consuming labour is the realization of surplus value as profit; the object of repressive labour is class domination (which is never fully achieved); and for reproductive labour, the replenishment and revitalizing of a workforce of sufficient quantity for capital to exploit. Reproductive labour is primary here; not only because it produces a workforce but, what I want to stress, the mutilation of the psyche for the three aforementioned purposes. It is the reproduction, in other words, of the masculine disorder. The four vectors are distinctive and also interconnected parts of the historically specific form of masculinity necessary to capital.

A masculinized subject is needed to compete for a wage and moreover, to be libidinally invested in the status a job affords. A subject who is invested in commodities for their phallic value is necessary to ensure sufficient quantities are purchased which here I conceptualize as consuming labour. The most brutalized form of masculinity has a premium for capital which depends on this subject to fight its wars, police the streets and imprison dissenters. Repressive labour is primarily the work of those typically recruited by the state to serve in the police, prisons and the military, the repressive state apparatuses as Althusser calls them. It is also the kind of labourer recruited to serve at the top of the corporate ladder and neoliberalized institutions. While reproductive labour is typically the work of women, my emphasis here is not on the biological reproduction of the species but the mutilation of the psyche. Once again, I should stress that none of these labours presupposes a sex. However, due to the effects of gendering and pressures placed upon the sex, repressive labour is predominantly male and reproductive labour predominantly female. Waged and consuming labour are more evenly distributed between the sexes (however many there are), but still nonetheless masculine.

As Marx (1973: 99) wrote, 'A definite production' determines 'a definite consumption, distribution and exchange as well as *definite relations between these different moments*' (italics in original). But each of these determinations fold back onto one another and cannot be apprehended in isolation. There is the production of value for exchange and also, returning to an earlier reference from *Grundrisse*, the production of consumption. To this, I add the production of repression or war and social reproduction. These four labours, then, mark the contradictory, co-evolving and interdependent ways in which the masculine form specific to capitalism adapts to its various phases, crises and transformations. They correspond to the different moments of circulation and expansion – namely, production, distribution, exchange and consumption – that this formation contributes its libido to.

I described the object of these labours from the point of view of capital. The object differs from the point of view of the labourer. For the waged labourer the object is employability; for the consuming labourer, hunger; for the repressive labourer, the obstacle to nirvana; and for the reproductive labourer, man. The need to render oneself employable is endless. The need to satiate a hunger for consumer products is endless. The need to rid society of what is ideologically conceived as the obstacle to nirvana is endless. The need to man up is endless. This is the case at least under capitalism.

For waged labour, the paid job is the means for making a living, but as the job itself cannot satisfy nor provide security, relative to the position of the worker in the division of labour, there is always another job to which libido must be competitively oriented. This is the function of employability (Cremin, 2011). It signifies a gap that the worker must close. However, because no job is ever secure or fully satisfying, closing this gap is impossible. Be it a job or promotion or the attributes that are said to secure either, there is always something missing: always a motive to obtain what capitalism designates as value. The subject must remain in permanent competition to make themselves useful to capital over and above other workers with whom they compete (usually under conditions in which jobs are scarce). There is always a vacancy for the worker to fill. The demands that capital places on the worker are themselves insatiable and impossible fully to satisfy. Through training, networking and so forth, this locks the worker into a perpetual need to prove themselves employable and more exploitable than others. Employability is in essence the managerial term for exploitability. The student who writes passionate essays criticizing capitalism is invested in the personally enriching intellectual endeavour and, also, in developing the credentials to make themselves more exploitable than others. Alienated labour not only pits one worker against another, but in our alienated condition esteem is derived from being valued and rewarded by the employer as exploitable over and above others.

'The corporate hierarchy,' Brownmiller (1994 e-book – section 507, unpaginated) writes, 'has no compelling motivation to modify what it demands of its career employees, and the prizes at the top of the heap go to those who pursue them with single-minded devotion.' The masculinized subject is at an advantage in this respect. It is worth stressing here that while women are frequently at a disadvantage because of the breaks they take to have and raise children or because of structural discrimination in the workplace, they are also disadvantaged in that, unlike men, they have not typically been primed from an early age to be libidinally invested in winning. But whether out of necessity or because of a libidinal compulsion, women also want a piece of the action. As Jessa Crispin (2017: 33) puts it, to succeed, women became the patriarchs themselves: 'In order to win in this world, we had to exhibit the characteristics the patriarchal world values and discard what it does not.'

The object of consuming labour is hunger. Consumerism is frequently confused with femininity and its libidinal dimension is easier to conceptualize. For these reasons I'll discuss consuming labour in more detail.

A ceaseless consumption is essential to a ceaseless production. Hence, why it is essential to capital that, even if sold on the premise, the object cannot satiate hunger. Its social use-value lies in its phallic function. Hence why for all its feminine associations, consumption is primarily masculine. The superego of late capitalism, the marketing industry functions as the conduit that tells you to abandon yourself to your desires. But it all feels rather stupid after you've done so. Consumption, however, is guilt's greatest emollient and guarantee of the consumer's repeated custom. The work of consuming labour is never complete. This is a point that, drawing on Lacan, Todd McGowan (2004) makes. Whereas once the superego commanded the subject to repress their desires, now it commands them to enjoy. In this 'society of enjoyment', the promise, as Adorno and Horkheimer noted, is a ruse. But it is one the consumer is nonetheless in on. They are not duped. As Adorno (2005: 103) later observed, 'People are not only, as the saying goes, falling for the swindle; if it guarantees them even the most fleeting gratification, they desire a deception which is nonetheless transparent to them.' They know full well the purpose for which the object is manufactured, but there is no choice when all political avenues of escape appear closed and the ego comes to depend on the object for status and security. As Ratner's faux pas confirmed, it is not that we do not know that products are 'crap'. Either due to our diminished wages there is no choice other than to purchase crap products or, because a modicum of enjoyment can be obtained through them, to be told that they are crap spoils the enjoyment. Like the commodity produced by exploited labour, to live in this world and not be weighed down by the injustices of it, the subject acts as if faeces are gold nuggets.

It is not in the acquisition itself wherein pleasure is to be found, for it is at best fleeting, but rather, constitutive of drive, in the anticipation. It is the fact of being hungry and craving for whatever it is imagined will satisfy the hunger. Consider, for example, the famous episode of the 1980s soap *Dallas* in which at the season end, arch villain JR Ewing is shot. A cliffhanger to beat all cliffhangers, audiences had to wait an agonizing six months or so to find out who in fact did shoot him. It was Kristin. So why not give audiences what they wanted and put them out of their misery by revealing the secret straight away? Because as soon as you know who did in fact do it the enjoyment is indeed spoiled. There is nothing more to look forward to. The retail commandment 'The Customer Must Be Satisfied' reflects a conscious demand. The truth, however, is that both for the capitalist and the consumer 'The Customer Must *Not* Be Satisfied'.

Consuming labour was only nascent and specific to the wealthier classes when Marx wrote that consumption produces production and the subject itself. It came of age at the beginning of the twentieth century when production techniques enabled capitalists to manufacture high quantities of goods at low prices. It established the need for what is now called the consumer economy. As businesses expanded, larger markets for their products were required – not only in terms of the quantity of consumers with sufficient wages to purchase them, but also in terms of consumers to desire commodities for the sake of desiring commodities. What capitalism produces at times is designed to fill a gap in the market, but more often than not, it produces the gap itself. The gap of course signifies castration. This is the function of what Adorno and Horkheimer (1997) termed the culture industry. It represents impossible ideals that reveal to the consumer the inadequacies that they were unaware of. The idol functions as the mannequin on which draped commodities intimate the secret of their success. By owning them, your face will be blemish free too. The larger-than-life idol functions in place of the paternal authority through which anxieties are evoked and manipulated. The corporations of today that increasingly monopolize cultural production also monopolize the production of subjectivity.

Against work, which is seen as productive and which 'creates' social use-values for exchange purposes, consumption by comparison is seen as destructive, wasteful, superfluous and thereby superficial to society's needs. In this topsy-turvy world in which masculinity is positive and femininity negative, it has the appearance of being feminine. Yet in a capitalist society, waged labour is anything but productive. Operationalized for exchange value, its social benefits are limited and its environmental impact is huge. Under these alienated conditions, where satisfaction at work cannot be obtained, the shopping mall, as Marcuse (2002) noted, becomes the imaginary oasis of enjoyment. Consumption promises a desublimated pleasure that is nonetheless repressive. Pleasures here are always superficial and fleeting yet make alienated labour easier to tolerate. But to pay for the pleasures and finance debt, the labour is all the more necessary, hence 'repressive desublimation'.

At a time when the white suburban classes could survive on the wage of a man, it was the wife who often did the shopping. This is the reason why, even when the product was designed for men, much of the advertising of the 1950s targeted women. Her task was not only to purchase the provisions the family needed to survive, but also the various accoutrements to adorn her body with to make herself attractive to the men her husband needed to impress. Floyd (2009: 98) notes that the male equivalent of *Vogue* and *Cosmopolitan*, glossy magazines like *Esquire* and *Face* which launched in the 1980s, contributed to the establishment of a 'consumer masculinity' that could be distinguished from feminine consumption. What I am arguing here, however, is that the so-called consumer society was always masculine. In the conditions of masculine domination, be it a car or whatever, the object is a compensatory phallus. Pilloried for being slaves to fashion, feminine consumption to various degrees is in service of the masculinized ego – the kind of ego that depends on a partner to make up for what he, or she, lacks. Women are thus reduced to the equivalent of a car, a signifier of status: his phallic prop.

The object of repressive labour is the obstacle to nirvana. Atavism and nostalgia, the Aryan race and the idyllic childhood that never was, the nirvana principle in Freudian theory is the principle of (a return to a state of) minimal tension. The work of repressive labour is to divest society of those elements perceived to have robbed the subject of their enjoyment. Capital and the state apparatuses set up in its defence recruit the most brutalized and brittle of men. Violence is their mode of cathexis. But what is a danger to society in some contexts, preserves society when put to service in the military, police and prison. Burns (2007: 178) describes his own experience as a US marine and 'the finely-honed curriculum and pedagogical processes of dehumanizing others, particularly toxic patterns of violent masculinity'. These techniques, he argues, are 'necessary for radicalizing individuals and creating bonding communities that embody an official hatred of others'. Bourdieu (2002: 29) draws parallels between 'the assassins, torturers and "hit men" of all dictatorships and all "total institutions"' and modern management. These neoliberal 'hatchet men[,] themselves often subject to ordeals of physical courage, manifest their virility by sacking their superfluous employees'. Repressive labour sometimes occurs under the veil of humanitarianism but is always rationalized in view of some perceived threat to society. It is mobilized by resentment of those who are the greatest victims of colonization, imperialism and, at home, policies geared towards enlarging the wealth and power of a billionaire class. Capitalists cannot guarantee the flow and expansion of capital without a class of borderline psychopaths with a powerful need to prove themselves manly. They repeatedly affirm this through legally sanctioned opportunities to strip others of their freedom, dignity, humanity and even their lives. Those with no moral compass to thwart their ambition are best equipped to act ruthlessly and decisively to further their own interest. They are the CEOs of large corporations and the vice chancellors of even the humblest of universities. They are found amongst the managerial elites. Repressive labour requires people from all class backgrounds and is served best by the paranoid psychopaths and pathological narcissists. The Oedipal narratives of the industrialized entertainment complex or culture industry service the fantasies of every would-be assassin.

The object of reproductive labour is man, not man in flesh and blood but a person capable of carrying out any of these labours, as well as being libidinally invested in the objects corresponding to them. Reproductive labour is the work of reproducing a psyche fit in its pathologies for capital. The reproductive dimension is central to the feminist critique of value production, a feminism that is at least worthy of the name, which I'll dedicate the next section to.

What I have described in each of these instances are the ideal types on which capitalism relies. A corporation or state institution may promote values at variance to these descriptions, but capitalism in the more abstract sense must, by necessity, feed off a pathology that it also breeds. It may not require everyone to exhibit such traits, some of which, like those necessary to repressive labour, would be destructive to its interests in many circumstances. Hence why what Connell describes as the hegemonic form of masculinity can be represented – as I have suggested – in figures such as Obama, who stands for values that the most toxic of men would likely consider feminine yet still functional for capital. Capitalism requires that a number adequate for its needs are sufficiently damaged to ensure surplus value. The most damaged are recruited into repressive labour, whereas ARMS can function in a multiple of capacities. REMS are the most ill suited to repressive labour but nonetheless may enjoy a premium in spheres of impression management wherein the humanitarian veil serves instrumental purposes. Affluent, compliant and class complicit, REMS can serve as the face of corporations such as Apple. At the university I work for, large banners and posters promote 'zero tolerance' of racism, sexism, transphobia and so forth. But as we learnt when I, (other) female colleagues and tutors of colour were targeted by a white supremacist cell, 'zero-tolerance' turned out to be an 'aspiration' not a policy. The deliberations with management painfully exposed the university's white supremacist and patriarchal heritage and leanings. The banners and posters, the best face of the institution, were quickly removed and its teeth bared.

The final section of the chapter is specifically about the fourth vector, the labour of reproducing the masculine disorder. The fourth vector is essential to the three other labours.

Do androids have castration anxieties?

Catherine Malabou (2009: 94) states that minimally 'woman' denotes an 'overexposure to dual exploitation' in the home and in the workplace. Venturing tentatively for the first time into gender politics, I quoted this uncritically in *Man-Made Woman* (2017). It seemed reasonable after having spent the majority of my adult life as a cis man that I had not encountered or contended with such 'overexposure'. But if 'minimally' this is what it means to be a woman, not only does it invalidate my identity as a woman now, but takes no account of the considerable variations between the kind of work women do and presumes that domestic labour is 'exploitative'. Is a woman who does the washing up being exploited? What if the man does all the domestic work? Is she no longer a woman? Can a CEO of a large corporation or one that hires domestic servants be a 'woman'? Patriarchy and the 'women' in it cannot be thought apart as a separate entity from capitalism. Rejecting the 'dual- systems' logic of feminist critiques of patriarchy, Lise Vogel proposes a unitary theory of women's oppression under capitalism.

Biological factors do not determine gender. It was first necessary, in the words of Christine Delphy (2016: section 395 of ebook), to turn 'an anatomical difference (which is in itself devoid of social implications) into a relevant distinction for social practice'. Vogel (1983: 159) writes, for 'the reproduction of labour power to take place, both the domestic and the social components of necessary labour are required'. Capitalism relies on a worker with sufficient wages to purchase the commodities that as a class they have produced. However, in order for this to happen, domestic labour must first be performed. Marx does not give much consideration to the social processes enabling the existence of labour power as a commodity. This is precisely what Vogel aims to make up for. This form of labour is produced within the 'kin-based site' of the working-class family. As there is no underlying logic why household labour needs to be undertaken by women, Vogel considers what distinguishes a male from a female. The latter's unique bio-physical capacities for pregnancy, childbirth and lactation come into focus. As Vogel stresses, the state plays a decisive role in ensuring that females perform this function. But Vogel is clear also to stress that bio-physical qualities do not in themselves explain women's oppression.

Biological reproduction is vital to capitalism. But, Vogel argues, it does not constitute a separate sphere of exploitation, nor is it encountered as exploitation by some women: 'Even in the most egalitarian hunting and gathering society, a variety of tasks is accomplished every day, requiring a division of labour. Differences arising out of biological and social development also characterise every society' (Vogel: 153). If that is the case in these egalitarian societal structures, how does it differ under capitalism? Vogel here provides a materialist explanation for masculine domination. The relative position of men and women to one another differs in respect to surplus labour. That is the labour given over to capital in excess of remuneration but also 'the two components of necessary labour': social labour, which involves the purchasing of commodities; and domestic labour of care, on which capital relies in order for people to work and purchase commodities. These categories more or less map to what in the previous section I described as waged labour, consuming labour and reproductive labour. Instrumental to the systems of 'male supremacy', repressive labour is also inferred.

These systems are the legacy of the oppressive divisions that existed between labour in previous class societies. The divisions that obtain through them are exacerbated under capitalism. Because capitalism, uniquely as a mode of production, relies on the exploitation of labour power to generate surplus value which, thrown again and again into circulation, leads to an ever-expanding need for additional labour, the organization of a domestic labour is essential to it. The state plays a vital role by intervening to ensure this happens. It relates back to Federici's claim that housework 'underwent' a process of 'real subsumption', hence 'for the first time becoming the object of a specific state initiative' that bound it to the needs of capital. As Vogel (1983: 160) writes, 'Domestic labour increasingly takes place in specialised social units [the atomized family], whose isolation in space and time from wage-labour is further emphasised by male supremacy. These conditions stamp domestic labour with its specific character.' What I have added in respect of the four discerned labours is the libidinal dimension and the objects of acquisition necessary to ensuring capitalist circulation and expansion.

Use value and exchange value are sometimes conflated by feminist critics of the wage relation. Cooking a nutritious meal is useful to capital because by eating it the waged labourer is revitalized for the next day at the office or factory. But cooking the meal does not produce exchange value. In other words, it is not a commodity that capital can hawk to consumers. While the work of servicing one's own home is no different to being employed to service someone else's, the crucial distinction here is that only in the latter is there (potentially) a capitalist to directly profit from the labour. A domestic labourer under the employment of a capitalist produces both use values that the rich client relies upon and also exchange value through the service that has been monetized which the employer directly profits from. The domestic labourer in this arrangement would receive a wage from the capitalist boss but the value of that wage would be lower than the value of the commodity the owner of the household pays the latter for. There is no equivalent surplus that capital profits from when household labour does not take place under the employment of a capitalist. When Marx says that only 'productive' labour produces value and it is only the waged labour that is 'exploited', he means precisely this. The terminology can be called into question. The material basis for making this distinction cannot. Thus, while unpaid domestic labour is often exploitative, the term 'exploitation' in Marx specifically refers to the capitalist's direct (rather than indirect) exploitation of the worker's surplus labour under their employment.

When domestic labour that is not under the employment of a capitalist is considered to produce exchange value, we arrive at the sort of absurd proposition like that of Cooper and Waldby. They claim that capital exploits the production of stem cells in vitro. In their words, the bodies of women produce cells that 'always exceed the finite possibilities available to the developed organism' that capital 'extracts' (quoted by Floyd, 2006: 71). The iconic awakening scene from *The Matrix* comes to mind here. The truth is revealed that humans are living in suspended animation pods filled with putrid green liquid feeding their energy into a monstrous machine. But according to the authors, stem cell generation is valorized 'retroactively'. Oedipalization is valuable and necessary to capitalism but, either immediately or retroactively, does not in itself directly make profit. The reproductive labour of psychic mutilation ensures that the child fits into the form that capital demands but is also a labour of love. What it isn't is a labour that commands exchange value. Labour that is considered feminine such as caregiving is essential to capital. It is mostly invisible in the sense that it does not command a wage and does not therefore 'count'. Like the masculine ego-formation, capital freely leaches from and depends upon the feminine. But if it were to 'recognize' this labour by monetizing it, it would be another object that the labourer is alienated from. The alienation that occurs in paid labour would in Marx's precise usage of the term encompass the whole of life. One can imagine the technologies integrated into the home to measure its value (metrics in the current corporatized university jargon) and how the mother would be incentivized to carry out certain tasks – for example, if breastfeeding was monetized, to keep little Johnny permanently wedded to her breast.

The pressure to gender a child may come from the grandparents, aunties and uncles whose attitudes are more conservative, from friends, social media and eventually of course institutions such as the school. But that pressure is brought to bear most of all on the primary caregiver, which in the capitalist patriarchy typically means (cis) women. Put another way, it is women who bear much of the responsibility for masculinizing the male. This relates to the subordination of women to their bio-physical capacities which place them on the frontline when it comes to caring for and socializing a child. To take a personal example, up until I was around ten or eleven years of age, my own father was a nominal member of the household to which he contributed some of his wage but was rarely present in my life. In this respect I'm typical of many kids who, regardless of whether it was a single-parent household, the mother played an instrumental role in our upbringing. But this kind of work could obviously be carried out by a man. The question I want to pose is whether in a hypothetical situation in which androids (man, of course, invoked in this word) performed all the bio-physical functions of female bodies, would androcentrism still be essential to capital?

Technology engenders new possibilities and new enslavements. Donna Haraway's *Cyborg Manifesto* (1991) is lyrical on the potential of the technological augmentation of bodies for their and our collective liberation. There isn't the space here for an exegesis on the 'post-human'. Inspired by a talk that Nick Dyer-Witheford gave at a conference I attended, instead I want to conduct a thought experiment in which all of the labours described in this chapter are done by non-human machines.

Nick Dyer-Witheford and colleagues (2019) conducted a thought experiment in which, under capitalism, machines have entirely replaced the function of the human labour force. I put it to him that for capital to continue to circulate and expand, a consumer would still be required. He suggested that the machines would consume oil. But this would be the equivalent of the consumer only purchasing commodities such as food, consuming only to replenish themselves. But as we by now know, capitalism cannot simply stand still. It requires a consumer to purchase commodities in excess of what they biologically require. It also requires a worker to have a motive for exceeding their own capacities. Capitalism is a libidinal economy and it cannot be otherwise. It requires machines, organic or inorganic, that have an inbuilt need and desire to constantly improve and upgrade themselves and consume for its own sake. In such a scenario a machine would need to be fabricated that in essence has castration anxieties and a need for phallic supplements. The masculine disorder would prevail, not least amongst capitalists themselves with their insatiable drive to make a profit for profit's sake. Hypothetically, a world could exist in which biological humans are made entirely redundant. But if not a simulacrum of all the complexities of being human, such a world would not be capitalism. The repudiation of femininity must in any event prevail under capitalism.

But what if, at the very least, machines took over the bio-physical functions of females, or male bodies were augmented to serve the same reproductive purpose? Except for those affluent enough to make such choices, no such condition is likely to emerge under capitalism. Firstly, because capital has no incentive to liberate the female from their bio-physical function and every reason, given that they do not pay for it, to ensure via the state that women continue to service it with an exploitable workforce. Not only would the costs of ending the dependency of capital on female bodies be prohibitive, capitalism is not a force for liberation. Moreover, there is nothing inherently enslaving or exploitative about any aspect of bio-social reproduction – only how it is operationalized under capitalism and the limitations therein placed on women within this socio-economic relationship. All of this is, of course, moot. Capitalism will destroy itself before such a possibility arises. In my 2012 book *iCommunism*, I questioned the idea that human life as such was the cause of climate catastrophe. We are not living, I suggested, in the Anthropocene. Ours is the age of the *Capitocene*. It is capital that renders the world unliveable. The second point, then, is that, as per Marx, the class relations of capitalism are a fetter on the technological means available either to liberate bodies from various reproductive functions or to prevent catastrophe. For such reasons, patriarchy cannot be overcome under capitalism. Thus, returning to my initial claim, a capitalism without masculine domination, and therefore patriarchy, is as inconceivable as a capitalism without class domination.

The next chapter is all about the libidinal dimension of transgender. Discussing my personal orientation and experiences of being trans, I consider why in particular the pleasure of wearing women's clothes is so frequently disavowed. If accorded the status at all, the male-to-female transvestite is perhaps the most marginalized and denigrated of all transgender subjects. This makes the transvestite the ideal subject through which to argue that, short of ridding ourselves of the capitalist patriarchy, 'perversity' may be our greatest ally in the struggle to mitigate the effects of the masculine disorder and signal the potential for liberating all subjects from the material need to identify themselves as a gender or sexuality. The principal point is to rid ourselves of the conditions whereby it is necessary to negate the gender that is given us, not to act as arbiters to legitimize or delegitimize an individual's identity as a gender. Whether a person regards their gender expression authentic to who they are ought to be of no concern. It is of concern to all of us only in respect, once again, of the material effect of gender identifications under the capitalist patriarchy. At the end of the chapter I will pick up on a point made earlier about the dangers of defining women as victims of patriarchy at the expense of men, a trademark of trans-exclusionary (but not necessarily (adical) feminists.

5

Queervestism

'Tights on babies are comfortable and adorable,' writes *Guardian* columnist Chitra Ranaswamy, 'which is why my son, when he was a baby, sometimes wore hot pink tights.' Ranaswamy is defiant and spirited in her refusal to box the kid in the usual garb. Putting a boy in tights is an 'issue' worthy of debate. But so, too, it seems, is dressing your daughter like a 'girly girl'. This in fact was the headline of Ramaswamy's piece: 'Should I feel guilty about dressing my daughter as a "girly girl"?'[1] Feminine dress is a strange kind of chemistry. We get high on it during playtime and pantomime but nonetheless feel the need to justify it. Whenever did the love of feminine things become such a guilty pleasure? Alexandria Ocasio-Cortez's declaration that 'femininity has power' puts a different perspective on this.

There's nothing frivolous about beauty and fashion, she says. It is all too serious and involves 'some of the most substantive decisions that we make – and we make them every morning'.[2] Femme is affirmative. This chapter is not, however, about the politics or otherwise of femme women; nor about the staging of femme by queer performers. It's about the implications of a socially defined male dressing in feminine styles in their everyday lives. More specifically, it's the libidinal pleasures of feminine dress which, countering a moralism that considers such pleasures perverse, this chapter affirms. It discerns in this desire the capacity for breaking out of a self- and socially imposed masculinity. REMS (reflective/experimental masculinities) are on the borderline. The pleasures obtained in feminine dress is a libidinally-charged incentive for crossing that line. Reflecting on the pleasure that from early childhood

I've derived in dressing 'as a woman', I discuss the effect of putting my libido out there: on my sleeve.

Coining the term transmisogyny, Serano (2007) drew attention to the particular abuse encountered by feminine trans women. The androcentric unconscious recoils at the sight of a trans woman, but the problem is perhaps more general than Serano supposes. A mere evocation of femininity is enough to stir revolt. In a recent survey involving 5,000 gay men, 71 per cent of respondents said that feminine attributes were a turn off. Some 41 per cent thought that gay men who are effeminate 'give the gay community a bad image'. Worse than dressing in feminine ways is getting off on dressing in feminine ways. Transvestites are perhaps the most maligned of transgender subjects. They are not very interesting in themselves. It's what they reveal about the self that make them worthwhile subjects for this chapter to focus on.

In the previous chapter, I introduced the formula LGBT+[ ]/. The brackets denote a rejection of identity but registration of unity with those who in their gender and sexuality are in breach of social norms and conventions. The forward slash politicizes the chain to denote antagonism to the capitalist patriarchy. This chapter is about the 'T' for transgender, transvestite, the T that I placed in brackets to denote a minimal difference in the sameness of woman: [T] woman.

People look and stare at me. I'm frequently the topic of conversation. However, here I want to invert the gaze. The more interesting and relevant question is not why I dress as a woman but, thematically linked to the book, why so many people follow convention and disassociate themselves from any signifier that in our society connotes femininity. I have already theorized why this is the case. Here I take this theory to the streets and argue for a street – better still, barricade – therapy that involves introspection and reflection on the potentiality that inheres in all of us to overcome our aversions and inhibitions in respect of the feminine. Transgender people often describe feelings of gender dysphoria, a disconnect from the gender given, one might even say forced upon them. They speak to the truth of gender – that whether it is recognized or not, gender dysphoria is a condition held in common. Gender is forced on all of us. It boxes us into routine styles, behaviours and affects. Transvestism is not merely a symptom of gender repression. A kaleidoscope of colours, patterns and affects to shuffle up and rearrange, the transvestite is a fragment of that once beloved toy now gathering dust in a box stored in the cellar. The transvestite is a reminder in distorted form of the playfulness and sensuality that is lost but which can also be recovered.

The transvestite's gender presentation reflects their desire to wear women's clothes. A term coined in 1910, the transvestite, according to Hirschfeld's (2003) definition, is someone who has an urge to wear clothing of the 'opposite sex' but does not necessarily identify as or want to be that sex. The word, as Stryker (2008) notes, originally served the same purpose as 'transgender' today, a label for all 'gender variant identities and behaviours'. Though sometimes deployed interchangeably with 'transvestite', by comparison the term 'cross-dressing' is more ambiguous and, as Stryker remarks, considered 'neutral'. This is because a libidinal motive pathologized by the medical establishment cannot be inferred in the term cross-dressing. I was once a transvestite. Today I'm a trans woman. Nevertheless, my love of wearing feminine things is undiminished. When is a transvestite not a transvestite? When do they become cross-dressers or trans women? This is one of the riddles this chapter seeks answers to.

The best way to answer this question is by examining my own feelings towards the items and experiences of wearing women's clothes. The chapter is closer in this regard to the more autobiographical *Man-Made Woman* (2017). A lot has happened since I wrote that book and over the space of these three years my attitudes have changed. We talk a lot about identity, but it is the process that really counts when it comes to being trans. Here that process is documented. My feelings, experiences and interpretations are in some ways, of course, unique, but nonetheless of sociological relevance. They are an index of desires that dwell inside of us, the prohibitions on expressing them, and the consequences, both individual and collective, when you do express them openly. A means through which to inspect and interrogate the norm, the symbolic exception is the proverbial swan to cast in ugly lights a world overpopulated by ducklings who mock the feminine.

Cis men like to don frocks. They snap up the enlarged opportunities available to them to act the trans. They wear our shoes – but they cannot see the world through our eyes. Fredric Jameson, in his signature obliqueness, offers an explanation for the unique perspective being 'other' affords:

> Owing to its structural situation in the social order and to the specific forms of oppression and exploitation unique to that situation, each group lives the world in a phenomenologically specific way that allows it to see, or better still, that makes it unavoidable for that group to see and to know, features of the world that remain obscure, invisible, or merely occasional and secondary for other groups.
>
> Quoted in FLOYD, 2009: 11

Transvestites are as common as chips. But in feminist and LGBTQI+ scholarship they hardly get a mention. The negative connotations of the word are undoubtedly a factor here, as too is the prominence of voices from a US context in the scholarship where, in contrast to Europe, the term is largely eschewed. In Britain, for example, you have celebrities such as Eddie Izzard who once openly identified as a transvestite, and cartoonist Steven Appleby who recently wrote about his transvestism when promoting a book in the *Guardian*.[3] In 2014, Allen published an article in *Feminist Theory* entitled 'Whither the transvestite?' Whither indeed? Noting the earnest and erotic identification of transvestites with normative dress codes, it is difficult, she argues, to 'situate them in a feminist theoretical tradition that places a premium on the subversion of gender binarism' (Allen, 2014: 53). Even in the medical journals that are sympathetic, she notes, transvestism is described as a sexual paraphilia.

However conventionally they dress, or what perspective they take on gender, I argue that what the transvestite does is queer masculinity and sexuality. They are the standout exception of the rule, not only of the general aversion towards femininity but also that normative sexuality is itself a myth. For two important reasons, my focus here is on male-to-female transvestism: first, because I can speak with authority from this position; and second, because this book is about androcentrism and the problem society appears to have is with the feminine. The reasons may seem obvious, but in the sphere of gender politics, the obvious sometimes need stating.

Perversity gets a bad rap. I open by rapping in affirmation of the perverse.

Perspective on perversion

The signifier 'woman' brings together a vast array of disconnected signifiers. From dresses through to fabrics, colours and shapes, it begets the lexical set 'women's clothes'. Women dress in many different ways of course, but when we talk of 'dressing as a woman', the image likely formed in the mind is of items that signify 'femininity' and that are arbitrarily associated with female bodies in Westernized cultures. So, when I say that I like to wear women's clothes, you are probably thinking of a male who wears dresses, tights, lingerie and make-up rather than jeans, pullovers, t-shirts and socks that are staples in a woman's wardrobe. A style that over time has become me, the clearly delineated feminine articles are precisely what I wear daily. It denotes a twofold wish to represent an image of a woman that is consistent with social conventions and to indulge an erotic pleasure. But whether it is tights, any other feminine accoutrements or the whole ensemble, such pleasures, perverse ones according to some, places one's desire in contradiction to the reality principle, the social norms and arrangements in which the male is expected to dissociate themselves from anything held as feminine. Not only does the desire to wear women's clothes place the sexed male at odds with gender norms, the 'perversity' of the pleasure is a perversion of genitally focused heterosexuality. The desire of the male to dress in conventional feminine clothing is by definition queer, a queervestism.

Freud, to recall, claimed that we are born polymorphous-perverse and through stages of socialization, oral, anal and phallic, particular zones of the body are eroticized. Libidinal energy is concentrated, displaced and, most of all, repressed through the unconscious assimilation and introjection of the reality principle. Libido is desexualized or sublimated in the unpleasant activity of labour which Freud considered essential to the development of civilization. Moreover, because procreation is essential to the reproduction of the species, it is essential that, after a period of latency, this undifferentiated drive ultimately in late adolescence focuses on the genitalia of the opposite sex. In the most conservative tracts of Freud, and those in particular who practise psychoanalysis in his wake, the idea that libido ought to go anywhere except into work and procreation is considered a problem.

Gozlan (2015: 24) stresses that 'the polymorphous perversity of the drive aligns with non-conformity'. We possess a capacity 'to play with the signifier in ways that escape the determinisms of culture'. Our 'perversions' denote a capacity therefore to 'transgress and shape the signifier'. And this, I am suggesting, is precisely what happens with the male for whom the signifier to which he is libidinally attached stands in negation to his masculinity. Only in the myth of normal sexuality does identity and desire align. Žižek (2020: 20) puts it another way: 'Far from providing the natural foundation of human lives, sexuality is the very terrain where humans detach themselves from nature: the idea of sexual perversion or of a deadly sexual passion is totally foreign to the animal universe.' Our perversions, it could be said, make us human. Normality is a condition of alienation.

Freud's interest is not in those who deviate in their sexuality from the norm. As Dany Nobus stresses, Freud's question of interest is 'Why and how does anyone ever become sexually normal?' (quoted in Gherovici, 2017: 67). 'Normal' is weird. Quoting Freud himself (2016, unpaginated), 'Nothing at all is achieved by the mere expression of indignation and personal disgust and by the assurance that we do not share these lusts.' They are, he writes, a 'very frequent and widespread phenomena'. He further elaborates:

If we fail to understand these abnormal manifestations of sexuality and are unable to relate them to the normal sexual life, then we cannot understand normal sexuality. It is, in short, our unavoidable task to account theoretically for all the potentialities of the perversions we have gone over and to explain their relation to the so-called normal sexuality.

Marcuse (2006) takes this to the next level. Born from a need to sacrifice pleasure in the collective interest in an alienated society, the subject rebels against their discontentment in destructive ways. In a non-alienated society where it is no longer necessary for pleasure to be sacrificed to the performance principle of instrumentality and exchange, the polymorphous drive is recovered. But as the conditions themselves are radically transformed, erotic energy (Eros) is no longer unconscious and destructive. It is self-consciously and creatively articulated in socially beneficial ways. Under prevailing conditions in which sexuality is genitally focused for procreative purposes, the pervert stands apart. Because their sexuality is not instrumentalized in this way, according to Marcuse it signifies a refusal of the performance principle and anticipates a world that is to come.

It is not surprising, then, that self-declared 'part-time' transvestite Mario Mieli (2018) saw the basis of a gay communism in Marcuse's pleasure-focused description of a more egalitarian and non-alienated society. Invoking the mythical Narcissus and Orpheus, the transvestite exemplifies the erotic life Marcuse (2006) envisioned of one dedicated to beauty and contemplation, poetry and play. If there is a general transvestism, as Mieli proposed, it is in the sensuality denied to us in both our gendering and alienated labour. It is denigrated through the androcentrism that repudiates femininity as a mark of castration. The repudiation of femininity is not only an obstacle to therapy; for Mieli and Marcuse, it is an obstacle to our collective emancipation from alienated society. The transvestite does not so much overcome this obstacle as demonstrate its presence within and outside of us.

Mieli's book was published over forty years ago. Aside from Allen's article, Torkild Thanem (and Wallenberg, 2016), a professor in the field of organization studies, co-authored an article published in 2016 on transvestism. Preferring the male pronoun, Thanem described himself as a transvestite. Ekins (2002) interviewed and wrote about transvestites. Garber (2011) theorized them. Published over twenty years ago, the absence of competing texts ensured that *Vested Interests* remains the touchstone for anyone discussing transvestism. Butler (1990) famously wrote that drag artists cause 'gender trouble', Bornstein (2012) railed against labels and Serano (2007) praised femininity. But none of these authors have elaborated what could be called a theory of transvestism. Garber declares that the transvestite confounds and thereby queers categorization. By this she means that the transvestite does not fit into a gender box. I am not unsympathetic to this claim. But even here, the transvestite is simply a foil by which to deconstruct gender, and not, as Namaste (1996) points out, an identity in and of itself.

If Mieli was a 'part-time' transvestite, today I am a 'full-time' one: I only dress as a 'woman'. Even though it has now been five years, the pleasure remains undiminished. It is not my aim, nor intention, to cast aspersions on the activities of many transvestites who only dress occasionally in private or, if publicly, typically in the company of other transvestites. There are many good reasons for keeping the activity hidden. However, when space and time are no longer an obstacle to dressing as a woman, when one refuses the reality principle by dressing openly everywhere and at all times, the effect on both one's own identity and relationship to others is likely (though not necessarily) more profound, disruptive and potentially life-affirming. Formerly repressed, due to the necessities of maintaining a masculine persona, the erotic dimension is, in degrees, recovered. Context must in any event be stressed. As Butler (1988: 527) notes, 'the sight of a transvestite on stage can compel pleasure and applause while the sight of the same transvestite on the seat next to us on the bus can compel fear, rage, even violence'. In the wrong place and at the wrong time – unhomely and untimely – on the bus or at work, the transvestite cuts an uncanny figure. Being in this position, as many trans women are, is both unnerving and revitalizing.

The transvestite is a contradictory figure. Typically, the desire to dress as a woman is in contradiction to the identity as a man. As their propensity is also typically hidden, their private life is in contradiction with their public image. When dressed as a woman, gender is queered via appearance, sexuality via desire, but they do not necessarily identify as queer or have any interest in campaigning for LGBTQI+ rights. The identity of a transvestite appears to depend on a spatial and temporal separation that my own identity also now appears to confound. As there is no masculine gender that I now default to, dressing as a woman is not an act of cross-dressing. It is a process of becoming a woman via the image, held in the mirror and thereby in my imagination, of a woman I now (also) identify as. But is it possible to be a transvestite and a woman when the pleasure of wearing 'women's clothes' is still a motive? What I mean by this is that the identity of being a transvestite enters into a contradiction with the identity of being a woman. If I am now, as I assert, a woman, I cannot be a transvestite, as this would imply that my desire is to dress as a man. We can imagine the absurdity of the situation in which publicly I wear women's clothes but, when at home, I prance around in men's clothes pulled from under my bed where hidden. It would be as if my masculine 'essence' is repressed and herein recovered. But if I see myself as a woman and dress according to convention, if no longer a transvestite, at which point did I cease being one? Or does the very fact that the items are a source of libidinal gratification invalidate my identity as a woman? In order to be considered a legitimate woman, must the erotic dimension be disavowed? Which begs the question, are women who get off on wearing women's clothes, make-up and so forth, women? By some accounts, such women are not feminist. As beings that derive sensual gratification in fabrics, colours, fragrances and the creative process of dressing, are we not, here thinking of Mieli, all in such respects, transvestites? 'Our transvestism,' Mieli (2018: 210) contends, 'is condemned because it shows up for all to see the funereal reality of general transvestism, which has to remain silent, and is simply taken for granted.'

In the film *Tootsie*, Dustin Hoffman's character, Michael, disguises himself as a woman in order to land an acting role. The evident pleasure he derives from wearing the items goes unnoticed by the film critic, says Garber (2011). They see a man dressing instrumentally as a woman for an acting part, not the perverse pleasures of the transvestite who is invisible to them. At home, I was self-evidently a transvestite to those who saw me dressed as a woman. Only in public, dressed as a woman in plain sight, is my transvestism hidden. Translating as force or intensity in Deleuze and Guattari's (2003a and b) terms, what is hidden is the affective dimension. It is at the level of affect that the act of 'cross-dressing' can be transformative. When you are in the world of random encounters, people react – sometimes in subtle ways, sometimes not, sometimes hostile, sometimes just differently. It is something that you sense. You affect them and they, in turn, affect you. Friends open up, become less guarded. Affinities are struck. Connections that would never have been made, now cohere into new and exciting networks of association. These open up new possibilities for being and becoming. In such respects, you do not become a man when taking off the clothes. Becoming a woman is indelible. Sliding into the Lacanian register, your symbolic identity changes when you dress publicly as a woman. However, of critical importance is whether there is a change of object at the level of the imaginary. What changes is not only how we see ourselves but, subsequent to this, the pathways we now trace. Evoking de Beauvoir, instead of becoming man, we are now becoming woman. I return to this shift in the imaginary and symbolic identity later.

The word 'transvestite' does, however, come with a considerable amount of baggage, enough to make even those with an erotic interest in the clothing to dissociate from the word. Despite politicizing the term transgender and considering transvestites to be 'transgender warriors', Feinberg (1996: xi) felt it necessary to use the term 'sparingly in the book' hir wrote. As hir notes, 'many people who are labelled transvestites have rejected the term because it invokes concepts of psychological pathology, sexual fetishism, and obsession'. While the fetish a man has for motor cars is unlikely to cause much concern, the male with a fetish for sheer tights is another matter. The problem society has is not with fetishes as such. In this case the 'problem' is with objects here connoting femininity that males fetishize, a 'problem' that psychoanalytic practitioners, imposing their own moral judgements, are at least in part responsible for (Gherovici, 2017). The transvestite is doubly guilty. They are guilty for their feminization and for declaring what is a given of human subjectivity: the polymorphous perversity of the libidinal dimension.

The failure of the majority of men to breach gender dichotomous styles – even in minor ways – ensures the continuation and reproduction of relationships that are in multiple ways detrimental to all of us. Femininity is coded female and associated with a range of signifiers presupposed negative. Only, though, from the perspective of a society predicated on the masculine. However, there is potential in a desire liberated from guilt for an exit from the masculine assemblage – liberated to question, to confound, confuse and scramble codes that in Westernized societies are reified as a reflection of nature.

Pleasure as principle

In the hostile environments negotiated by those whose gender identity contradicts the one assigned at birth, explanations are demanded as to why such an identity is adopted or transformative process embarked on. We like to justify our pleasures or desires to undergo transformative changes which is really just a conversation with the internalized superego authority. But whatever justification or explanation is given, it is never enough to satisfy those who demand one. In this context, pleasure would likely be considered the least legitimate reason for presenting and identifying as a woman. In opposition to a reality principle that demands the male's predisposition towards women's clothes be kept hidden and, if revealed, an erotic motive disavowed, pleasure can be considered a principled and even a noble motive for presenting openly as a woman. To declare oneself a transvestite and follow through on this declaration by openly dressing as a woman requires the rejection of a moralism in which suffering, sacrifice and bodily dysphoria is the criterion of acceptability that, metonymically, as Armed (2016) notes, is permanently shifting. It is a moralism that transvestites are not alone in being victims of, but which encompasses all trans women. Fearing hostility, pleasures many cis women declare, must be kept hidden or disavowed. However we are sexed, pleasure is part and parcel of what it means to be human. Pleasure humanizes us. It makes our womanhood real. But as Freud through to Lacan have observed, the pleasure-seeking drive is also a conservative one in that while pleasure is the ultimate aim, the process is, if anything, one of pain avoidance. I return to this in a moment.

'Desire, as an autonomous and polymorphous force,' writes Hocquenghem (1999: 77), must 'in the eyes of the psychoanalytic institution' disappear. Homosexuality, he notes, becomes not only a symbol of lack but also, accordingly, of men's hatred of women. Transvestism is characterized in much the same fashion, namely that transvestites have a problem with women.

Fitting Freud to his own moral perspective, Stoller claims that women's clothes are the means by which the transvestite enjoys and also disavows a fear of castration; in other words, representing a fear, even a hatred and disgust, of women. The pleasure, writes Stoller (1968: 176), 'is in tricking the unsuspecting into thinking he is a woman, and then revealing his maleness (e.g., by suddenly dropping his voice)'. It 'is not so much erotic as it is a proof that there is such a thing as a woman with a penis'. As a phallic woman, the transvestite tells 'himself that he is, or with practice will become, a better woman than a biological female if he chooses to do so'. Put differently, in staging their castration, the transvestite demonstrates they are better than women because, unlike him, women are in fact castrated.

While I reject this sweeping and empirically indefensible interpretation, there is no denying the reactive tendencies and misogyny amongst some cross-dressers. Despite deriving pleasure from the clothing, this was made apparent to me by the reactions of some men to my style of dress. I wrote an op-ed piece for the conservative British newspaper the *Daily Telegraph* in which I was pictured in women's clothes. My hesitation about publishing an article in such a newspaper was outweighed by the desire to agitate and provoke the reader. The comments, as one might imagine, were universally hostile. But it was the reactions of men who like wearing women's clothes that proved more revealing. A contributor to 'Skirtcafe', a forum for men who like to wear skirts, writes, for example, that 'The problem that I have with that story is that in the pictures he looks like a woman. The hairstyle, makeup, clothes are all intended to impersonate a female.' Another agrees: 'On this board, we identify as men and don't seek to pretend in any way to be women (whereas, I think, many cross dressers do).' Another remarked, 'The only way I would ever consider myself a woman would be to submit to SRS (sexual revision surgery). The thought of it makes me shudder.'

Acknowledging that such attitudes are out there does not validate the argument that those who derive pleasure from dressing as women are misogynistic. It does, however, avoid digging oneself into a hole by claiming the opposite. Misogyny may as well factor into the pleasure some transvestites derive in dressing as women, but it cannot be assumed. Rather than seek 'evidence' to refute Stoller's claim, which is difficult to obtain given the unconscious nature of repression, a more pertinent question consistent with Freud's own thinking is why men derive no satisfaction in dressing as women. Put another way, why speculate on the misogyny of transvestites when it is easier to detect amongst those who disavow and denigrate femininity, not reify it as many transvestites do? Paradis (2006) observes this tendency in the biographies of cross-dressers for whom clothing functions as a means through which to articulate what they conceive as a feminine essence. Instead of being a masturbatory prop, the clothing is the means through which to experience the oceanic feeling of being at one in body and mind that their masculine egos deny to them. As one cross-dresser puts it, 'What I find appealing about being a woman is being able to show my feelings, cry when I want, smell lovely flowers, have lovely soft, feminine things around, just be myself.' It can be put another way. What the transvestite here experiences, is how liberating it is not to be themselves. As another from a survey in Suthrell's book *Unzipping Gender* (2004: 56) puts it, 'I have a lot of femininity inside of me . . . I hate my male image as a "macho" guy in a macho job.' The 'macho job' is not, however, placed in jeopardy, and, as conversations I have had with cross-dressers appear to testify, is justified as a way to hide their proclivity.

Cross-dresser Jess Jones is a case in point. In Jones's words, 'I experience feminine emotions and desires each day. I suppress them in order to function in the culture I live in. I do not feel comfortable displaying these mannerisms or emotions in "guy mode"; or dressed as men typically do in our society.' But just to be clear:

> Be not confused though; it isn't just about the clothes. There is a feminine component to my personality and who I am at my deepest core. This is a huge contrast to who I am on the outside most of the time. Most of the time I am as stereotypically male as the next husband, father, endurance athlete, hunter, shooting sports enthusiast, car mechanic, or infantry combat veteran. I am all of these things all of the time.[4]

The third edition of the *Statistic Manual of Mental Disorders* (DSM) was the first in which transvestism was defined as a paraphilia rather than a fetish. By the most recent edition, DSM 5, transvestism was further 'downgraded' to that of a 'disorder', only if causing the individual 'significant distress or impairment'. Blanchard's influence on the manual is notable here and elsewhere in the entry on autogynephilia, an invention he defines as the sexual pleasure men derive 'by the thought or image of themselves as women' (Blanchard, 2005: 439). This differs from transvestism in that it is not the clothes as such but the idea of being a woman, clothed or otherwise, to which the desire is oriented. In her survey of the science on gender, Tosh (2016) demonstrates that there is no consensus that the effects of chromosomes and testosterone levels can neatly be mapped to sex. This also goes for autogynephilia. Not only is there no empirical evidence for such a condition, it could just as equally describe the relationship of cis women to their bodies. Tosh refers to a study conducted by Moser who claims that over 90 per cent of gender-conforming women derive a narcissistic gratification in their feminine appearance. While often associated with self-obsession, when libido is not exclusively self-centred, narcissism, as Freud made clear, is important for self-esteem and self-preservation. As Moser suggests, pleasures obtained in appearance is a banal and non-pathological condition of being human.

As with anything concerning the inner workings of the psyche, the pleasure a woman does sometimes derive in dressing in feminine ways is complex. The standard psychoanalytic reading is that women dress in feminine ways to function as the male's phallic prop. But as with the presumption of misogyny in the transvestite's 'staging' of castration, nothing can be presumed from the fact that a woman loves wearing make-up, pretty dresses and heels. The psychoanalytic reading tells part of the story and no doubt does apply in many instances. But there is more to this, I argue. Dressing, experimenting, adorning the body in silky fabrics, the art of a transformation – there is a sensual and affective dimension to this that is integral to being human but which in this androcentric order is phallicized and turned into a fetish.

If the psychiatric establishment bears responsibility for giving transvestism such a bad name, it is one that, despite its change of heart, still carries weight in society and amongst transvestites and also people more generally who have questioned and negated the gender given them at birth. A libidinal motive is understandably disavowed. While from a psychoanalytic perspective, libido factors into everything, it is the association of pleasure with sex that seems to be the issue here. Transgender Amelia, quoted in Hines (2007: 76), for example, casts aspersions on those who dress only part-time as women. But while the implications may differ from that of a trans woman who always presents in feminine clothing, the issue I have

with the following statement is the aspersion cast on dressing being
a turn on.

> I just think those groups [transsexuals and transvestites] have got
> nothing in common. What have I got in common with a heterosexual
> guy who gets off on wearing a dress? Not a lot really. I've got no
> objection to him doing that if that turns him on, but please don't
> expect me to call you 'Gloria' and 'She' because you're not. Please
> don't ask me to treat everyone as my brothers and sisters.

Getting off on wearing a dress appears here to invalidate your identity
as a woman. Even assuming that by this she is thinking of
masturbation, there is no escaping the conservatism of the statement.
Whether you are a cis woman with an extensive shoe collection or a
trans woman with a thing for knee-length boots, whatever is done
with the items in private – stored in the cupboard perhaps? – becomes
a moral issue. But in respect of the pleasure males derive from
feminine things, eroticism is conflated with masturbation and sexual
congress and the thought that one might indeed get off on the items
in private, as many people, male, female and intersex, undoubtedly
do, is enough to warrant erasure.

'Cross-dressers are a largely misunderstood group,' an article
explains.[5] 'Most of these men followed the typical path of playing
sports, chasing women, striving to be a success in a career and
having a wife and family. They were all male, except for their need to
dress and express themselves as a woman, sometimes.'

The pleasure of dressing as a woman does in this sense preserve
rather than negate the symbolic identity. It is saved for those
moments when it can be indulged without having negative
consequences. Pleasure is postponed in the workplace, which is
made more tolerable by the prospect that home, in one's suburban
oasis, the pleasure can be indulged without consequence. The
pleasure principle is the principle of pain avoidance, hence why for
both Freud and Lacan it is a self-conserving and essentially
conservative drive. Crossing the lines, putting the perversion in the
place that the veneer of normality is thickly coated – the workplace,
pub, school, whatever – is a common fantasy of the transvestite, but,
if realized, a disaster in that it would have deleterious effects on their

capacity to live and be identified as men. Dressing at home is a tonic, not a detoxifier. The feminine praxis must cross thresholds. Perhaps because the magnitude of desire reaches a pitch of intensity akin to the death drive, those thresholds are passed when caution is abandoned.

The compartmentalization of pleasures is sustained by the idea that there is an external impediment to indulging them either openly or, at home, freely and whenever one likes. Those who have corresponded with me after reading about me in newspapers and magazines describe lifelong repression, in many instances to the point that they have not been able to dress at all. Typically, the problem is with the 'wife' but also the children or the boss. While there are consequences if openly declaring one's interest, such justifications cannot be taken at face value. They function as a means to go on living as a man without having to reconcile with the repudiation of femininity.

The point here is that however true it is that there are negative consequences in declaring an interest or coming out in public, it is sometimes an alibi for preserving whatever benefits are afforded by living as men. Recalling Žižek's (2020: 1) point about anti-Semitism, many Jews did, as the propaganda claimed, occupy positions of power prior to the Nazi takeover. But the 'reason' given to justify anti-Semitism was simply a device onto which to deflect inner anxieties and justify prejudice. There are always good and legitimate reasons to hide one's desires when they are not reflective of social norms or one's social identity. But it is important also to look beyond them and what it is in us that is at stake, what is feared and how those fears are projected.

The discourse on perversion that psychologists promulgates not only shames people whose pleasures do not align to the norms, but can also have the effect of defining us. Nobody understood this better than Michel Foucault (1978). His rejection of the Freudian 'repressive hypothesis' notwithstanding, a scene in Sacha Baron Cohen's social satire *Borat* perfectly captures the effect that naming has on perception.

A projection of American presuppositions about what someone from another culture is like, here Kazakhstan, Cohen goes on a journey across America, sending up various individuals who think

Borat, the character Cohen plays, is a genuine person. Casually describing a game that he plays with male friends involving getting into the shower and having one of them thrust a rubber fist into his anus, Borat is horrified when Republican Alan Keyes, whom he is interviewing, describes the friend as homosexual. What was for Borat a playful game of male bonding, now acquires a different meaning. It can go one of two ways. Either Borat now either recognizes himself as homosexual or disavows it and stops playing a game that he derived pleasure from. According to Foucault (1978), nineteenth-century sexologists were responsible for the naming and shaming of bodies and pleasures. In doing so, they invented perversion. Unlike Freud's position, then, there is no unconscious dimension to repression. Repression for Foucault is discursive and interpersonal.

Pleasures that Borat considered harmless fun are labelled non-normative and these in turn come to define the individual. Specific pleasures thereby acquire a special significance for the subject and legitimation is sought for them. Thus, the subject comes to define themselves as a 'homosexual' or, in my case, 'transvestite'. Through demands for recognition, these terms are subsequently politicized. An effect of this is to establish hierarchies of acceptability. In her influential article, Gayle Ruben (2011) placed monogamous homosexual men at the top of a sliding scale, whereas transvestites are from society's hypocritical moral angle amongst the 'lowest of the low', which also includes fetishists, sadomasochists, sex workers and 'those whose eroticism transgresses generational boundaries'.

As far as Foucault is concerned, the labelling of pleasures has negative consequences. What this appears to miss, or is at least insufficiently theorized, is that names, as psychoanalysis recognizes, provide us with a bearing. They are our positive answer to the void in being. In other words, without a name we would appear to ourselves and to others as empty. It is impossible, as Žižek earlier noted, to escape the law of signification. Names cannot be avoided. But names can be adopted that negate social prescription. 'Ciara' is my *nom de guerre*. It is one of several means by which a rejection of gender conventions is affirmed and by which I live according to the principles authentic to me as a subject of desire. The term transgender and the discourse associated with it is crucial in this regard. It is the means through which, formerly unable to make much sense of their feelings of gender dysphoria, the proverbial ugly duckling recognizes themselves to be the very fine swan who now proudly takes flight amongst their flock.

The reaction to a random set of signifiers we label as feminine is a textbook example of what Lacan is referring to when he says that desire resides from outside of the self in the discourse of the other.

Lipstick is life

When I was five, we moved out of the house I was born in, in Sutton, South London. It was the house in which my sister, who was nine years older, forcibly put pink lipstick on me. It was also in this house that I looked out of an upstairs window onto the street and staring back at me was a giant Goofy-like figure. These memories are real but at least one of the events my mind recalls did not take place. I don't know why I remember the giant: a paternal authority, perhaps? However, the reason I remember the lipstick is plain enough. It's chained together in a long line of memories of wanting to wear feminine things and sometimes even doing so. I remember it because the signifier was retroactively indexed to a narrative of being a transvestite. The desire is real and so too the pleasure. But why transvestite? Why not transsexual?

'I was three or perhaps four years old,' Jan Morris (1974: 9) writes, 'when I realised that I had been born into the wrong body and should really be a girl. I remember the moment well, and it is the earliest memory of my life'. It's not without coincidence that our earliest memories are from around the same time, when, as children, we enter into the symbolic order of language. It's when we become aware of our self-image and also gender differences. Every transgender person has a story to tell involving desire, recognition, repression, reconciliation; the tentative steps towards coming out and many of the consequences of doing so. Whether stories of joy or sadness, pleasure or pain, they're the ones we find comfort in and which give meaning, and sometimes even direction, to our lives. Being a transvestite gave me direction. It meant that my desire to dress as a woman could be satisfied at home without ever having the need to become a woman by stepping out of it. The irony here that by avowing the pleasure that people are often made to feel ashamed about, I was able to avoid asking myself the more difficult question of whether the desire to dress as a woman reflected a deeper need to live as a woman. By avowing the pleasure and regarding this to be the only reason for wanting to wear women's clothes, I was able to disavow anything that, if acknowledged, would have a more derailing effect on my life. My pleasure conserved my masculinity.

My memories have not changed, only my interpretation of them. What I considered a rational perspective on my desire, I now recognize to be a device through which to disavow and protect myself against the more socially disruptive effect of recognizing I was transgender and making the necessary moves to live as a woman. The word 'transgender' was not part of my vocabulary. The identification with the word was instrumental in leading me to the path I subsequently traced. This testifies to the point that labels can sometimes have a positive and emancipatory effect. In respect of transvestism and 'masculinity', it also testifies to the fact that some labels we adopt can also, with the benefit of hindsight, reduce our capacity to develop and flourish. Signifiers are in this sense meaningful and of material importance to our lives – not empty as such.

Today the desire to dress as a woman is consistent with my identity as a woman to the point that it no longer makes sense to say that I like wearing women's clothes. I wear women's clothes because I am a woman. It's both a tonic and a thrill to get up every morning, put on a bra and knickers, slide into a silky pair of sheer tights, a snug fitting dress, and spend twenty minutes or so applying make-up. I love my dresses and shoes, my make-up drawers full of lipsticks and eyeshadows, my drawers packed with bundles of tights. I had no desire to go on HRT (hormone replacement therapy) when writing *Man-Made Woman*. Now, at the time of writing, I am awaiting an appointment with a consultant to gain approval for HRT. And if not achieving my desired size, I fully intend to have breast augmentation surgery. Currently, I have no desire to have 'the' operation but perhaps even this will change in due course. I've at least searched information on it.

I used to see a man in the mirror and construct an image that was compatible with how I wanted others to see me. Now I see a woman.

It's a dress, not a pair of trousers that becomes me. I put on my make-up the first thing in the morning and take it off the last thing at night. I feel bare without my lipstick on and uncomfortable in public if I'm not fully made up. This shift from a masculine self-image to a feminine one was gradual. At first, I was too self-conscious to feel comfortable as a woman and at times, when putting make-up on, I paused to reflect on who this person was, like that of an outer body experience. My self-image has changed. The first month of COVID-19 lockdown also reinforced the fact that my identity is also contingent on others. It is not enough to see myself dressed as a woman. I depend for my sense of self on others seeing me in women's clothes and this, for a while, was not possible, at least were it not for Facebook and my posting of images of me in various dresses.

The image that I construct is comprised of a number of objects that have nothing intrinsically in common. My make-up, dresses, tights, heels, jewellery and handbags have only one thing in common, the linguistic signifier of 'woman'. The signifier places this random assortment of objects into a recognizable constellation. The desire to dress 'as a woman' must then at some level originate from outside of me in the symbolic order of language. The transvestite is proof of Lacan's thesis mentioned earlier; that desire originates outside of us. Lacan calls this the 'extimate' cause, the cause external to the self but which is also an intimate one. It is like that of the creature which impregnated itself in the unfortunate character, Kane, in the film *Alien*. The estimate cause is also an intimate one in the sense of being more in us than the self-conscious self. Tickling the senses, sending us along pathways that by normative standards are considered perverse, it does things to us that we have no agency to stop. If what Kane experienced is real death, what I experienced, when the desire to dress openly had finally gotten the better of me, was a symbolic one. The masculine image was erased and a woman was born.

Recalling Lacan, Schuster (2016: 44) puts it nicely when writing that 'Life, like language, is not something that we intrinsically possess and that flows naturally from the inside, but something that we "get caught up in," a foreign element in which we are uncertainly entangled.' A chocolate lover concerned about their waistline can repress the desire but not with the same degree of ease get rid of it. While the stakes are not as high for the chocolate lover, it was possible and even necessary for me to self-consciously repress the desire to wear women's clothes. But as the lover of chocolate knows, repression does not necessarily make the desire go away. If anything, the desire intensifies. Conscious repression enters into a contradiction with the symptoms of an unconscious repression and which, far from having a deleterious effect, has enriched my life. The symptom of wanting to dress as a woman was, and remains, a source of pleasure. It is the cause of a permanent itch I love to scratch.

There was a shaking of the coordinates of the masculine imaginary which occurred, not through therapy, but by being in the world as a woman. Gender was not negated by doing this. Gender was a means through which to negate my masculinity. This was not primarily due to wanting to challenge social conventions and politicize my body. I have my libido to thank for this. The breaching of the gender divide was, in other words, libidinally charged. This is the positive effect of that alien inside of us. Sometimes we need to let it breathe. Sometimes, when having a deleterious effect on the capacity for others to flourish, it needs to be repressed, even suffocated. The psychoanalytic therapy does, after all, have its uses.

At the time of writing this, I have now experienced the effects of HRT for two months. To be honest, I didn't detect any emotional changes. The changes I did detect were physical. My breasts started to enlarge but to the point that if seen bare chested, one could be forgiven for thinking I had been lifting weights. The biggest effect, however, was on my libido. I could no longer orgasm and my desire to do so, at least at the time, diminished. But I was troubled more by something else. Dressing as a woman became ordinary. Aside from the creative, and in degrees sensual, aspects, I derived no greater pleasure in doing so than dressing as a man. A transgender friend said that for her this effect was a positive one. It normalized her relationship to the items. For me, though, this was a crisis of ontological proportions. (That said, I cannot be sure that HRT was the cause. Adding this note some months later, I suspect it may have been more to do with a depressive state at the time. Nevertheless, the idea that I had a choice through HRT to rid myself of the pleasure is worth pursuing.)

For me, the desire to dress as a woman anchors my identity as a woman. It also means that I put a lot of effort into my style. Now, however, I was going back to the habits of old. I 'slung' on whatever skirt and jumper was lying around and simply to keep my legs warm, a pair of tights (now tending towards thicker opaque ones). It didn't make me want to go back to living as a man. I've gone too far on my journey to even contemplate that. I see myself as a woman and this is how I want others to see me. That didn't change. This underlines how living as a woman has positively affected my relationship to others and helped me to overcome inhibitions related to being masculinized that I recognize now were debilitating. Put another way, to desire once again to live as a man is to desire one's own enslavement. Dressing as a woman before was an authentic expression of my desire which I had no agency to determine. But if HRT now offers the 'choice' to rid myself of the desire, given that choice I'd sooner choose to preserve it. I would no more want to rid myself of the pleasure than I would the pleasure from listening to Miles Davis's *On the Corner*. Hence why I came off HRT.

Whatever its origin, the desire (to wear women's clothes) is a real material aspect of my subjectivity and in that respect my identity as a woman is an authentic expression of the desire – for which I never had and do not have determination of – to wear women's clothes. The desire is an ontological foundation to my womanhood that as a man was obscured. If, therefore, as I conceive it, gender is not something we are born with, my gender as a woman is nevertheless a more authentic representation of who in a sense I am, want to see myself and others to see me, than that of a man.

The man I once recognized in the mirror was a masking effect, an act of misrecognition (*méconnaissance*), as it is according to Lacan (2004) with all identities. The imaginary, to recall, functions to mask the void in being or pre-symbolic, pre-human, Real. Men have problems coming to terms with their 'castration'. As a woman, it is far easier to bear. Tussling my long blonde hair, smoothing the creases in my skirt, adding blush to my cheeks; this process of crafting an image on this mirror double is a submission to the judgement of others. Gherovici (2017) speculates that the reason young people regularly post selfies on Facebook is because their identities are nascent. They're learning and experimenting with styles, putting it out there and developing a stable sense of self. Because many trans men and women undergo transition in adulthood, there is a comparable need to do the same. I rarely posted images of myself on Facebook when a man. My identity as a woman is also nascent, however, and so to develop a stable sense of self that I can believe in and feel confident about, I do exactly what the young do: post selfies on Facebook. Far from being individualistic, it affirms us as social beings.

Gender is not simply, as Butler appears at times to claim, a product of iteration, nor is it one of habit. It is intimate to our being, not simply 'performative' (an affirmative speech act like the marriage vow 'I do') or the outcome of a discourse that names gender. However habituated I was to my masculine image, the alien was always there inside of me, threatening to burst out. This was the constant that I repressed but never forgot, and one which always rubbed up against me. Butler seeks the dissolution of gender categories. Far from enabling the subject to queer their gender, in my case this perspective was a way to trivialize the desire. For all my sympathies with the idea of getting rid of these categories, the feminine gender was the only means available to me through which, dialectically, to loosen my phallic attachments to masculine signifiers. It is not a move against a presupposed heteronormativity as such, but against the androcentric masculine disorder.

But this still doesn't answer why I developed a libidinal interest in the feminine in the first place. I can only speculate. Language, returning to the quotation from Lacan (2007: 124), 'cannot be anything other than a demand, a demand that fails'. This recalls the obscene demands of the superego authority and the impossibility of 'being a man'. What Lacan calls *jouissance* – again to recall, the fleeting satisfaction a subject derives from the repeated failure to acquire the non-existent object of desire, *objet (petit) a* – relies on prohibition. Fascinated by vibrant colours, silky fabrics, flowery scents, shiny objects and different shapes, the infant is oblivious of any gender signification. Their interest is a sensory one. It is only later when the child enters the symbolic order that these items are seen as gendered, and the fascination now met with disapproval. If the drawer in which my mother housed all her colourful make-up was, for me, both a source of fascination and fear, it was because for no obvious reason they were prohibited to me. What unfathomable injustice when girls and women wore make-up freely without being ridiculed or told no.

It was a mystery that I unconsciously wanted to solve. Perhaps I was and still am trying to resolve the mystery of my Oedipalization which has no rational foundation. Why other boys do not have this relationship to femininity that I have is a mystery to me. But the mystery is simply that I do not know what occurred in my life at that time for these signifiers to take on such significance that eventually I wanted to change my gender designation. It is the outcome of contingencies that are buried deep in my psyche.

When the pleasure is a source of stress and disruptive to one's life, psychoanalysis can help with the removal of that itch. Recalling my earlier analogy, by the end of the treatment when the fantasy is 'traversed', the drive to catch the ball at all seems rather stupid. But I want to chase the ball. In other words, I don't want to sacrifice the enjoyment. For it is this that has given me the strength to breach the gender divide. My femininity feels authentic to me for this reason. That I am no longer consciously prohibited from dressing as woman does not retroactively change the fact that pleasure derives from the unconscious relationship with prohibition. Notwithstanding the effects of HRT, the desires and pleasures are locked in and I am happy to keep them there.

Trans people have all, at a certain stage in their lives, been compelled to reflect on their social identity and recognize 'that isn't me'. We are the 'hysterics' of Lacan's discourse theory, not the now discredited clinical hysteric. Like the boy who shouts that the emperor is naked, the hysteric questions the master's knowledge – and his symbolic position as the legitimate authority with the capacity to name. It is the hysteric, as Žižek (2020: 253) explains, who says to the master, 'Why am I what you are telling me that I am?' But the hysteric, according to this theory, isn't someone who has no need of a master. Like the woman whose man is never man enough, they want a more adequate one. The trans woman calls into question the name they are given. But, contrary to the hysteric as so conceived, it doesn't mean that the name they subsequently adopt represents a submission to a new master. Their desire to wear lipstick as confirmation of their identity is not the equivalent of the (phallic) desire a male has for a car to confirm theirs. Not only do the implications differ – the feminine accoutrements are instrumental to a process of becoming not of closure; not of a need to disavow one's castration or function as another phallic supplement. Moreover, identifying as a gender is not the same thing as subscribing to a binary notion and thereby wanting to reinforce the patriarchy. Žižek's perspective is that of a cisgendered man. A trans person gets to view gender from a different angle. More than one angle, in fact.

Trans eye view

The real cannot be directly encountered but appears to us through a multiplicity of symbolic fictions. What Žižek (2006; 26) refers as the parallax Real is the 'hard bone of contention which pulverizes the sameness into a multitude of appearances'. The parallax perspective is our subjective take on reality, the angle from which we observe the world that is only ever partial but nevertheless objective to us. My metaphor of the valley in *Man-Made Woman* is worth repeating. As a man I stood on one side of the valley. I saw a large boulder in the middle, not the cottage shielded behind it. Living as a woman enabled me to switch sides. Now I could see the cottage. However, unlike the cis woman, my memories of what I saw on the other side remained. A more complete perspective of the gender scene is afforded. It affords a perspective on gender as the dialectically unified concept of opposing masculine and feminine terms. A comparison can be made with the opposing perspectives of the consumer and capitalist towards the commodity. One evaluates the article in terms of whether it is useful to them, the other in terms of whether it is exchangeable. Use value and exchange value are present in the same article but the perspective, while objective from these class standpoints, is also subjective. To get the 'whole' picture, what in Hegelian terms is called the dialectical unity of opposites, both perspectives need to be taken into account, hence the commodity as an expression of value is an article of use and of exchange.

At the end of the film from which Žižek takes the title of his book, *The Parallax View*, Joseph Brady, who is played by Warren Beatty, discovers that the conspiracy he thought he had exposed was in fact planted. Instead of thwarting an assassination at the hands of the shady 'Parallax Corporation', positioned in the rafters with a rifle to take out the assailants, he instead is framed as the assassin. The plot affords the viewer the perspective of Brady but by the end places the entire film in a different light. The script, perhaps the narrative of one's own life, is redrafted. This relates to the way my personal narrative changed when I came out as a trans woman. My life as a man was comprised of a number of memories that confirmed me for who, at the time, I saw myself as. The story I told myself as a man now, from the perspective of a trans woman, appeared full of plot holes. Memories that had little significance to my narrative as a man now became significant to my narrative as a woman. Now I see myself differently and want others to see me in the same light. The things that I identified with also underwent a shift. A transgender person has a third eye. They have a perspective on what it is to live as a man and as a woman. They experience how people react differently according to your gender presentation and, crucially, being transgender. It is why I think a transgender person has the most complete perspective on gender and, in particular, masculinity. From a third-eye perspective, the binary is itself objectified in abstraction.

Žižek was rightly pilloried for a badly articulated article in which he intimated equivalence between a trans person who declares they are a woman and a cis person who declares they are an animal such as a dog. In *Sex and the Failed Absolute*, Žižek appears to want to make amends. He describes the transgender position as the exemplary Other to the gender binary. Žižek (2020: 146) refers to Zupančič, who, in his words, suggests that 'the minimal formula of sexual difference is simply M+: masculine (phallic) identity plus something to be added'. Importantly, 'Femininity is not another identity, a counter-position to complement the masculine position, but it's possible supplement.' The feminine position is both the supplement of, and precursor to, a (phallic) masculine sexuality. Moreover, the + of feminine sexuality is exhaustive of all possible variations in human sexuality that cannot be phallicized, the real as it were eliding signification. As Žižek explains, '+ stands for subjectivity itself as the [hysteric] questioning of every identity'. It's here that he makes amends for his apparent trivialization of transgender.

He adds a 'third element' of sexual difference, the 'difference as such' (Žižek, 2020: 131). Thus the transgender position is substituted in place of the + (feminine) on which the gender binary is symbolically constituted. Žižek gives the formula MF+ for this. Whereas Zupančič is describing the real of sex, Žižek appears here to be describing how the other, here T for transgender functions as +, the supplement to a symbolic gender binary. If T was added to make MFT, three genders would be confirmed. By positioning T as the supplementary +, the binary itself as denotive of all possible genders is called by the 'other' into question. This is precisely what those who do not fit into or who negate these categories do call into question. It is why, as I show at the end of this chapter, far from wanting to erase trans, TERFS or 'gender critical' feminists require the other in order to define themselves as the authentic female. They need what they in themselves disavow: that gender cannot neatly be delineated according to sex.

If, then, + denotes in the M+ formula the real of sexuality, the + is fully exhaustive of all possible sexual orientations. Žižek's qualification that a 'third element' can be added has the effect of gendering sexuality while also calling into question a binary concept of gender. The 'third element', the Other to man and woman, is what he suggests registers difference as such, the 'three sexes are masculine, feminine and the difference itself' (131). Difference (+), he avers, precedes this difference (MF) which itself cannot be reduced to a difference between sexes. The transgender subject is thus the enigmatic Other whose desires are unfathomable to the cisgendered, including no doubt himself, without which there would be no contrasting concept of a gender 'binary'.

In respect to capital, the class on which it depends for surplus-value functions as its necessary but mystified supplement: the bourgeoisie, B, and the + of the proletariat. As with the relationship of the feminine to the masculine, the exploited is both the supplement to and the precursor enabling the augmentation of value. Simply put, there would be no capitalism without a working class to exploit (no masculinity without the Other of feminine sexuality). The full subsumption of society to a capitalist mode of production first requires a 'free' labourer whose only means of survival is to sell their labour power to the capitalist. The capitalist class cannot include the working class as its equivalent and share the dividends of production accordingly without undermining the very premise on which it is based. A BP formulation (B for bourgeois, P for proletariat), denoting equivalence, would simply be a mystification of the real relations of production. And for the same reason, here in respect to gender and the Oedipalization of polymorphous sexuality, the formulation MFT is incompatible either with a binary notion of gender or a multiplicity of genders. The + that replaces the T intimates a radical and inexhaustible plurality of 'genders' that the binary obfuscates.

The same can be said of the position of black people in respect of capitalism. The demands of the BLM movement for structural transformation is antagonistic to a capital which, historically and unconditionally, is founded on a white supremacist ideology. Hence why BP (bourgeois and proletariat), MFT (man, woman and transgender/third gender) and WB (white and black) are structurally impossible. It is also why, at an intersectional level, the black working-class trans woman (woman because the order is androcentric) is the antagonistic subject (the radically Other) par excellence, (hysterically) questioning all other claims to marginality.

I was once a part-time transvestite. I became a full-time one. The effect of this and the marginal position it placed me in was sufficient to cause me to abandon the label altogether and henceforth declare myself transgender, a woman no less. But subsequent to coming out, I met self-defined transvestites who do sometimes dress as women openly, even in the workplace. I've been out with them too. For example, I recently dined at a restaurant with one such friend dressed as a woman. The waiter nevertheless addressed us both as 'Sir'. Breaching symbolic protocol, my friend was righteously indignant and was mindful to leave. While I also felt offended, it did not seem to affect me as much as it did him. The waiter had called into question his symbolic identity which he adopts only when dressed as a woman, thus spoiling the performance and his enjoyment of it. My speculation is that it did not affect me as deeply because I was not, from my perspective, putting on a performance. The only thing it revealed to me was the waiter's ignorance, possibly even bigotry. There was nothing for the waiter to expose. A transvestite flaneur and REM, my friend can affect people in public as I do. Unlike me, however, his dress does not represent for him what it does for me. My clothing does represent my gender *as a woman*. It represents how I see myself and want others to see me. Such that, whether at a restaurant or at home, clothed or naked, in every circumstance and whomever I am in the company of, I am a woman.

Late in life, Lacan shifted his position. Therapy was no longer about abandoning the rules of the game but to come to terms with one's symptom. Patricia Gherovici's work with transgender patients is the stepping stone in the next section of this chapter towards the theorization through Deleuze and Guattari of the transvestic affective figure.

Transvestic figure

Reflecting on her transsexual analysands, Gherovici (2017) argues that desire operates for them at the level of 'sinthome'. In Seminar XXIII, Lacan (2018) describes the sinthome as a fourth 'ring' that holds together the Real, Symbolic and Imaginary to make life liveable. It is not a phallic supplement but the Real condition of existence. According to Lacan's interpretation of James Joyce, it is the writing process itself not a phallic ideal that the artist is in their desire oriented to. *Jouissance* is now like the relationship the artist has with their craft. It is not a frustrated means for compensating for inadequacies nor is it one that serves an instrumental purpose. Gherovici (2017: 116) makes this comparison then with the process of body modification that transsexuals undergo. The joy derives from the process in which there is no objective of occupying a masculine position and thereby disavowing castration. It is akin to a non-orientable feminine *jouissance* that is not available to the masculine. From a certain perspective, my desire now to wear lipstick represents a symbolic attachment to the idea of woman and could therefore be construed as phallic. Through Lacan's late work, Gherovici's intervention affords a different and less reductive perspective. Neither my gender as a 'woman' nor my desire to wear 'lipstick' are phallic. They are integral to my being a woman and the multiplicity of pleasures that in an endless process of becoming are now afforded to me.

The notion of becoming is more readily associated with the work of Deleuze and Guattari. I have no interest in pondering on the tedious question of whose version of desire is correct, theirs or Lacan's. The relevance of concepts is the use that is made of them. And for my purposes, what Deleuze and Guattari do afford is a way to conceptualize a therapy that takes place on the streets. Rather than deploy their theory to negate Lacan, here it is deployed as a productive addition.

By linking desire to castration, or lack, which requires phallic substitutes, Deleuze and Guattari charge Lacan for making desire acquisitive. This is essentially what I am arguing in respect of the function of masculinity to capitalism. In other words, the masculinized subject is, in a manner of speaking, the slave in their libido to the objects that capitalism derives value from and that guarantees surplus value. Lacan describes the condition. Deleuze and Guattari's disagreement lies in the presumption of Lacan that the desire is born from signification and which I have now, via Gherovici, qualified. Psychoanalysis is not indifferent to the damage that society inflicts on the psyche. Therapy, however, focuses on the individual and those who can pay for it. By contrast, Deleuze and Guattari invite the subject to abandon the couch and take their therapy to the streets. This is where for me their ideas can be deployed productively in addition to Lacan.

What Deleuze and Guattari call 'schizoanalysis' is collective and thereby social. The schizophrenic, Deleuze and Guattari (2003a) argue, does not lose grip on what is real in the sense of what is materially encountered and must be contended with. Lacking the psychological means through which to gain distance from it, reality is all too real and overwhelming. The object of schizoanalysis is to destroy the Oedipal myths, beliefs and representations we become invested in and entrapped by and thereby to break apart the unconscious resistances and blockages that 'territorialize' desire for the purposes of capitalist and patriarchal reproduction. Through Oedipalization, a molar line is traced, a line in which defined as male or female we conform through life to a normative idea of gender. 'Gender' is here a 'molar' representation not affect. Affects in their usage, to recall, is an intensive force not an emotion. Cis gender is normative. Akin to the Imaginary ideal that functions as a masking effect of the lack of being, it is a molar tracing taken from a normative idea of what a 'man' or 'woman' is supposed to be, look like and do. Like the nomad sat stationary astride the horse that gallops across the open plain, breaking up the ego and its molar identifications is a process of deterritorialization (Deleuze and Guattari, 2003b), a molecular affect. Like lines drawn in the sand, the plain is a smooth space open to creation that was once segmented and striated. But first we need to learn how to ride that horse. We cannot liberate ourselves from the ego or the masculine assemblage in a stroke. Try to do so and the horse may buck, and a line of flight becomes a line to oblivion. 'Deterritorialization' is not, therefore, necessarily positive. Nor does it omit the need for an identity. Hence in view of circumstance, the stress is on experimentation, not abandonment:

> Lodge yourself on a stratum, experiment with the opportunities it offers, find an advantageous place on it, find potential movements of deterritorialization, possible lines of flight, experience them, produce flow conjunctions here and there, try out continuums of intensities segment by segment, have a small plot of new land at all times.
>
> DELEUZE and GUATTARI, 2003b: 161

Deleuze warns of the common temptation and error in categorizing by appearance. For example, I dress as a 'woman' but the style itself is not what defines me. What defines me is something more profound. I am affected by the different ways that people now interact with me which clothing does not in itself signify. In other words, you can see that I represent in my dress an idea of 'woman'. You cannot see, though, how dressing as a woman has, in a multiplicity of ways, affected me. You may sense that I'm different and note how your relationship to me has changed. However, if there was nothing more profound to dressing as a woman than the fact that I enjoy doing so, then there would be no reason if staying on HRT to continue dressing this way. In view of the difficulties one encounters in dressing at variance to gender norms, there'd be every reason to dress again as a man.

Deleuze and Guattari explain the difference between representation (molar) and affect (molecular) in terms of what a racehorse is capable of in contrast to a plough horse. Representationally, a racehorse and plough horse can both be considered a 'horse'. A male who wears a dress, sheer tights, stiletto shoes and make-up can be considered dressed as a 'woman'. But if we think about different creatures in terms of their affects or intensive capacities, these comparisons no longer apply. The racehorse and plough horse, Deleuze (1988: 124) writes, 'do not have the same affects nor the same capacity for being affected; the plough horse has affects in common rather with the ox'. In terms of their usage of affect as intensity, the part-time transvestite is sometimes of a different species to that of the full-time transvestite. In the world, the latter encounters the same problems as any trans woman does. They have to deal publicly with the desires and demands of others. They are affected by those who they randomly encounter and who they in turn affect.

What Deleuze and Guattari call 'becoming-woman' is an affective process through which (phallic) dependencies on the patriarchy are loosened. It is because 'man' is the dominant or 'majoritarian' identity under patriarchy that this molecular politics is couched in feminine terms. As Stark (2017: 29) explains, 'Becoming goes through "woman" rather than "man" because of the position that women are afforded within patriarchy – because woman is minoritarian – not because of some innate quality that women possess.' It is not a process from living as a man to living as a woman but for discovering the capacities within you that were plugged up and repressed because of your masculine molar identification or assemblage. This applies to the sexed male as it does to the sexed female. Recalling Freud who detected a repudiation of femininity in both males and females, becoming-woman is a process that, as defined here, everyone can benefit from, and which does not depend on how we dress. It is a process without beginning or end but which is always in the middle. A kind of contagion, it is not an individuated process but intimately social, through which the ego is made supple and light. Thus, relative to the socio-historic context and masculine formation, it becomes possible at last to take flight. Names such as transvestite, trans woman, woman and so forth matter in a society that casts us as inferior, as freaks or as a minority. It is why I identify as transgender and as a woman. Names are like stabilizers on a child's bike, a means to orient ourselves and gain our balance until such a time, should we choose and as the situation affords, they can be removed altogether. Becoming-woman is a process that augments a capacity to live and flourish towards what Deleuze and Guattari call becoming-imperceptible. Names can be abandoned when the weight of history is lifted. But it is not necessary to abandon gender terminology altogether, just to deprive it of its power to contain, control and delimit, in a Deleuzian sense, the flows of desire.

In contrast to figurative portraits attempting verisimilitude, Deleuze (2008) explains why the distorted self-portraits of Francis Bacon exceed representation. The distortions that appear like craters on the face are produced by forces that are not represented, only intimated. This helps to further qualify the difference between representation and affect. Representations or molarities can be counted. You are a 'woman' or a 'man'. By contrast, intensities or affects such as heat, gravity, speed and so forth are not in themselves seen but, like those that Deleuze says distort Francis Bacon's self-portraits, have the capacity to affect. It is like the difference between the abstract commodity and the multiplicity of concrete determinants that the commodity as a quantifiable object of exchange obscures. This distinction can also be made between what I have so far called the 'part-time' transvestite and the 'full-time' one. The former is a figurative transvestite and, the latter, the transvestic figure. The former is nameable and their femininity, if spatially and temporally compartmentalized, is in the order of representation, taken off before stepping into the beyond. You can count the number of transvestites in a room. You cannot count how they are transformed through affective encounters. While dressing in the same fashion (the level of representation), the transvestic figure is 'distorted' or transformed by the force of encounters through their being in the world and at symbolic variance to the norms people by and large subscribe to. It produces molecular affects that are likely – though circumstance matters hugely – to be more disruptive to the ego and their symbolic position than that of the part-time transvestite. Analogous to the application of heat to ice, at a certain threshold of intensity the masculine image starts to melt away and a feminine image gradually reveals itself. But this 'image', to be clear, comes with affordances – affordances for freeing the self from the masculine assemblage and embarking on an entirely new and vitalizing trajectory through life. Trajectories that augment rather than have a diminutive effect on our capacity to act and crucially, in a kind of contagion, others to act too.

Some like me say fuck it, let's do it. Others sneak out at night. But many keep their pleasures hidden. But libido has a tendency to overreach and accidently expose itself. Perhaps it was the overlooked stocking left on the bed, or the mascara thought cleansed that smudges that others notice, like a Freudian 'slip', the desire to dress as a woman is difficult to fully contain and control. When a part-time transvestite, I harboured the fantasy of dressing openly, daily, in the workplace, as a woman. But fantasy realized, as Lacan says, is fantasy no more. The very coordinates that gave structure to life changes. This can be seen as an opportunity to embrace the new or a disaster requiring everything in one's power to disavow or excuse. Desire burns holes in the imaginary delusion. Transvestites who are not afraid to be seen or known for having the desire join the ranks of those like myself, who also dress openly but identify as trans women. As they do so, instead of stitching up those holes, more people will proudly display them. They pronounce that there is nothing shameful about being feminine. Masculinity is the symptom of those who are unable to accept or cope with the insignificance and frailty of being. Individualism is born from this condition. To own and affirm femininity is a pathway to freedom.

One thing that both Lacan and Deleuze and Guattari do share in common is that 'woman' for them does not automatically denote 'female'. A female can be inferred only in respect to how sociologically those who are sexed female are compelled along certain pathways. In the final part of this chapter I take to task the idea that 'woman' can serve the same political function as 'class' and 'black', here politically to denote an antagonism to the capitalist patriarchy. Nowhere is the problem with this term more apparent than in the hostility of a certain kind of feminist towards trans women. I'd sooner not give space to TERFs. However, as with the worst of men, they cannot be ignored. The calibrated masculinity, which a certain kind of 'progressive' acts as the ambassador of, makes this excursion necessary, as I show in respect of the *Guardian*'s equivocations about who gets to define themselves 'woman'.

What is woman good for?

Lauded internationally for her response to Covid-19, Jacinda Ardern's style of leadership sharply contrasts to Trump, Johnson and Bolsonaro. Put bluntly, her feminine touch and willingness to defer to the scientific consensus saved, and continues to save, lives. It is said that science is a masculine endeavour. What this claim doesn't take into account is the ego that feels diminished by those who grasp facts better than they do. Trump, Johnson and Bolsonaro pointed their fingers, invoked conspiracies and babbled incoherently on television. Rather than base their policies on the scientific consensus, as with the consensus on the catastrophic effects of production on the environment, their policies reflected their own self-interest. Not only does the denigration of science serve instrumentality in their class interest, but it also certainly in respect of Trump and Bolsonaro, served their ego. Ardern's message, by contrast, was clear and precise. It was conveyed with warmth, compassion and humility. We felt confident in her leadership and acted in unity to contain the virus. In a nation of 5 million, six months after the outbreak, twenty-two people have died. Initially pursuing a strategy of 'herd immunity', in Sweden, a country of 10 million, 5,783 people by contrast have succumbed to the virus. A study comparing 194 countries with similar populations and GDPs confirmed that those led by women who were 'risk averse with regard to lives' but 'more willing to take risks in the domain of the economy' achieved significantly better results than those led by men.[6] Rather than suggest an innate capacity of females for empathy, what this goes to show is how systemic the imposition of a binary notion of gender is on sexed bodies and the profound effects on human life. Even though women appear to have responded better to Covid-19 than men, as Thatcher through to Ardern demonstrate in respect of their free market agendas, having a feminine touch does not in itself negate the interests of capital. One statistic puts this in perspective. Out of the 11,000 jobs lost as a result of the lockdown in Aotearoa, women accounted for 10,000 of them.[7] In respect of any policy to address this problem, Jacinda Ardern is characteristically silent.

The concepts of 'man' and woman', even the 'distinction between them', are always, as Hennessy (2000: 20) puts it, 'sites' of struggle in a capitalist society. Such naming, she notes, 'can and have been used to justify, legitimise, authorise, and explain away the contradictions on which capitalism's relations of production rely'. It functions to ensure the disorder on which capitalism depends. The question I now turn to is whether 'woman' can function to name an antagonistic position against patriarchy through which to organize against it. The problem with 'woman' as a political category is underlined by the denial of TERFs or feminists who self-define as gender critical that trans women are women.

Although they are never entirely dead, Voloshinov (1986: 23) spoke of how signs lose force when no longer part of a class struggle. 'Feminist', a label that the former Conservative prime minister of the UK, Teresa May, once brandished on her t-shirt, could be considered one such example. Arruzza, Bhattacharya and Fraser's (2019: 8) *Feminism for the 99%* is an attempt to resuscitate the sign which they connect to a multiplicity of struggles. These centre primarily on the 'activities from which capital benefits, but for which it does not pay'. They stress the mutual interests of women whose unpaid but economically essential work is rendered invisible and, beyond fighting for better wages and shorter working hours, those of strikers 'targeting sexual harassment and assault, barriers to reproductive justice, and curbs on the right to strike'. By redefining what constitutes 'work' and who the 'worker' is, 'capitalism's structural undervaluation of women's labour – both paid and unpaid' is challenged. Part of the struggle, as they see it, is overcoming the false dichotomy of identity and class, which has proven so divisive on the left. Here, I propose that, in many instances, the sign 'woman' has not only lost force as a term by which those who are oppressed under the patriarchy can unify, but that it is deployed as a means by which to exclude and divide. The clearest example of this is the exclusionary language of those variously called TERFs (trans-exclusionary radical feminists), LRFs (lesbian radical feminists) or, their own preference, 'gender critical'.

To be clear, there are many struggles in which the sign 'woman' is of material and political significance, such as in some of the most oppressive and patriarchal regimes on the planet where women are denied basic rights and freedoms. Also, for example, in particular organizational contexts, be it workplaces or political parties, in which women are at a structural disadvantage, and also of course unvalued domestic work. My issue is with how 'woman', like the use of 'feminist' by certain celebrities and establishment politicians, is appropriated to serve agendas that exclude, discriminate and privilege a certain class of individual with the authority and institutional power to influence and shape the discourse on patriarchy, who the victim of it is (invariably themselves) and thereby the kind of struggles to prioritize which distracts from those that are of material importance to women's lives.

Many would argue that there is no such a thing as a 'real man'. There are only masculine ideals, such as those you find in advertising, blockbusters and video games. Boys and men do of course try to live up to those ideals and some react violently when their efforts are exposed as wanting. But when it comes to the idea of a 'real woman', an inversion takes place. There *is* such a thing, it seems, as a real woman – and trans women are not it. The line taken by former *Guardian* columnist Suzanne Moore is nothing less than that women's liberation from patriarchy is at stake when it comes to defining what a woman is. In order to be able to organize and take a unified stance in opposition to patriarchy, clear categorical distinctions are, she claims, required.[8] The Black Lives Matters movement forges alliances with white people whose interests align with its material aims to dismantle white supremacist capitalism. In contrast, the dismantling of the capitalist patriarchy for TERFs is at best secondary to the struggle for ownership of 'woman'. When 'women' are the de facto, and narrowly defined, victims of patriarchy, the white affluent professional woman has a reason for bearing a chip on her shoulder and, under no illusion who the enemy is, declaring herself the enlightened victim.

In holding to a rigid binary definition of sex and crude notion of gender oppression, TERFs do the same as sociopathic right-wing men hostile to the merest of attempts to blur the lines between masculine and feminine. They are RAMS (reactive/aggravated masculinities) in the female form. These women share many of the characteristics of RAMS. They are emotionally brittle, dogmatic, hostile to difference, aggressive and, oddly, though not surprisingly given what we know about the repudiation of femininity, misogynistic. They are in certain respects at the reactive end of the masculinities continuum, which may explain why they have on occasion aligned themselves with right-wing conservatives.

On the surface, I share some of the positions that TERFs take. I too want to 'abolish' patriarchy. I want to deprive gender categories of their power to mark, constrain and direct us towards certain behaviours, activities and positions within the division of labour. I want to 'abolish' gender in this prescriptive sense and rid society of the effects of a pathological masculinization. The similarities end there. Where I come from on the question of gender and patriarchy, my personal orientation and identity, and where I take my thinking on it is in all meaningful respects incompatible with the views of TERFs.

In October 2017, New Zealand granted a fifty-seven-year-old trans woman residency on 'exceptional' humanitarian grounds. In contrast to the country she came from, where due to her gender, she suffered years of 'persecution', since arriving in Aotearoa in 2009 she has experienced no discrimination or abuse. It may be a surprise to some that the country she came from was none other than the United Kingdom.[9] In 2018, an anti-trans activist group was permitted to lead London's annual Pride march. Signs bearing slogans such as 'transactivists erase lesbians' were carried and leaflets distributed that denounced proposed changes to the Gender Recognition Act.[10] The changes, which were subsequently abandoned, would have made it easier for trans people to legally change their gender and for young people in particular to embark on HRT. Academics, most of whom are based in UK universities, weighed in to oppose them by adding their name to a collective statement published in the *Guardian*, recognized as one of the most progressive mass circulation newspapers in the world. They used the platform to announce their 'newly formed network of over 100 academics' and to share their concern 'about the suppression of proper academic analysis and discussion of the social phenomenon of transgenderism, and its multiple causes and effects'. Academics have the least to be concerned about but with their certificates in hand they legitimate an underlying hostility towards trans people. Signatories included Sheila Jeffreys, more on whom momentarily. Ever keen to act as the voice of reason in this polarized debate, the *Guardian* added, without the attribution of an author, its editorial 'view':

> While campaigners for trans rights are entitled to push for laws that they believe advance equality, feminists are entitled to question whether such changes could adversely affect other women. Neither group is a homogeneous bloc and there are more than two points of view.[11]

'Gender identity,' they moreover declared, 'does not cancel out sex.' Implying that a trans woman is still a male, but also reinforcing the notion that males are naturally more aggressive, and thereby a threat to women, the article continued, 'Women's oppression by men has a physical basis, and to deny the relevance of biology when considering sexual inequality is a mistake.' The editorial also reinforced the idea, which TERFs often repeat, that trans people think there is nothing biologically to distinguish a male from a female.[12] Accordingly, we are all deniers of basic science. Once again, in view of the singular focus on 'toxic' masculinities in their editorials, this should come as no surprise. In aligning themselves with TERFs, they also position themselves and their sympathetic readers in between the toxic RAMS and the REMS, who stoke confusion with their ambiguous use of pronouns, but most of all trans women. Of a singular voice, the editorial team are the calibrated masculinity affording those who by extension can consider themselves reasonable and moderate to veil and legitimize a transphobia that is normative to ARMS and RAMS.

Soon afterwards, a rebuttal was published in the letters page. As it pointed out, no reference was made in the editorial 'view' to the vulnerability of trans people in the community, the high levels of poor mental health and incidences of attempted suicide. It highlighted that there was no mention of the hate crimes trans people daily contend with, nor the ostracization from friends and loved ones.[13] Comparable to the tabloid press, which justifies through recourse to a single example its painting of Muslim men as violent abusers and rapists, the *Guardian* used a similar tactic regarding TERFs who, as one blog piece notes, obsessively spotlight the tiny number of incidences in which trans women commit violence against cis women.[14] Trans author Juliet Jacques notes the peculiarly British obsession with trans people and that US readers of the publication may well be baffled that the centre-left Labour Party is failing unequivocally to support transgender rights. Jacques makes the point that it is not only radical feminists who are transphobic but also, whether or not aligned to the Conservative Party, the media establishment. That a left-leaning publication with considerable influence in shaping progressive debate in the UK does the same underscores the depth of the problem.[15] It explains why a New Zealand tribunal considered that it would be 'unduly harsh' to force a trans woman to be returned to the UK.

However, the courting of anti-trans rhetoric is not only a UK phenomenon. Writing for the *New York Times*, Elinor Burkett has castigated Caitlyn Jenner, whom she repeatedly misgenders, for proposing that she has a female brain. 'People who haven't lived their whole lives as women,' Burkett thunders, 'shouldn't get to define us.'[16] The statements of ill-informed and self-serving celebrities that I, as a trans woman, would also question become here an alibi for hatred. It propagates what any reasonable person who is not invested in the ideology would challenge. The tactic of lumping us all together and presuming that we deny biology is a recurring one amongst TERFs and a tactic commonly used against minorities of all kinds.

Radical feminists have long held notoriety for their dogmatism, extremism, authoritarian tendencies and violence. In the US during the 1970s, they sought to shut down feminist conferences and silence academics for their seeming equivocation about the 'evils' of porn. One conference, as Stryker notes in *Transgender History* (2008), demanded that transsexual lesbian singer and activist Beth Elliot be barred from giving a scheduled performance. It was during the 1970s, Stryker writes, that grassroots lesbian networks began circulating the 'transsexual rapist' trope.

The history of transgender struggles, the founding ideas of radical feminism and the movements they gave rise to will have to be parked to one side. Of more relevance to the discussion are the more recent interventions of TERFs or trans-exclusionary-feminists, on trans issues. What this broad selection of work demonstrates is a deep and self-loathing antipathy towards women, and the need, for all their protestations, of a paternal authority. They bear the symptoms of Freud's female patients who he lamented were unable to overcome their repudiation of femininity and demand, in turn, for a penis.

Endorsed by TERF poster girl Janice Raymond, who wrote *The Transgender Empire*, and crackpot eco-primitivist Derrick Jenson, *Female Erasure: What You Need to Know about Gender Politics' War on Women, the Female Sex and Human Rights* contains over fifty articles from academics, medical practitioners and activists. Including a forward by Germaine Greer and an epigraph from Sheila Jeffreys'

Gender Hurts, this recently published volume neatly condenses the argument.

The collection, according to the blurb, 'shows how transgenderism is erasing the reality of what it means to be a woman'. Starting with the editor's introduction, this is framed as a 'gender-identity ideology' which, it is charged, 'avoid[s] discussing the vast differences in sex-based biology' (Barrett, 2016: xxvi). Rather than stress the different effects of our socialization that cut across a number of divides, the authors lay emphasis on biological differences, including distribution of chromosomes, hormones and so forth, the effects of which, as Tosh (2016) shows, are not clear cut at all and vary amongst the same sex. They make no mention of intersex. 'Transgender activists dismiss biological sex difference as irrelevant' (Barrett, 2016) is a typical sweeping and misrepresentative statement.

Despite enormous variations amongst the trans community and the wildly divergent perspectives on what it means to be trans, we are uniformly presented as sharing the same ideological perspective. Thus, as Barrett (2016) insists, 'We are being told that we must accept without question or concern that males who identify as transgendered are to be considered equivalent to females in every way.' Who exactly is this authority she speaks of, whose demands, which if they were being made, should rightly be challenged? Analogous to declaring that someone with conservative leanings is a Nazi, absolutism combines with hyperbole, with one contributor even comparing the effect of transgender politics to that of 'witch burning' (Barrett, xxvi). Culpable for perpetuating the idea that 'women can only be defined within the paradigm of male authority' is the 'progressive left'. The suggestion that 'progressives' are the enemy appears to confirm the ideology to be reactive. Patriarchy is not the obstacle to liberation but the means through which the middle-class academic can position themselves as the rebellious child in respect of the superego Law. This way, they create for themselves an identity of being Other to which they narcissistically cleave as a means to dominate and silence those in whose name they claim to be fighting. As Rachel Ivy (Barrett, 2016: 13), a contributor to the collection, declares, 'In order to be an outlaw, there has to be a law. In the case of gender outlaws, that law is patriarchy, that system of values and that law is the class oppression of females.'

The antagonism is between the sexes and those who are sexed female all suffer the same fate. They are gendered and have no agency to do anything about it. Without nuance, 'Gender *is* sex-based oppression of female people, who as a class are systematically oppressed for the benefit of male people' (Barrett, 2016: 21). The synergies with right-wing paranoia are evident in the repeated suggestion that there is some kind of conspiracy amongst men 'to facilitate the exploitation of female people' (Barrett, 2016: 21). Irrespective of their class position or political power, men are seen as the exploiters. No consideration is given to how patriarchy and capitalism intersect or the negative effects of being gendered masculine. 'For radical feminists,' Ivy declares, 'the ideal number genders would be zero' (Barrett, 2016: 19). But such a goal, which would require the elimination of males, is of course impossible. And this is precisely the point. A system of oppression regarding which there is no effective agency to oppose it means there is always something to kick against and derive *jouissance* from.

While insisting that transgender ideology conflates sex and gender, TERFs systematically conflate the two by denying any agency either to themselves or to trans people. Only those born female can legitimately be called women and all those born male will only ever be men. As Stryker and Bettcher (2016: 7) point out, the ideology 'completely ignores the question of transgender agency – that is, of trans people making conscious, informed choices about the best way to live their own embodied lives – and instead represents trans people as having no will of their own'. In other words, there is agency, an agency that TERFS must disavow to sustain the ideological perspective in which they are libidinally invested.

Animated by the notion that transgender 'ideology' threatens to undermine the hard won victories of feminists against patriarchal oppression and, furthermore, to women in general, there is a fundamental contradiction in the claim that we have no agency and that whatever personal changes we make they are not political. According to one of the contributors to *Female Erasure*, Kathy Scarbrough (Barrett, 2016: 33), that 'Certain individuals may make the personal decision that they can't wait for that new day to dawn . . . the decision is a personal one . . . not a political act'. If there is nothing political in transgressing gender norms, one has to wonder why transgender people are regarded as such a threat?

Sheila Jeffreys' *Gender Hurts* (2014: 2) provides a distillation of the anti-trans perspective that once again insists that 'transgenderism' is predicated on the idea that there is an essential gender. It 'disappears', she claims, 'the fixedness of sex, the biological basis that underlies the relegation of females to their sex caste'. These 'men who adopt the "gender identity" of being female' homogenize the 'experience' of women. 'Transgender' is here, as elsewhere, the necessary supplement to the idea of 'woman' without whom the signifier, and their own identity as 'real' women, would be empty. The protest is itself a sign of how dependent TERFs are on the gender designation they fetishistically disavow. All trans people, according to this logic, are 'cross-dressers' and share the same sexual 'excitements and interests' in the clothes (Jeffreys, 2014: 28). There is a fundamental moral conservatism and disgust for feminine sexuality in the idea that libido invalidates your status as a (trans) woman.

Elliot and Lyons' (2017) symptomatic reading of Jeffreys' book identifies a number of important themes of anti-trans radical feminism. A symptomatic reading, they explain, looks for the truth contained in the text. It is an 'immanent reading' that 'strives to uncover a knowledge that does not know itself as such' (2017: 359). Like the Freudian slip, this is discovered 'through an analysis of its major signifiers, repetitions and fantasies, all of which point to the unconscious of the text' (2017: 360). Disregarding difference, what is at stake for the RLF (radical lesbian feminist), they note, is 'an imagined harmonious and egalitarian community of women' (2017: 360). In their transgressions of gender norms which they both question and threaten, trans women in particular 'are the source of fear, disgust, and rejection' (2017: 363). Trans woman function for the RFL as the 'unwoman' who represents a paternal authority with the capacity to judge, expose and shame. The trans woman is therefore a symbol of the all-powerful authority who monopolizes and deprives the RFL of their enjoyment, but which, as rebels, they derive enjoyment in.

Given how accurately the description fits that of TERFS, 'licensed psychotherapist' Laura Anderson (Barrett, 2016: 87) demonstrates a complete absence of self-awareness when she says of trans people:

> Of course, I'm describing the pull of all cults; that deep human desire to be known through and through and through. The cult experience seeks to end the frustration that naturally comes when we mature and begin to see ourselves as separate beings. In our separateness, we must do the hard work of truly learning to know another. Group thinking reduces the fear that comes when we are unsure if we will be located by another, when we remain unable to locate *ourselves*.
>
> 89

Medical professional Kathy Mandigo MD writes about a 'man transitioning to a female' who sought her counsel. 'He' began, she writes,

> . . . by being all girl-friend-ly with me, like we were two girls together in this crazy world, behaviour I assumed he had seen and adopted as how women get what they want (had he ever read me wrong! He was mimicking behaviour without having the years of lived experience by which a woman learns, if so inclined, when to use that tactic).

Of course, she questioned 'him' about 'his' health background, which revealed 'inconsistencies in his story (suggesting psychological problems)'. She describes how 'he got angry and leaned forward into my personal space and flashed that "you fucking cunt" look' (Barrett, 2016: 84).

TERFs are a death cult of the psychologically damaged. Typically white and middle class, they are women in need of a father to punish them, which they freely volunteer themselves for. Far from wanting to rid the world of the patriarch, they marshal every resource available in order to support it. By encountering joy in their femininity, trans women are resented for having what is denied to the RLF, and for showing that change is possible. Trans women demonstrate that the male is not the problem at all but the gender order that RLFs claim they want to abolish. Psychically, affectively, in their attitudes and in their actions, TERFs, as suggested, are to all intents and purposes at the RAMS end of the gender spectrum.

While the grounds on which trans women are categorized as male differ, Luce Irigaray's description of a feminine essence effectively does the same. Summarizing her position, Alison Stone (2006: 69) writes that since Irigaray 'believes that all women, qua women, have a certain bodily character, and that this character shapes women's experience, she seems obliged to conclude that all women's experiences will exhibit certain shared patterns'. It is a conclusion, Stone adds, 'which is falsely overgeneralised'.

bell hooks (2000) declared that 'feminism is for everybody'. The category of 'woman' is not, however, I want to stress, for everybody. In the constellation of late capitalism, the term serves to divide and privilege a certain class of women who have the most to lose in ridding the world of patriarchal structures. The invocation of the term as a rallying cry in the fight against patriarchy comes up against so many complications that it lacks political saliency. It's not only a problem of the various intersections of class, race and so forth, that are frequently elided, but that there is no strict way to delineate what it actually means to be a woman. Any attempt to do so comes up against the sort of problem I earlier discussed with Malabou, which leads to the erasure of trans women and intersex.

Returning to the example of race, in the United States racial discrimination and oppression is emphatically linked to slavery and segregation. Moreover, and this is crucial in respect of gender, there is a clear class dimension to race but not, in the United States and Britain at least, to gender. It is a different matter entirely of course in countries such as Saudi Arabia or in gender segregated institutions in which politically the signifier woman is hugely important. I have argued that patriarchal oppression has a class foundation and in respect of colonial history, a racial dimension too. By blurring such distinctions, gender- or queer-centred politics is fatally compromised. I sought to rescue LGBTQI+ from this fate by adding the forward slash to denote antagonism to the capitalist patriarchy. The question is not one of whether you are queer or what it means to be a woman, but whether in addition to identifying as cis, trans, queer, man or woman, you also politically and in respect to your material relation to capitalism identify with the sign /. My contention throughout this book is also that those who are masculinized have ample reason to oppose the patriarchy too. As the authors of *Feminism for the 99%*

recognize, there is no prospect of overcoming the gender-based forms of oppression unless people unite on the basis of class and, while not dismissing the importance of identity as some Marxists do, overcome the narcissism of minor differences. Trans women are not responsible for depriving the term woman of its political saliency but depriving those in denial of their divisive and anachronistic platform. The fight against patriarchy is necessary. In the contexts that TERFS typically operate in, defining it in gender terms as a fight in the name of women is not.

It is perhaps ironic that given the hostility trans women encounter, I as a trans woman get a clearer insight into how misogynistic society is and how deeply invested people are in a binary notion of gender. Translating as hatred of trans people, transphobia is not a word to be used lightly but I deploy it nonetheless as symptomatic of the general repudiation of femininity.

Living in an affluent and liberal part of Auckland, represented in parliament by a member of the left-leaning Green Party, and being a tenured academic in the field of sociology comes with many advantages. I do not encounter on a daily basis the level of hostility that many trans people do. If there is hostility, it is typically more discreet. But whether it is being addressed 'he' or 'sir', or the evident unease in the way that people mouth your preferred pronoun, from even my limited and somewhat cushioned experience, I would suggest that there is a deep and pervasive unease with people who transgress gender norms. Why, after having dressed consistently and unambiguously in a feminine style for over five years, do some colleagues in the so-called 'liberal' arts still regularly slip and refer to me as he? Some women colleagues, openly to my face and in front of students, scorn the idea that I am a woman by constantly and wilfully misgendering me, even making snarky remarks when called out because of it. Why rather than address me as Ciara, do some people in text communication now address me as 'C' (my masculine name was Colin) or, affectionately perhaps, just by my surname? Why is it certain that if I dress tomorrow in men's clothes, people will start querying my gender and be affronted if I use the women's lavatory? Clothes, they say, do not make a woman and women should not be judged according to whether they dress in feminine ways or not. People do not consider being dressed as a woman a valid reason for being called a woman either, but despite doing so for five years and adapting to the many consequences of this, dressing as a man does in the eyes of many remove any legitimacy in my claim of being a woman (perhaps I am getting a sense here of the pressures of those designated female to perform femininity). It takes only the slightest of provocations and the flimsiest of excuses for the unease that many people harbour to reveal itself in more unambiguous ways. The veneer of tolerance is, after all, a thin one.

In a society unconsciously invested in an androcentrism that privileges the masculine and denigrates the feminine, there is also an unconscious need for categorical gender and sex distinctions. As the masculine position is the 'neutral' gender default of the society with which we are all intimately acquainted, trans women who are unable to pass as cisgender have a jarring effect on this sensibility. Sensibilities recoil against what appears alien to them. Some, such as TERFS, will feed on this sensation and feel emboldened by it. Others will be discomforted by this feeling and, to their credit, compensate for their guilt by supporting transgender rights. I was brought up in the same world. I am not immune. But I am repulsed by any residue of transphobia that can sometimes be detected. Through every conceivable means available to me, I am, like every trans woman, thinking and acting against this socially impregnated reactive impulse. As this phobia issues from an unconscious repudiation of femininity, trans women are particularly difficult for people to come to terms with. It is not only trans women, however, who experience transmisogyny. In advertising their agency to determine their gender, or affirm a gender at variance to anatomical presumption, trans men do too. It follows that in a society in which a fear and revulsion towards the feminine is psychically installed, that transmisogyny is in various magnitudes a general symptom. But this is not in itself the basis on which to be hostile to those who recoil in the presence of a femme cis or trans woman. It is a question of whether the reaction-formation is consciously being checked and negated. It is a question of whether we act against these installed sensibilities or aid and abet those that feed on them or are silent when, even if only subtly, their problems with femininity are manifest. Transphobia needs to be called out in others and in our selves. The anecdotal evidence that young people are more accepting of gender varied identities and behaviours may have more to do with their conscious response to this general sickness that resides within. We are what we are, subjects to a sickness that is not of our choosing but one for which there is the capacity at least to ameliorate. If there is no capacity to purge the self and society entirely of the condition, there is at least the possibility to progressively negate it.

The final chapter summarizes the various arguments I have developed throughout the book and concludes with what Freud considered a 'riddle'. The solution to the problem of the masculine disorder is in the feminine.

6

Obsolescent empire

Masculinity is an obsolescent empire. Whatever benefits to society were accrued through this strange ego-formation were long ago spent. Defined by the repudiation of what in our society is held to be feminine, the masculine disorder is the condition on which capitalism depends and, knowing only this sickness, the subject in turn becomes dependent on too. The worst manifestations are there for all to see but which by comparison render its more general ones invisible. Masculinity is obsolete in the way that a new operating system renders a serviceable device obsolete. That system is a society in which production is organized to serve our collective interests not the interests of the few – a system in which sensibilities now regarded as feminine that strike fear into many men are nourished in each and every one of us. It is a hypothetical possibility but not for all the factories in China will it be manufactured on our behalf. Yet the materials are already available to us in fragmented, sometimes shattered, parts. To salvage and make them serviceable requires tools and the skills to utilize them. By mapping the condition, this book has aimed to identify where the problems lie, and having done so, propose ways that they can be overcome. The inadequacies of the capitalist mode of production and the subject who in their psyche is crippled by it are increasingly, however, transparent. They can be disavowed, decentred, or worse attributed to shadowy conspiracies, immigrants, metropolitan elites, women, LGBTQI+ or whatever conveniently a resurgent far right blames for our universal predicament. It is in their twilight that empires are at their most dangerous. Their fall is inevitable. But if barbarism is not to be the outcome, we need to be the engineers of its replacement. Femininity is the material from which an alternative can be forged.

The central claim of this book is simple: masculinity is a toxic ego-formation, *period*. Like the word femininity, the term is loosely associated with a range of character traits, behaviours, activities and so forth, many of which are not in themselves negative. Being competitive in a game of tennis is one thing. Feelings of anger and humiliation when losing the game another. I made a similar point about aggression. Although difficult sometimes to tell apart, ethically motivated aggression is entirely different to aggression motivated by ego. What makes masculinity toxic and even a disorder relates to what bell hooks (2004) aptly describes as 'psychic self-mutilation' and the mutilation of the psyche through external pressures. I identified these pressures with Oedipalization, the process whereby those who, defined male, learn to associate their sex with figures who in this androcentric society appear to dominate. These figures are distinguished in their style, manner, behaviour and activities from those who, in contrasting ways, are labelled feminine. These masculine figures are not simply role models. They represent a largesse to which the male is socialized to feel entitled but nonetheless, never the equal, has a need to compete for. Females have feminine role models too, of course. However, subordinated to the masculine there is no largesse to compete for. In this cruel and twisted set-up, the male competes with other males for ownership of the signifiers that represent status and authority. Normatively, the female competes with other females, not to dominate but to serve. Masculinized males have ideals to live up to, points to prove, but essentially, inadequacies to mask. The male may not consider himself entitled. Dwelling in the unconscious, it can nonetheless be detected in the ways that the ego is staked to symbols of power and authority, the feelings of humiliation that arise when revealed to be lacking or a loser, and the anger towards those who, whether intentionally or not, act the boy who declares that the emperor is naked. Like a black hole, others get drawn into the gravitational vortex of the masculine need to prove themselves adequate.

Wars are fought. Lives are destroyed. Sometimes veiled by the feminine, look closely enough and from domestic violence to climate change denial through to the authoritarian state, you will find irreparably damaged men. One article notes that, as masks are considered unmanly, masculinity is a barrier to containing Covid-19.[1]

Traits we associate with masculinity clearly predate capitalism, but the form of masculinity Westernized societies are habituated to and which is woven inextricably in its fabric is of a most peculiar nature. But the disorder is not the cause of capitalism. Rather, it is a consequence of the material conditions that depend on it and the institutionalized arrangements that ensure it. Ours is a sick society. It is a society plagued by a contagion that the state has no interest in either containing or eliminating. It aids and abets it. None of us are immune, not even women who in many ways are either afflicted by it themselves or addicted to those who display the symptoms.

We need to purge ourselves of this disorder. Like the virus we are combatting at the time of writing, this can only be achieved collectively. We cannot wait for others to do this on our behalf. We cannot wait for a revolution that may never happen. Even if it does, the sickness will still be amongst us. I proposed a feminine praxis. Why feminine? Because in our society the qualities that are identified as feminine are not only anathema to many men – if universalized, they would be anathema to capitalism. It thrives on an ego-motived and a libidinally-invested need for status and domination. The standard feminist strategy of rejecting femininity on the basis that it represents weakness, passivity and subordination does not negate androcentrism. It merely confirms it. There is every reason for a woman to want a piece of the pie, but it's a losing strategy. Not only are the obstacles, both material and psychic, formidable. It requires self-mutilation.

With my focus on the male, I haven't spoken much about the appropriation by women of femme styles as a mode of resistance. There is nothing political about being femme in itself. As I proposed with the LGBT+[ ]/ formula, unless we stand in opposition to capitalism as a class, being 'non-normative' is dietary fibre to capitalism. It is a system that today thrives on politically denuded modes of individual expression and identity. Marcuse comes to mind here. He said that in a one-dimensional society difference is fully embraced. Different styles of living are 'the ceremonial part of practical behaviourism, its harmless negation, and are quickly digested by the status quo as part of its healthy diet' (Marcuse, 2002: 16). There is a weaponized form of femme. It can inspire and give confidence to those who desire to articulate a femininity on their body and, in a challenge to androcentrism, put femininity into practice. But the forces of reaction to repel such strategies are far greater and more powerful than we are. Hence why femme must enter the class struggle and the materially braided struggle against white supremacy. The reality principle needs testing and its institutions transforming. Marcuse describes the instrumentalization of life to the logic of exchange as the historically specific performance principle, a diagnosis as relevant as ever and which we must find ways to combat.

Four indisputable truths as to why masculinity is a generic disorder have been outlined. These were not drawn from surveys, but appeals to common sense. I reasoned that anybody who lives in a society comparable to the one in which I was raised would testify to these truths through observation and reflection.

One truth is that those who commit violent acts and massacres are in almost every instance male. For some, this suggests that males are inherently violent. But with a few exceptions, why it is those who are sexed male and *also* identify as men that commit such acts is not difficult to explain in sociological terms. The most brittle and damaged of men, some of whom can accurately be described as sociopaths and pathological narcissists, I labelled RAMS (reactive/ aggravated masculinities). They pose the most immediate and present danger to all of us, especially since, with no moral compass, many of these men occupy positions of high office, are chairs of boards and are the agents of 'law and order'. Exhibit number one in the case for the prosecution is the *extreme*.

Exhibit number two is the *exception*. To take a personal example, I know from experience that even fully dressed as a man, my long and painted red fingernails are enough for people to look, stare, reflect and remark. You do not have to deviate far into the terrain of feminine representation to stand out as the exception to the rule that the vast majority of men do not deviate in any meaningful sense from the default and generic masculine norm. Sure, men sometimes wear pink shirts and affect feminine airs and graces. Those who do the latter are typically singled out as gay and, as the survey I referenced shows, even this act is considered a turn off for many gay men and in their eyes gives the gay community a bad name. The exception is proof of the rule that femininity is generally repudiated. Men fear and recoil against the feminine. Their very identity as men depend on it. The tragedy of this for Freud, for which without a critique of patriarchy he had no answer to, is that men cut themselves off from emotions that are essential to their wellbeing. Not only that, but women come to depend on and demand this crippled psyche that they themselves are so often victim to. The capitalist patriarchy drums into the female the idea that the feminine is inferior and unable to compete on the male's terms, that they need their own 'penises'. This can be translated as a need for men and babies as a means of gaining security, not necessarily for a literal penis. But women recognize that men suffer. They are all too acquainted with but often accommodating of their sickness. Women are not diminished. Society compels them to act as if they are.

Rather than polymorphous-perverse, through the process of socialization, sexuality becomes fixated on genitalia and the procreative function. The reproduction of and caring for the species are essential to all societies, but in specific ways to capitalism. A mode of production in which profit is derived from the value waged labour produces in excess of remuneration requires an endless supply of bodies to carry out this task. If not simply to be discarded and driven to their grave, women are tasked not only to resupply capital with workers but also through caregiving to revitalize them. However, as Vogel (1983) shows, there is no bio-physical basis for women's subordination but a capitalistic one. Capital needs women to hold the male's hand as they are taken through the process of Oedipalization. Femininity contains its own dialectic. It is both the problem and solution to this sorry state of affairs. It is the problem that society is unable to reconcile itself with but also depends on, and also the solution in that, when positively affirmed, what is characterized as feminine negates the disorder. Our personal and collective liberation lies in this and liberation, moreover, from this binary terminology altogether and the implications of it.

The third exhibit and perhaps the most banal piece of evidence is the *fantasy*. So routine is the Oedipal formula of the entertainment industrial complex that one could be forgiven for thinking it a natural representation of who we are as human beings. And in some ways, it is. It is the reproduction on the screen of the masculinized unconscious. It is the palliative for the little man inside of us who cannot in life live up to the ideals to which libidinally they cleave. The liberal press celebrates the increasingly common casting of women in the role of the hero. The hero, now the heroine. But such figures are the empty placeholders onto which the same masculine fantasies are projected. The 'strong woman' is the woman who has learnt, perhaps the hard way, how to be a man. There is no negation of androcentrism in these female-centred narratives. It is why video games such as *Tomb Raider*, considered progressive for making the avatar the female Laura Croft, can appeal to even the most sexually frustrated and inadequate of boys and men. The culture industry would not invest their many millions of dollars into these forms of entertainment if, for a second, they thought it would alienate its largest audience. They are not stupid. The same goes for Gillette and all those companies in on the #MeToo movement. They talk the talk. Nothing structurally changes.

The fourth exhibit in the chapter 'Vectors of androcentrism' was the *economy*. Androcentrism operates, I suggested, on four libidinal vectors of labour: waged, consuming, repressive and reproductive. The historically specific form of masculinity peculiar to capitalism is here discerned. These labours serve specific and interrelated functions. While repressive labour predates capitalism, it is integral to the totality of labours of androcentrism specific to it and also therein acquires its own distinctive form. Capitalism is inextricably libidinal. It requires a subject that not only works out of necessity but who derives meaning through competition and the accolades that may or may be tossed to them in their alienated occupations. Employability/ exploitability is ceaseless. Our need and desire to make ourselves useful and pliable to capital is the catastrophe upon catastrophe.

If things were purchased to satisfy basic material needs, the modern form of consumerist capitalism would not exist. Production would be ground down to a halt. There is use-value in the phallic function of the commodity to which we now appear to be addicted. It is convenient to pin the blame for consumerist excesses on women. This is simply another one of those masking effects, in this case to conceal the masculine dimension to and androcentric basis of mass consumption.

Sociopaths have many uses, most of all in what Althusser calls the repressive state apparatuses. Repressive labour demands the most brutalized of men, sometimes women, who are recruited to serve in the police, prison service and the military. Without such men, capitalism would not survive the many uprisings that occur periodically – such as the ones in the United States triggered by the police execution in Minneapolis of forty-six-year-old George Floyd. White supremacy is not only institutionalized, it is instilled in the unconscious. But repressive labour does not necessarily come with weapons. It is a weaponized form of masculinity that primes the male for leadership roles. Capitalism breeds psychos. It rewards those who are willing to act ruthlessly and without compassion to crush organized labour and compel people to act in their image.

Given the necessity for a psychically damaged subject and the subordination of females to their bio-physical functions, it is women who are typically burdened with the task of ensuring that boys are primed for such labours. The material disadvantages of unpaid domestic labour combined with the disadvantages of institutionalized discrimination and, a disadvantage only in a society that rewards those who aggressively pursue their own interests, the psychic effects of feminization. In each of these respects, women are at a competitive disadvantage. But it would be entirely wrong to conclude from this that patriarchy serves the interest of men. It is an ideologically false dichotomy that pits women against men or that, through appeals to compassion, recruit men into a kind of charity. My claim that capitalism is a libidinal economy is not original. But following from this, it is evident that capitalism, in whichever scenario, requires a subject, maybe even a machine, to desire a phallus in order to compensate for engineered feelings of inadequacy. Specific to my mapping of masculinity to capitalism, it is the function of Oedipalization that in my usage of the term reproductive labour, which hypothetically could be carried out by anyone or thing, I lay stress on. In any event, the feminine must be repudiated and androcentrism prevail. Capitalism is for these reasons inextricably patriarchal.

If all masculinities are toxic, some are more toxic than others. Taking issue with some of the presuppositions about what in our society today represents the masculine ideal, I suggested that the hegemonic form of masculinity is represented by corporations that support LGBTQI+, which is embodied in figures like Barack Obama, *not* Trump. It is not necessarily a reflection of how men are, but, whether due to pressure or a revulsion for men who are openly misogynistic, sexist and racist, how they want others to see them. I indexed toxicity to three core types: RAMS (reactive/aggravated masculinities), ARMS (avoidant/restrictive masculinities) and REMS (reflective/experimental masculinities). RAMS and REMS are the polar opposites, one reactively counter-hegemonic and the other progressively counter-hegemonic. From RAMS to REMS, the boundaries separating ARMS, which lie between the two, are porous and constantly shifting. They are not impermeable nor are they neatly delineated. ARMS on the outside may just as easily be RAMS on the inside, their rage, which may well be encountered by those in the home, kept in check but vulnerable to exposure should their material conditions change. I presented the fictional Walter White/'Heisenberg' as an example. ARMS are 'moderate'. Their masculinity is calibrated by the shifting tides that gravitate either towards the RAMS or the REMS. Calibrated masculinity is my preferred term for what, noting the problems with the way it is conceptualized, Connell calls hegemonic masculinity. ARMS calibrate their masculinity to changing attitudes and trends. They acquire the lingo. Under pressure from the #MeToo movement and its accompanying critique of RAMS, they become the good but 'flawed' feminist. Feminism and femininity are phallicized. Perhaps reluctantly and with dead eyes, ARMS grudgingly address those who are trans or non-binary by the appropriate pronoun. They may yearn to dress as I do but are too invested in their masculine persona or deterred by the material implications. We need to free these men from their self-imposed cages and the cages that society also locks them into. On the cutting edge between the masculine and feminine, REMS are stretching the definition of what a man is and challenging the idea of a naturally given binary. There is agency here, an agency that through these three typologies I have given theoretical form to. They embolden those who harbour the desire but lack the confidence to break free from their cage and take flight.

However, as I have sought to stress throughout, masculinity is not only a male phenomenon. Some of the worst of men are women. TERFS act like RAMS, appear to have the same complexes as RAMS and in many ways they are RAMS. Along with the intersections of class and race, the battle to own the signifier 'woman' raises the question of whether 'woman' can function as a signifier for all those who are oppressed under patriarchy. The struggle for ownership of this term and for it to define an antagonism through which to politicize the subject to rise up against patriarchy is divisive and counterproductive. Except in specific circumstances, in the most Westernized of societies at least, ontologically and epistemologically, the struggle to determine 'woman' must be abandoned. There is a feminism for the 99 per cent but not a woman for the 99 per cent. Whether you are a cis man or woman, trans, non-binary or intersex, there are multiple reasons for taking sides to crush the capitalist patriarchy. We need to overcome our fixations on identity and, as Arruzza, Bhattacharya and Fraser (2019) have suggested, the idea too that class and identity politics are incompatible with each other. We need to become agents of the C.I.A. – class, identity, and affect – to affect a feminine praxis that connects dialectically to identity in antagonism to the capitalist patriarchy.

Chapter by chapter, let me summarize the book. Chapter 1, 'The general sickness', set the scene. Chapter 2 theorized the disorder as a libidinal condition. Ranging from the most brittle and aggressive to the most reflective and open, chapter 3, 'Toxicity index', developed a schematic for theorizing a continuum of masculinities; the formula for all masculinities: RAMS–ARMS–REMS. Chapter 4, 'Vectors of androcentrism', placed the disorder in its material context. It not only showed why the disorder is indispensable to capitalism but that it also, in its peculiar form and function, has its roots in European colonization and white supremacy.

In chapter 5, 'Queervestism', my particular relationship to, interpretation of and reflections on dressing openly as a woman became the 'data' through which to explore the relationship between identity and desire. My point is that desires that are perceived as perverse can potentially in degrees, and in respect of a feminine praxis, liberate the subject from its masculine designation and affects. I described how through the practice of dressing publicly as a woman a change is affected in one's imaginary and symbolic egos, leading to a change of object and direction. I focused on the figure of the transvestite who it was reckoned is the most maligned of transgender subjects (if counted as transgender at all) and whose desire to dress as a woman unambiguously originates outside of them – though nonetheless integral – through what the term woman is linguistically associated with.

That is the basic summary. Now for some final thoughts and reflections.

A lack less ordinary

'Castration' is the unfortunate word Lacan uses to refer to the effect of signification. As the subject is formed by language and language is full of ambiguity and imprecision, we are never as subjects 'whole'. There is a hole at the core of subjectivity that puts desire on a train of hopeless quests for whatever object is imagined will fill that hole. Lacan called this missing 'thing' *objet (petit) a*. The phallus is what symbolically, for the subject, constitutes closure, in masculine terms to be the Real impossible and perfect 'man'. Only in death are we no longer subject to the symbolic law. This suggests that desire will always be phallocentric, always in need of a phallic substitute. Lack, in this sense, is not only 'ordinary' but, as Deleuze and Guattari say, acquisitive. It is ordinarily and hopelessly capitalistic and androcentric. But if there is such a thing as an artist who derives pleasure in the creative process itself and which is integral to their *being*, then, as Gherovici (2017) points out in respect of her trans analysands, desire can operate without recourse to a phallic supplement. In this reading, Lacan begins sounding like Deleuze and Guattari, for whom 'becoming' is a process that has neither a beginning nor an end, neither an object nor an identity, a desire that is not phallicized.

Gender is one of many means through which subjects gain a sense of consistency and direction. Masculinity is fraudulently predicated on the idea that man is not castrated in the Lacanian sense. This is the basis of a universal delusion complex. There is no such exception with feminine sexuality. The former is dominated by a need to have the phallus representing the signifier that would foreclose this gap between what we are and would ideally be. The latter's need for a phallus is tempered by the fact that there is no equivalent ideal. Feminine sexuality is open in this respect and not, as is the case with masculine sexuality, fixated. Being fixated, however, comes with many benefits. My fixation on women's apparel helps, as I freely confess, to stabilize my sense of womanhood. Perhaps one day I won't feel this need, but that will be the day when femininity is the universal default of a society freed of the masculine pathology. A society in which without a masculine referent the term femininity itself serves no purpose.

Parallels can be drawn between my 'fixations' and those of the artist, scientist, intellectual and musician. If, as suggested, there are elements of what we think of as masculine that can be salvaged to serve in our collective interests, whatever drives such figures to succeed is the mana that I imagine many of us would want to sample. But as with everything, this is a double-edged sword. Moreover, it is something of a myth that such productive endeavours, from which we derive many benefits, are the work of individuals. Just as waged labour obscures the vital function of unwaged labour in maintaining the capitalist economy, the attribution of a work of art or scientific discovery to a single individual has the effect of obscuring the collective efforts of those who make such achievements possible.

If there is any one individual who embodied the many contradictions this book explores, it is my hero and idol Prince. Exemplary of the problem of and solution to the masculine disorder, he poses for me the question of whether society could indeed thrive, or if it is even possible, without this mutilated psyche. If what Prince achieved was symptomatic of the disorder, then isn't the disorder something we may want to preserve?

Prince refused to box himself into categories. 'Am I black or white, am I straight or gay?' he teased on *Controversy*. He famously posed naked on the iconic cover of *Lovesexy*. Whether clothed or naked, in nothing but stockings and panties or face colourfully painted in make-up, he is the closest representation of androgyny in the Westernized imaginary. This could be said of Bowie too. But whereas Bowie's femininity was worn on stage, Prince, as many who knew him have noted, dressed in private as he did in public. When in Minneapolis I put it to his former wife, Mayte Garcia, that I always suspected Prince was a closet cross-dresser. She beamed a smile and said that he always used to borrow her clothes. Prince actively and self-consciously sought to scramble up the signifiers of masculinity and femininity. He adopted an unpronounceable non-gendered symbol and scrawled 'SLAVE' across his cheek in protest at the fact, as he put it, that 'Prince' had become a commodity owned by Warner Brothers. They owned the aptly named master tapes. He didn't use the word, and probably never read Marx, but it was a protest against his alienated condition. It was an alienation not only from the product of his labour but also, under commercial pressure to produce the hits, the process of artistic creation itself.

He stated this through his art, most notably the *Around the World in a Day* album which was released in 1985, less than one year after the mega hit *Purple Rain*. The psychedelic funk that fused together with Middle Eastern influences was outside the register of the funk-rock behemoth that preceded it. He described an 'FU attitude' when making it and the outcome as a 'gift' to his fans. It was a fuck you to Warner who wanted a *Purple Rain* mark 2. Through repeated listens, fans would come to appreciate the broader palette of colours it presented. This was the 'gift'. My musical tastes matured with Prince. Through the jazz-influenced 1986 album *Parade*, I learned an appreciation for the most experimental and challenging work of Miles Davis. Prince was a gift to me on many different levels. Most of all, his imaginary *Paisley Park* utopia in which there weren't any 'rules'. It was a place, as stated in the song, where people of many colours could live freely and play. It populated my imagination with a world far removed from the one I was brought up in and inspired me to go in search of. It's no exaggeration to say that were it not for Prince I would not be writing this book now or be in my profession. Prince was, and is, the exemplar on the very cutting edge of REMS. He reflected on, and from his position of influence, pushed every boundary and pressed every button to challenge norms and expectations. He was the sparkling confetti of an altogether more colourful masculinity.

Unlike figures like Hendrix, who at the time of his death was producing his best work, Prince hit his peak and crashed from it many years ago. Yet the outpouring of grief upon his death was profound. It happened in the darkest of moments. It wasn't that Prince's death marked the end of hope but that he reminded us that there is hope – that we are capable of being so much more than what society has turned us into. He was and, even more in death, is the subjective antithesis of what Fisher (2009) called capitalist realism. A negation, in other words, of the idea that not only is there no alternative to the prevailing order but also no alternative to the self-interested and sociopathic subject neoliberal ideology presumes us to be.

Prince was a virtuoso on lead and rhythm guitar and bass, a formidable drummer and also an accomplished pianist. His live performances were electrifying. A master of many different musical forms, his creative output during his 'imperial' phase spanning *Dirty Mind* in 1980 through to *Lovesexy* in 1988 is without parallel. In many respects, he was the total artist. But all of this comes with caveats. His passion for music came at heavy price. It cut him off from the world and ultimately from his loved ones. Former partner, Kim Basinger, complained that Prince was 'married' to his music. Every woman in his life played on second fiddle. Mayte (2017) documents in her autobiography attitudes, behaviours and characteristics of Prince symptomatic of the masculine disorder. Prince's success afforded many riches, so many in fact that he could isolate himself in his own Paisley Park world, the studio complex built on the outskirts of Minneapolis. He lived there in isolation. He died there in isolation.

Prince was a self-cultivated enigma and also a myth. For all his many preternatural talents, the unparalleled catalogue of musical riches was effectively closed at the end of the 1980s. He continued to mesmerize audiences with his live performances, but after the patchy 1988 *Lovesexy* album, as a songwriter he produced little of artistic merit. Many have pondered on the creative cliff that he fell off. One explanation is the distractions of the Paisley Park complex; another, the disbandment in 1986 of the aptly named Revolution.

His best work was produced under constraint, the constraints of the collective –in particular, key members of the Revolution: Wendy Melvoin and Lisa Coleman. Unlike most who surrounded him, they were bold and confident enough to say to his face, 'I heard that before', 'You can do better' and, more importantly, 'Here's something to inspire you.' Rarely credited, they provided him with some of the most memorable of melodies. It was Lisa's brother, David, who introduced to him the melody and textures to the song 'Around the World in a Day', the signature sound of that album. When the Revolution was disbanded in 1986, the album that followed in 1987, typically thought his masterpiece, *Sign o' the Times*, was considered proof that he could make it alone. Many of the songs were in fact written while with the Revolution, to which Wendy and Lisa contributed but for which they were not credited. Put simply, and taking nothing away from his genius, in his heyday, Prince was the name of a mystified collective.

While it's impossible to know how instrumental Wendy, Lisa and many others in his wider entourage were in ensuring Prince's creative vitality, they were certainly key contributors during that 'imperial' phase. I visited Paisley Park in 2018. My most poignant memory of the visit was the studio in which Prince spent much of his life. Working in isolation, he derived a method by which to record vocal tracks in the console room. To project their voice, vocalists usually stand beside a mic when singing. Prince devised a contraption that placed the mic over the console and a method for projecting his voice while sat working the nobs and sliders. It obviated the need for a sound engineer, an engineer like Susan Rogers who worked closely with him during his imperial phase.

She recalls Prince's peculiar behaviour during the *Sign o' the Times* recording sessions, after the Revolution was disbanded. Not only had he cut himself off from his closest friends, but his relationship with his lover and muse, Suzanne Melvoin, twin sister of Wendy, had also ended. Yet many of the songs from those sessions were upbeat. Prince, Rogers observes, was unable to express himself emotionally: 'He did not like admitting any kind of a weakness.'[2]

What do we learn from this? First, that the heroic compositions, creations and scientific breakthroughs of those who in our society we revere are never achieved in isolation. There is a hidden abode that women such as Wendy and Lisa commonly occupy. The potential for such greatness resides in our collective capacities not through the work of individual egos. Furthermore, to accomplish such achievements in an alienated society involves personal sacrifices that are beyond what should be expected of anyone. There will never be enough Prince in a free society but a multiplicity of Princes, Princes that are composed by an ensemble, the compositions not of a person but of a multitude. Masculinity is a form of constraint that in a capitalist society can produce great things but only relative to such a society. In a feminized society, in which the subject is under no such constraint, libido spreads in many different directions and, lacking inhibition or a need for recognition, connects productively with a multiplicity of forces. Instead of being attributed to a single author, great works will be attributed to the collective. Such hypotheses do not need to be tested. They are documented in the many objects that in Westernized societies are revered. Heroism, scientific endeavour, great art, the strongest argument in favour of the preservation of the masculine ego-formation is based on a false prospectus. When freed of our psychically and materially imposed inhibitions, there will be many great artists and scientists. But none such as Prince.

In his short essay 'End of Utopia',[3] Marcuse writes about the means, both material and intellectual, available to realize a free society. The 'total mobilisation of existing society against its own potential for liberation' is the reason they are not marshalled to this end. 'The end of utopia' has a double meaning: that, reminiscent of Fisher's critique of 'capitalist realism', any alternative to capitalism is consigned to utopian fantasy; and, in regards to the above, that these conditions do not themselves mean that the idea of a free society is itself a utopian one.

And this is the point at which I arrive with Lacan. Given that masculine and feminine sexuality are not opposing gender norms but, emphatically according to the theory, the two possible ways in which the subject contends with the lack of being, there is no conceivable situation in which there is no masculine sexuality. The idea that a feminine sexuality, which has no object and therefore elides symbolic inscription, could exist without a masculine sexuality, which is entirely phallic focused, is as inconceivable to sexuation theory as a capitalism without a worker to exploit. Born of the signifier, androcentrism, like that of capitalism, is an historical anomaly that can hypothetically, however, be overcome. Gender realism states otherwise. To invoke Marcuse, our Great Refusal is the idea that androcentrism is the only game in town and that a masculine sexuality, while always a hypothetical possibility, must in practice exist as the psychic condition of any of us.

But to stress the point, why, when the phallus can represent anything whatsoever, is masculine sexuality a problem? In other words, the 'object' to which desire is oriented could be the book I'm currently writing, and having completed it, another and another, or, alternatively, by instrumentalizing research that the university values, to occupy the highest office and deploy the power it affords to crush all competition. One is benign and, one might hope, of sociological value, the other strengthens my position at the expense of others who are not so privileged to be afforded the opportunity to write such a book. The problem, certainly as I see it, is that under these conditions, in its phallic function, masculine sexuality is inextricable from capitalism and, more to the point, essential to it. While also, as its necessary supplement and, in its hysteric formation, demanding of a master (a real man), feminine sexuality is similarly bound and also thereby productive to capital. However, a feminine sexuality, wherein the libido is multidirectional and not, as with masculine sexuality, singularly oriented to the phallic function, affords a different prospectus.

It is a feminine sexuality that is in no part oriented to the masculine need for a supportive and supplementary phallus in which the potential that resides in us lies. Under the atomizing and alienating conditions of capitalism, and here recalling Lacan's claim that the superego today commands the subject to enjoy, libido finds its object at the shopping mall and the workplace. However, in a communistic society wherein we are no longer alienated as workers, the potential that inheres in the drive is realized through its collective and self-conscious reconstitution. Libido would here travel along non-instrumentalized and multidirectional pathways that collectively intersect to produce art, architecture, technologies and so forth that far exceed not only that what the Romans achieved, but in a single generation what even was achieved under capitalism. In a single generation, it can slow down, arrest and ultimately reverse the damage that humans have done to the planet. More than the flourishing of the human subject, the flourishing of all non-human species is also at stake. It is only through such arrangements that a new kind of subject is born. Only future generations will have a chance of living their entire lives without being subject to the sickness past generations have passed down to the present ones.

Born with unambiguous genitalia – a penis, in other words – whether or not it was my parent's intention, I was raised to be competitive. I was raised to be a winner, in contrast to which there are always losers. Losing rubbed me up the wrong way (it still does). I was raised to hide my emotions, which had a stunting effect on my personal growth and capacity to show love and empathy, to feel ashamed if ever tenderness was observed. Today I'm reconciled with and no longer feel ashamed to reveal what in our society are regarded as feminine expressions. I no longer feel pressurized to 'man up'. But this doesn't mean I am less competitive nor feel flushed with power and pride when achieving goals that in our society command status and authority. I am, however, more self-aware and better positioned to check my aggression, a violence of presence rather than a physical one. But I can no more extirpate these feelings than, notwithstanding the effects of HRT, the pleasure I derive from wearing women's clothes. Nevertheless, just as I would not want to expunge the fantasy that gives form and direction to my desire to present and live as a woman, neither would I want to withdraw from the game, returning to the earlier analogy, to stop chasing the ball and no longer be exploited by capital necessary to earning a wage. Circumstance necessitates this but does not omit the possibility of libido simultaneously tracing more revolutionary pathways. This is the dialectic of masculinity that enacts its own erasure through the progressive overcoming of the conditions that give rise to the disorder and the institutions and apparatuses that aid and abet it. The drive to transform our condition is, in view of the general sickness, paradoxically phallocentric. In class society, the unconscious is primarily androcentric. This is the condition that cannot consciously be overcome individually, only collectively through the course of time. Masculinity and femininity contain their own asymmetrical dialectics of enslavement and liberation.

I neither reify nor essentialize femininity. I spoke at the start of a *tactical reification* of femininity. These gendered terms cannot be ignored. We cannot rid ourselves entirely of the effects of our gender dysphoria nor the preternatural talent for clocking the masculine and feminine without reflection. We have to work with what we are and what we have. The feminine is both a form of enslavement and a pathway towards our liberation. Its dialectic lies in the function it serves to prop up the masculine disorder and also therein to negate it.

Femininity is the riddle of the masculine disorder solved, and it knows itself to be this solution

In the *Economic and Philosophical Manuscripts of 1844*, Marx wrote that 'communism is the riddle of history solved, and it knows itself to be this solution'. This can now be amended with a Freudian twist: Femininity is the riddle of the masculine disorder solved, and it knows itself to be this solution. The answer is not so much to the riddle of why a feminine subject develops attachments to father figures but the answer, which without a critique of the capitalist patriarchy, Freud would never arrive at. The answer lies in what must in this androcentric order be repressed and subordinated but also marshalled collectively in opposition to capital. Had Freud focused on the social arrangements he may have found his solution to the feminine barrier in men and women. But as a therapist, not a Marxist, his task was to find ways to help people cope with the damage that had already been done to them. This is perhaps as much as we can hope for in the present conditions. But if not for the self, then for future generations and the planet on which they make their home, it is vital that the therapeutic process is taken to the streets and onto the barricades. This means ditching our books on self-healing, crushing those crystals that New Age fascists find pious comfort in and telling our managers who recruit consultants to teach us about wellbeing where to shove it. The therapy that is both individually and collectively required is a feminine praxis.

There is no third gender that the binary has repressed. There are one, two, a thousand genders, genders to the nth degree. The trans man does not mutilate himself to live as a man. He affirms what the cis man denies in himself, that 'being' a man does not have to require the killing off of parts of himself on the basis of an erroneous association with the feminine. Trans women may in contrast have already been mutilated by the compounding effects of a masculinized socialization, but they have found ways, if not to entirely purge themselves of the sickness, to ameliorate its effects. They show to the world that femininity is not something to be feared but positively to be embraced. The idea of a positive femininity terrifies men and women. They are repulsed by what trans women represent and show to them. But this repulsion is itself a symptom of the disorder. The reactive formations of the mind are not ones that we consciously determine. Even if only to stand in solidarity with those who in their being and becoming do, as with Prince to an extent, remind us that it doesn't have to be this way, we are at least on the right side of history. A feminine praxis is the prefigurative move of a people who want to see an end to masculine domination. It is the move of a subject who knows from history that even a revolution that eliminates the capitalist class is no guarantee that, due to the dominant tendencies of the masculine sickness, it will not resurface in an even more barbarous form.

The future is feminine. Which is to say that there is no conceivable classless society that defaults to the masculine. If socialism marks a transitional phase between capitalism and the end of class society, then communism is the state of affairs in which there is no masculine subject – a collective withering away of a phallic sexuality towards a time when phallic sexuality has no economic function.

This is not the same as saying that there is no lack of being – whether there is such a thing I leave to others to speculate on – or that masculine sexuality is not a possible response to it. Just as in communism, capitalism will exist in memory and be described in history books, even that, perhaps due to some unforeseen catastrophe, a form of class society could resurface, a generic feminine sexuality does not omit the possibility for a masculine sexuality. Just as all available means are today mobilized to privilege the masculine, so too, dialectically, will the very same means, technological, institutional, legal and so forth, in such a scenario privilege the feminine. This is our lack less ordinary. This is our Deleuzian becoming-imperceptible. Why? Because in a future that has no referential use for the term masculine, like that of 'working class' in a classless society, the term feminine will cease to serve any ontological or epistemological purpose. None of this will determine in itself how as subjects we choose to dress, nor what gives us pleasure, or how as subjects we relate to one another. Except to say that in each of these respects, there would be no normative style reflective of a binary position nor any psychic need to represent one. All labels denoting a sexuality can finally be abandoned, if we so choose, and the perversity of our pleasures can multiply and flourish without detriment to either the individual or the collective. The artist, the scientist, the intellectual, whatever, the potentialities available in all of us would in a variety of ways find expression – but not in such individuated, atomizing and destructive ways as they do today. It would not require males who are unable to admit weakness. In such a society there would be no 'riddle' to solve, no normative gender or sexuality to puzzle over and trace to some formative moment in our lives. It's a utopian, perhaps in a literal sense impossible, prospectus. It is one nonetheless to which we can strive and that stands as an ideal-type or barometer against which to question and condemn the current state of affairs. This is our utopian 'no-man's land'.

Notes

1 The general sickness

1 R. M. Barton, 'On Femininity and Being a Fierce, Autonomous, Radical, Queer Femme', *WUSSY*, 19 February 2018, https://www.wussymag.com/all/2018/2/17/on-femininity-and-being-a-fierce-autonomous-radical-queer-femme.

2 Who's ur daddy?

1 https://www.theguardian.com/lifeandstyle/2018/jul/20/is-eating-bananas-whole-gay-fragile-masculinitys-bizarre-new-hetiquette.

2 *Breaking Bad*, directed by Thomas Schnauz; created by Vince Gilligan; first broadcast 26 August 2012. Produced by High Bridge Entertainment, Gran Via Productions and Sony Pictures Television. Original network AMC. ©2019 Sony Pictures Television Inc. All Rights Reserved.

3 R. Godwin, 'Men after #MeToo: "There's a Narrative that Masculinity is Fundamentally Toxic"', *Guardian*, 9 March 2018, https://www.theguardian.com/world/2018/mar/09/men-after-metoo-masculinity-fundamentally-toxic.

4 J. Perkiss and J. Serie, 'Obama's Covert Drone War in Numbers: Ten Times More Strikes Than Bush', *Bureau of Investigative Journalism*, 17 January 2017, https://www.thebureauinvestigates.com/stories/2017-01-17/obamas-covert-drone-war-in-numbers-ten-times-more-strikes-than-bush?fbclid=IwAR3hx0QgSt5qsD9NjMHkN1nAf7D3uDEcPNST8mKsdnBvi7HTFJfDIOphYCQ.

5 Unattributed, 'Coca-Cola Was Accused of Hiring Hitmen from a Prominent Paramilitary Group Between 1990 and 2002 to Kill at Least 10 Trade Union Leaders', *teleSUR*, 1 September 2018, https://www.telesurenglish.net/news/Colombia-Coca-Cola-Accused-of-Funding-Terrorist-Paramilitaries-20160901-0005.html.

6 https://www.cnbc.com/2019/07/30/procter-gamble-writes-down-gillette-business-but-remains-confident-in-its-future.html.

7 S. Fitzmorris, 'From Bond to Blonde: Daniel Craig Dresses Up in Drag to Help Highlight Inequality', *Mail Online*, 10 March 2012, https://www.dailymail.co.uk/tvshowbiz/article-1363866/Daniel-Craig-drag-International-Womens-Day-From-James-Bond-Blonde.html.

3 Toxicity index

1 D. Thomson, 'Toxic Masculinity and its Threat to a Caring Society', *Open Democracy*, 15 September 2019, https://www.opendemocracy.net/en/transformation/toxic-masculinity-and-its-threat-caring-society/.

2 S. Kale, 'The Rise of Arfid: the Truth about the Eating Disorder that made a Teenager go Blind', *Guardian*, 6 September 2019, https://www.theguardian.com/lifeandstyle/2019/sep/06/the-rise-of-arfid-the-truth-about-the-eating-disorder-that-made-a-teenager-go-blind.

3 S. Moore, 'If We Can't Define what a Woman is, How Can We Organise Politically', *Guardian*, 3 August 2020, https://www.theguardian.com/commentisfree/2020/aug/03/define-what-a-woman-is-organise-politically-suzanne-moore.

4 C. Cederström, 'How to be a Good Man: What I Learned from a Month Reading the Feminist Classics', *Guardian*, 2 October 2018, https://www.theguardian.com/world/2018/oct/02/how-to-be-good-man-me-too-month-reading-feminist-classics?

5 C. Mudde, 'Why is the Far Right Dominated by Men?', *Guardian*, 17 August 2018, https://www.theguardian.com/commentisfree/2018/aug/17/why-is-the-far-right-dominated-by-men?CMP=fb_gupeople are typically seduced by the far right but because of masculinity.

6 Unattributed, 'Video Manifesto Reveals CA Shooting Spree was Revenge for Social Rejection', *Aljazeera*, 4 May 2014, http://america.aljazeera.com/articles/2014/5/24/ucsb-mass-shooting.html.

7 D. Thomas, 'Elliot Rodger Wasn't Interested in Women', *Aljazeera*, 7 June 2014, https://www.aljazeera.com/indepth/opinion/2014/06/elliot-rodger-killing-sexism-20146219411713900.html.

8 Unattributed, 'When Women ar the Enemy: The Intersection of Misogyny and White Supremacy', *ADL: Fighting Hate for Good*, n.d., https://www.adl.org/resources/reports/when-women-are-the-enemy-the-intersection-of-misogyny-and-white-supremacy.

9 J. Moorhead, 'UK's Only Trans Philosophy Professor to JK Rowling: Harry Potter Helped me Become a Woman', 11 July 2020, https://

www.theguardian.com/education/2020/jul/11/uks-only-trans-philosophy-professor-to-jk-rowling-harry-potter-helped-me-become-a-woman.

4 Vectors of androcentrism

1 K. Muir, 'Jane Campion: "Capitalism is such a Macho Force: I Felt Run Over"', *Guardian*, 20 May 2019, https://www.theguardian.com/film/2018/may/20/jane-campion-unconventional-film-maker-macho-force?CMP=Share_iOSApp_Other.

2 Unattributed, 'Volkswagen to Stop Making its Classic Beetle Next Year', *Guardian*, 14 September 2018, https://www.theguardian.com/business/2018/sep/13/volkswagen-to-stop-making-its-iconic-beetle-in-2019.

3 https://www.uktights.com/tights/mens-tights.

4 L. Aratani, 'Jobless America: the Coronavirus Unemployment Crisis in Figures', *Guardian*, 28 May 2020, https://www.theguardian.com/business/2020/may/28/jobless-america-unemployment-coronavirus-in-figures.

5 Queervestism

1 C. Ramaswamy, 'Should I Feel Guilty About Dressing my Daughter as a "girly girl"?', *Guardian*, 21 May 2018, https://www.theguardian.com/lifeandstyle/2018/may/21/why-should-i-feel-conflicted-about-dressing-my-daughter-as-a-girly-girl.

2 J. Mason, 'Alexandria Ocasio-Cortez Knows that Beauty is Political', *The Mary Sue*, 21 August 2020, https://www.themarysue.com/alexandria-ocasio-cortez-knows-that-beauty-is-political/

3 S. Appleby, 'Why I Felt Liberated When I Started Dressing as a Woman', *Guardian*, 5 April 2020, https://www.theguardian.com/lifeandstyle/2020/apr/05/steven-appleby-why-i-felt-liberated-when-i-started-dressing-as-a-woman-.

4 M. Jones, 'Being Transgender without Transitioning: What Does Being Transgender Mean to Me?', *Medium*, 18 May 2018, https://medium.com/the-transition-transmission/being-transgender-without-transitioning-300fa3f10153.

5 T. L. Ryan, 'Where Do Cross-Dressers Fit into the Transgender Community?', *Chicagonow.com*, 4 August 2015, http://www.

chicagonow.com/shades-gender/2015/08/where-do-cross-dressers-fit-into-the-transgender-community.

6 J. Henley, 'Female-led Countries Handled Coronavirus Better, Study Suggests', *Guardian*, 18 August 2020, https://www.theguardian.com/world/2020/aug/18/female-led-countries-handled-coronavirus-better-study-jacinda-ardern-angela-merkel.

7 M. J. Vergora, '11,000 New Zealanders Have Lost Their Jobs – and 10,000 of Them Were Women', *The Spinoff*, 5 August 2020, https://thespinoff.co.nz/business/05-08-2020/11000-new-zealanders-have-lost-their-jobs-and-10000-of-them-were-women/.

8 Moore, 'If We Can't Define What a Woman is, How Can We Organise Politically?'.

9 E. A. Roy, 'British Transgender Woman Given Residency in "Safer" New Zealand', *Guardian*, 12 October 2017, https://www.theguardian.com/world/2017/oct/12/british-transgender-woman-given-residency-in-safer-new-zealand.

10 H. Southwell, 'Anti-Trans Group Allowed to Lead Pride in London March After Hijack', *Pink News*, 7 July 2018, https://www.pinknews.co.uk/2018/07/07/anti-trans-group-allowed-to-lead-pride-in-london-march-after-hijack/.

11 'The Guardian View on the Gender Recognition Act: Where Rights Collide', *Guardian*, 17 October 2018, https://www.theguardian.com/commentisfree/2018/oct/17/the-guardian-view-on-the-gender-recognition-act-where-rights-collide.

12 J. J. Gleeson, 'On The Guardian's Transphobic Centrism', *New Socialist*, 21 October 2018, https://newsocialist.org.uk/on-the-guardians-transphobic-centrism/.

13 'Transgender Rights Are Not a Threat to Feminism', *Guardian*, 18 October 2018, https://www.theguardian.com/commentisfree/2018/oct/18/transgender-rights-are-not-a-threat-to-feminism.

14 L. Finlayson, K. Jenkins and R. Worsdale, R. '"I'm Not Transphobic, but . . .": A Feminist Case Against the Feminist Case Against Trans Inclusivity', *Versobooks*, 17 October 2018, https://www.versobooks.com/blogs/4090-i-m-not-transphobic-but-a-feminist-case-against-the-feminist-case-against-trans-inclusivity.

15 J. Jacques, 'Transphobia is Everywhere in Britain: It's a Respectable Bigotry, on the Left as well as the Right', *New York Times*, 9 March 2020, https://www.nytimes.com/2020/03/09/opinion/britain-transphobia-labour-party.html.

16 E. Burkett, 'What Makes a Woman?', *New York Times*, 6 June 2015, https://www.nytimes.com/2015/06/07/opinion/sunday/what-makes-a-woman.html.

6 Obsolescent empire

1 D. Victor, 'Coronavirus Safety Runs Into a Stubborn Barrier: Masculinity', *New York Times*, 10 October 2020, https://nyti.ms/3iNITO8.

2 S. Rogers, 'The Story of Sign 'O the Times, Episode 5: It Be's Like That Sometimes', *Prince: Official Podcast produced by The Current 2019 American Public Media Group*, 2020.

3 H. Marcuse, 'The End of Utopia', *Marxists.org*, 1967, https://www.marxists.org/reference/archive/marcuse/works/1967/end-utopia.htm.

Bibliography

Adorno, T. (2005). *The Culture Industry: Selected Essays on Mass Culture*. Edited by J. M. Bernstein. London: Routledge.

Adorno, T., E. Frenkel-Brunswik, D. J. Levinson and R. N. Sanford (1950). *The Authoritarian Personality*. New York: Norton.

Adorno, T. and M. Horkheimer (1997). *Dialectic of Enlightenment*. London: Verso.

Ahmed, S. (2016). 'An Affinity of Hammers . . . on TERFS', *TSQ: Transgender Studies Quarterly* 3, Nos 1–2 (May): 22–34.

Allen, S. (2014). 'Whither the transvestite? Theorising male-to-female transvestism in feminist and queer theory', *Feminist Theory* 15, no. 1: 51–72.

Althusser, L. (1994). 'Ideology and Ideological State Apparatuses (Notes Towards an Investigation)', in S. Zizek (ed.), *Mapping Ideology*. London: Verso.

Anderson, E. (2009). *Inclusive Masculinity*. New York: Routledge.

Arruzza, C., T. Bhattacharya and N. Fraser (2019). *Feminism for the 99 Percent*. London: Verso.

Bannerji, H. (1995). *Thinking Through: Essays on Feminism, Marxism and Anti-Racism*. Ontario: Women's Press.

Barnard, S. and B. Fink (2002). *Reading Seminar XX: Lacan's Major Work on Love, Knowledge, and Feminine Sexuality*. New York: SUNY Press.

Barrett, R. (ed.) (2016). *Female Erasure: What You Need to Know About Gender Politics' War on Women, the Female Sex and Human Rights*. Pacific Palisades, CA: Tidal Time Publishing.

Bartky, S. L. (2002). *'Sympathy and Solidarity' and Other Essays*. Oxford: Rowman & Littlefield Publishers.

Beauvoir, S. de. (2015). *The Second Sex*. London: Penguin.

Bederman, G. (1995). *Manliness and Civilisation: A Cultural History of Gender and Race in the United States, 1880–1917*. Chicago: University of Chicago Press.

Blanchard, R. (2005). 'Early History of the Concept of Autogynephilia', *Archives of Sexual Behaviour* 34, no. 4: 439–46.

Bordo, S. (1995). *Unbearable Weight: Feminism, Western Culture, and the Body*, Berkeley/Los Angeles: University of California Press.

Bornstein, K. (2012). *A Queer and Pleasant Danger: A Memoir.* Boston: Beacon Press.

Bourdieu, P. (2001). *Masculine Domination.* Stanford, CA: Stanford University Press.

Bray, A. (2004). *Helene Cixous: Writing and Sexual Differences.* Missouri City TX: Transitions.

Brenner, R. (2020). 'Escalating Plunder', *New Left Review* 123 (May / June), https://newleftreview.org/issues/ii123/articles/robert-brenner-escalating-plunder.

Brightwell, L. (2018). 'The Exclusionary Effects of Queer Anti-Normativity on Feminine-Identified Queers,' *Feral Feminisms: An Open Access Feminist Online Journal* 7 (Spring): 15–24.

Brownmiller, S. (1994). *Femininity.* New York: Ballantine Books.

Buchanan, I. (2017). 'Assemblage Theory, or, the Future of an Illusion', *Deleuze Studies* 11, no. 3: 457–74.

Buchanan, I. (2020). *Assemblage Theory and Method: An Introduction and Guide.* London: Bloomsbury Academic.

Burns, J. (2007). 'Biopolitics Toxic Masculinities Disavowed Histories and Youth Radicalization', *Peace Review* 29, no. 2: 176–83.

Butler, J. (1990). *Gender Trouble: Feminism and the Subversion of Identity.* London: Routledge.

Butler, J. (1988). 'Performative Acts and Gender Constitution: An Essay in Phenomenology and Feminist Theory', *Theatre Journal* 40, no. 4 (December): 519–31.

Chatzidakis, A., J. Hakim, J. Litter, C. Rottenberg and L. Segal (2020). *The Care Manifesto: The Politics of Interdependence.* London: Verso.

Connell, R. W. (2005). *Masculinities,* 2nd edition. Berkeley: University of California Press.

Connell, R. (2012). 'Masculinity Research and Global Change', *Masculinity and Social Change* 1, no. 1: 4–18.

Connell, R. W. and J. W. Messerschmidt (2005). 'Hegemonic Masculinity: Rethinking the Concept', *Gender and Society* 19, no. 6 (December): 829–59.

Cremin, C. (2011). *Capitalism's New Clothes: Enterprise, Ethics and Enjoyment in Times of Crisis.* London: Pluto Press.

Cremin, C. (2012). *iCommunism.* London: Zer0 Books.

Cremin, C. (2016). *Exploring Videogames with Deleuze and Guattari: Towards an Affective Theory of Form.* London: Routledge.

Cremin, C. (2017). *Man-Made Woman: The Dialectics of Cross-dressing.* London: Pluto Press.

Crispin, J. (2017). *Why I am Not a Feminist?* New York: Black Inc.

Deleuze, G. (1988). *Spinoza: Practical Philosophy.* San Francisco: City Lights.

Deleuze, G. (2008). *Francis Bacon.* London: Continuum.

Deleuze, G. and F. Guattari (2003a). *Anti-Oedipus: Capitalism and Schizophrenia, Volume 1.* London: Continuum.

Deleuze, G. and F. Guattari (2003b). *A 1000 Plateaus: Capitalism and Schizophrenia, Volume 2.* London: Continuum.

Deleuze, G. and C. Parnet (2007). *Dialogues II: Revised Edition.* New York: Columbia University Press.

Delphy, C. (2016). *Close to Home: A Materialist Analysis of Women's Oppression.* London: Verso.

Demetrakis, D. (2001). 'Connell's Concept of Hegemonic Masculinity: A Critique', *Theory and Society* 30, no. 3: 337–61.

Drucker, P. (2015). *Warped: Gay Normativity and Queer Anti-Capitalism.* Boston: Brill.

Duggan, L. (2002). 'The New Homonormativity: The Sexual Politics of Neoliberalism', in R. Castronovo and D. D. Nelson (eds.), *Materializing Democracy: Toward a Revitalized Cultural Politics.* Durham, NC: Duke University Press.

Dyer-Witheford, N., A. M. Kjøsen and J. Steinhoff (2019). *Inhuman Power: Artificial Intelligence and the Future of Capitalism.* London: Pluto Press.

Ekins, R. (2002). *Male Femaling: A Grounded Theory Approach to Cross-dressing and Sex-changing.* London: Routledge.

Elliot, P. and L. Lyons (2016). 'Transphobia as Symptom: Fear of the "Unwoman"', *TSQ: Transgender Studies Quarterly* 4, no. 3–4 (November): 358–83.

Federici, S. (2004). *Caliban and the Witch: Women, the Body and Primitive Accumulation.* New York: Automedia.

Federici, S. (2017). 'Notes on Gender in Marx's Capital', *Continental Thought & Theory: A Journal of Intellectual Freedom* 1, no. 4.

Feinberg, L. (1996). *Transgender Warriors: Making History from Joan of Arc to Dennis Rodman.* Boston: Beacon Press.

Fiorini, L. and G. Rose (eds.) (2010). *On Freud's 'Femininity'.* London: Karnac.

Fisher, M. (2009). *Capitalist Realism.* London: Zer0 Books.

Fisher, M. (2017). *K-Punk.* Edited by Darren Ambrose. London: Repeater Books.

Floyd, K. (2009). *The Reification of Desire: Towards a Queer Marxism.* Minneapolis: University of Minnesota Press.

Foucault, M. (1978). *The History of Sexuality, Volume I.* New York: Pantheon Books.

Franklin, K. (2004). 'Enacting Masculinity: Antigay Violence and Group Rape as Participatory Theatre', *Sexuality Research & Social Policy* 2 (April): 25–40.

Fraser, N. (2016). 'Contradictions of Capital and Care', *New Left Review* (July–August), https://newleftreview.org/issues/ii100/articles/nancy-fraser-contradictions-of-capital-and-care.

Freud, S. (1989). *New Introductory Lectures on Psycho-Analysis*. New York: WW Norton & Company.

Freud, S. (2011). *Three Essays on the Theory of Sexuality*. Translated by James Strachey. Eastford, CT: Martino Fine Books.

Garber, M. (2011). *Vested Interests: Cross-dressing and Cultural Anxiety*. London: Routledge.

Garcia, M. (2017). *The Most Beautiful: My Life with Prince*. New York: Hachette Books.

Gherovici, P. (2017). *Transgender Psychoanalysis: A Lacanian Perspective of Sexual Difference*. London: Routledge.

Glocer, F. and G. Abelin-Sas Rose (eds.) (2010). *On Freud's Femininity*. London: Karnac Books.

Gozlan, O. (2015). *Transsexuality and the Art of Transitioning: A Lacanian Approach*. London: Routledge.

Halberstam, J. (1998). *Female Masculinity*. Durham, NC: Duke University Press.

Haraway, D. J. (1991). *Simians, Cyborgs, and Women: The Reinvention of Nature*. London: Free Association Books.

Harvey, D. (2007). *A Brief History of Neoliberalism*. Oxford: Oxford University Press.

Hennessy, R. (2000). *Profit and Pleasure: Sexual Identities in Late Capitalism*. London: Routledge.

Hines, S. (2007). *Transforming Gender: Transgender Practices of Identity, Intimacy and Care*. Bristol: Policy Press.

Hirschfeld, M. (2003). *Transvestites: The Erotic Drive To Cross Dress*. New York: Prometheus Books.

Hochschild, A. (1983). *The Managed Heart: Commercialization of Human Feeling*. Berkeley/Los Angeles: University of California Press.

Hocquenghem, G. (1999). *Homosexual Desire*. Durham, NC: Duke University Press.

hooks, b. (2000). *Feminism is for Everybody*. London: Pluto Press.

hooks, b. (2004). *The Will to Change: Men, Masculinity, and Love*. New York: Atria Books.

Irigaray, L. (1993). *An Ethics of Sexual Difference*. New York: Cornell University Press.

Jameson, F. (1990). 'Cognitive Mapping', in C. Nelson and L. Grossberg (eds.), *Marxism and the Interpretation of Culture*, 347–60. Chicago: University of Illinois Press.

Jeffreys, S. (2014). *Gender Hurts: A Feminist Analysis of the Politics of Transgenderism*. London: Routledge.

Kalish, R. and M. Kimmel (2010). 'Suicide by mass murder: Masculinity aggrieved entitlement, and rampage school shootings', *Health Sociology Review* 19, no. 4 (December): 451–64.

Karner, T. (1996). 'Fathers, Sons, and Vietnam: Masculinity and Betrayal in the Life Narratives of Vietnam Veterans with Post Traumatic Stress Disorder', *American Studies 37*, no. 1 (Spring): 63–94.

Kimmel, M. (2008). *Guyland: The Perilous World Where Boys Become Men.* New York: HarperCollins.

Lacan, J. (1991). *Freud's Papers on Technique, Book I.* Edited by J.-A. Miller. London: Karnac.

Lacan, J. (1993). *The Psychosis, Book III 1955–1956.* Edited by J.-A. Miller. London: Routledge.

Lacan, J. (2004). *The Four Fundamental Concepts of Psychoanalysis, Book XI.* Edited by J.-A. Miller. London: Karnac.

Lacan, J. (2007). *The Other Side of Psychoanalysis, Book XVII.* Edited by J.-A. Miller. London: Routledge.

Lacan, J. (2018). *The Sinthome, Book XXIII.* Edited by J.-A. Miller. Cambridge: Polity Press.

Malabou, C. (2009). *Changing Difference.* Cambridge: Polity Press.

Mann, B. (2004). *Sovereign Masculinity: Gender Lessons from the War on Terror.* Oxford: Oxford University Press.

Marcuse, H. (2002). *One-Dimensional Man.* London: Routledge.

Marcuse, H. (2006). *Eros and Civilisation.* London: Routledge.

Marx, K. (1973). *Grundrisse.* Translated by Ben Fowkes. London: Penguin.

Marx, K. (1982). *Capital: A Critique of Political Economy.* Translated by Ben Fowkes. London: Penguin.

Messerschmidt, J. (2010). *Hegemonic Masculinities and Camouflaged Politics.* Boulder, CO: Paradigm Publishers.

Messner, M. (2007). 'The Masculinity of the Governator', *Gender & Society 21*, no. 4: 461–80.

Mieli, M. (2018). *Towards a Gay Communism: Elements of a Homosexual Critique.* London: Pluto Press.

Mies, M. (1994). *Patriarchy and Accumulation on a World Scale: Women in the International Division of Labour.* London: Zed Books.

Morris, J. (1974). *Conundrum.* London: Faber and Faber.

Nagle, A. 2017. *Kill All Normies: Online Culture Wars from 4Chan and Tumblr to Trump and the Alt-Right.* Winchester: Zer0 Books.

Namaste, K. (1996). 'The Politics of Inside/Out: Queer Theory, Poststructuralism, and a Sociological Approach to Sexuality', in S. Seidman (ed.), *Queer Theory/Sociology*, 194–212. Oxford: Blackwell.

Nast, H. (2015). 'The Machine-Phallus: Psychoanalyzing the Geopolitical Economy of Masculinity and Race', *Psychological Inquiry: A Topical Journal for Mental Health Professionals 35* (November): 766–85.

Packard, V. (2007). *The Hidden Persuaders.* New York: IG Publishing.

Paradis, J. (2006). *Sex, Paranoia and Modern Masculinity.* New York: SUNY Press.

Penney, J. (2014). *After Queer Theory: The Limits of Sexual Politics*. London: Pluto Press.

Robinson, C. J. (2000). *Black Marxism*. Chapel Hill: University of North Carolina Press.

Rubin, G. (2011). *Deviations: A Gayle Rubin Reader*. Durham, NC: Duke University Press.

Sanday, P. (1990). *Fraternity Gang Rape: Sex, Brotherhood, and Privilege on Campus*. New York: New York University Press.

Scholz, P. (2009). 'Patriarchy and Commodity Society: Gender without the Body', in N. Larsen, M. Nilges, J. Robinson and N. Brown (eds.), *Marxism and the Critique of Value*, 123–42. Chicago: MCM Publications.

Schuster, A. (2016). *The Trouble with Pleasure: Deleuze and Psychoanalysis*. Cambridge, MA: MIT Press.

Sculos, B. W. (2017). 'Who's Afraid of "Toxic Masculinity"?' *Class, Race and Corporate Power* 5, no. 3: unpaginated.

Segal, L. (2005). *Why Feminism? Gender, Psychology, Politics*. Cambridge: Polity Press.

Segal, L. (2007). *Slow Motion: Changing Masculinities, Changing Men*. Basingstoke: Palgrave-MacMillan.

Serano, J. (2007). *Whipping Girl: A Transsexual Woman on Sexism and the Scapegoating of Femininity*. New York: Seal Press.

Stark, H. (2017). *Feminist Theory After Deleuze*. London: Bloomsbury.

Stoller, R. (1968). *Sex and Gender: On the Development of Masculinity and Femininity*. New York: Science House.

Stoller, R. (1985). *Presentations of Gender*. New Haven, CT: Yale University Press.

Stone, A. (2006). *Luce Irigaray and the Philosophy of Sexual Difference*. Cambridge: Cambridge University Press.

Stryker, S. (2008). *Transgender History*. New York: Basic Books.

Stryker, S. and T. M. Bettcher (2016). 'Trans/Feminisms', *TSQ: Transgender Studies Quarterly* 3, no. 1–2 (May): 5–14.

Stryker, S., P. Currah and L. J. Moore (2008). 'Introduction: Trans-, Trans, or Transgender?', *Women's Studies Quarterly* 36, no. 3–4 (Fall–Winter): 11–22.

Suthrell, C. (2004). *Unzipping Gender: Sex, Cross-Dressing and Culture*. New York: Berg.

Thanem, T. and L. Wallenberg (2016). 'Just doing gender? Transvestism and the power of undoing gender in everyday life and work', *Organization* 23, no. 2: 250–71.

Tosh, J. (2016). *Psychology and Gender Dysphoria: Feminist and Transgender Perspectives*. London: Routledge.

Vogel, L. (1983). *Marxism and the Oppression of Women: Toward a Unitary Theory*. Boston: Brill.

Voloshinov, V. N. (1986). *Marxism and the Philosophy of Language.* Cambridge, MA: Harvard University Press.

Žižek, S. (1989). *The Sublime Object of Ideology.* London: Verso.

Žižek, S. (2006). *The Parallax View.* Cambridge, MA: MIT Press.

Žižek, S. (2020). *Sex and the Failed Absolute.* London: Bloomsbury Academic.

Zupančič, A. (2017). *What is Sex?* Cambridge, MA: MIT Press.

Index